DIFFERING VISIONS OF A LEARNING SOCIETY

Research findings

Volume 2

Edited by Frank Coffield

First published in Great Britain in November 2000 by

The Policy Press
34 Tyndall's Park Road
Bristol BS8 1PY
UK

Tel   +44 (0)117 954 6800
Fax   +44 (0)117 973 7308
e-mail tpp@bristol.ac.uk
www.policypress.org.uk

© The Policy Press 2000

In association with the ESRC *Learning Society Programme*

British Library Cataloguing in Publication Data

A catalogue record for this book is available from the British Library

ISBN 1 86134 247 0 paperback
A hardcover version of this book is also available.

Frank Coffield was Director of the ESRC's research programme into *The Learning Society* from 1994 to 2000.

Cover design by Qube Design Associates, Bristol.

Photographs on front cover supplied by kind permission of Mark Simmons Photography, Bristol.

Printed and bound in Great Britain by Hobbs the Printers Ltd, Southampton.

Contents

Notes on contributors

Professor David Ashton is Professor of Sociology and Director of the Centre for Labour Market Studies, University of Leicester. He has published extensively on national systems of human resource development and various aspects of the process of skill formation. His latest book was written with Francis Green, Donna James and Johnny Sung, and is entitled *Education and training for development in East Asia* (Routledge). He is also currently researching the process of workplace learning.

Stephen Baron is a Senior Lecturer at the Faculty of Education, University of Glasgow. A former Raising of the School Leaving Age (RoSLa) and remedial teacher, his research interests are in the cultural studies of education, particularly the reproduction of marginal groups. He has published widely on the politics of education and of community and is currently completing *The politics of learning disability* with Paul Dumbleton (Macmillan, 2000: forthcoming).

Professor John Bynner is Professor of Sciences in Education and Director of the Centre for Longitudinal Studies, the Joint Centre for Longitudinal Research, the DfEE Research Centre on 'The Wider Benefits of Learning' at the Institute of Education, London University. He was national coordinator of the ESRC 16-19 Initiative (1986–91), and currently directs the National Child Development Study and the 1970 British Birth Cohort Study. He is a member of the Social Exclusion Unit's PAT 12 on disadvantaged youth and produced research for the Social Exclusion Unit on young people not in education, employment or training. His research interests include: transition to adulthood, basic skills, economic and political socialisation, life course research and comparative and longitudinal research methodology. Recent publications include an edited volume *Adversity and challenge in life in the New Germany and England* (with Rainer Silbereisen) and *Obstacles and opportunities on the route to adult life: Evidence from rural and urban Britain*.

Professor Frank Coffield is Professor of Education at the University of Newcastle and was Director of the ESRC's research programme into *The Learning Society* from 1994 to 2000. In 1997 he edited a *report A national strategy for lifelong learning* (Department of Education, University of Newcastle) and produced in 1999 *Breaking the consensus: Lifelong learning as social control* (Department of Education, University of Newcastle). Four reports on findings from *The Learning Society Programme* have been edited and produced so far: *Learning at work; Why's the beer always stronger up North? Studies in lifelong learning in Europe; Speaking truth to power: Research and policy on lifelong learning;* and *The necessity of informal learning* (The Policy Press).

Dr Pat Davies is Reader in Continuing Education at City University. She has a long-term research interest in access to learning for adults, both in the UK and in the rest of Europe. She is currently a member of the Expert Panel for Adult Education for the European Commission and of the Swiss National Science Foundation research programme 'Education and Employment'. She was co-director (with Professor John Bynner) of 'The Impact of Credit-based Learning on Learning Cultures' project within *The Learning Society* programme.

Susan English was Research Assistant on the 'Innovations in Teaching and Learning in Higher Education' project and is currently completing her PhD thesis about the process of change in teaching and learning at the Open University. She is based at the University of Plymouth.

Dr Alan Felstead is Reader in Employment Studies at the Centre for Labour Market Studies, University of Leicester. He has published widely in the field of Employment Studies, and has research interests in non-standard forms of employment, training and skills formation in Britain and elsewhere. He currently sits on the Research Group to the government's Skills Task Force. His books include *Global trends in flexible labour* (Macmillan, 1999, edited with Nick Jewson); and *In work, at home: Towards an understanding of homeworking* (Routledge, 2000, co-authored with Nick Jewson).

Professor Ralph Fevre is a Professor in the Cardiff University School of Social Sciences. He recently edited (with Andrew Thompson) a volume of articles on *National identity and social theory* (University of Wales Press, 1999) and forthcoming titles include *The demoralization of western culture* (Continuum, 2000) and *The sociology of economic behaviour* (Sage Publications, 2001: forthcoming). He is currently engaged on a study of devolution, social capital and active citizenship in Wales.

Professor John Field is Professor of Lifelong Learning at the University of Warwick; previously he was a Professor in the School of Education, University of Ulster. He serves on the Secretary of State for Education and Employment's National Advisory Group on Continuing Education and Lifelong Learning, and is an adviser to the Northern Ireland Assembly. He chairs the research committee of the Universities Association for Continuing Education. His recent books include *European dimensions: Education, training and the European Union* (Jessica Kingsley, 1998) and, with Mal Leicester, *Lifelong learning: Education across the lifespan* (Falmer, 2000). He is learning to speak Polish.

Professor John Furlong is a Professor in the Cardiff University School of Social Sciences (having recently moved from the Graduate School of Education at Bristol University). He has published extensively on the training and professional socialisation of teachers and on the role of mentors in teacher education. He has co-authored *Teacher education in transition: Re-forming professionalism?* (Open University Press, 2000: forthcoming). He is currently completing an ESRC-funded project on the uses of ICT by children in their homes.

Dr Stephen Gorard is a Reader in the Cardiff University School of Social Sciences. In addition to his work on participation in lifelong learning, he has published extensively on the marketisation of schools and the determinants of differential educational attainment. His latest book, *Education and social justice* (University of Wales Press) will be published in 2000. He is currently completing an ESRC-funded project on the impact of marketisation on the social composition of schools and a study of the effects of new ICTs on patterns of participation in adult learning, funded by the Spencer Foundation.

Professor Francis Green is Professor of Economics at the University of Kent at Canterbury. He has published widely on political economy and on labour economics, with special attention to the economics of skills acquisition, and to the role of trade unions in the labour market. He is a research advisor to the government's Skills Task Force. Among his recent books are *Education, training and the global economy*, co-authored with David Ashton (Edward Elgar). He is currently researching the links between increasing skills and the intensification of work effort in Britain and Europe.

Dr Andrew Hannan is Reader in Education and Research Coordinator in the Faculty of Arts and Education of the University of Plymouth, and was co-director of the 'Innovations in Teaching and Learning in Higher Education' project. He was formerly Director of the MA Equal Opportunities programme at Birmingham Polytechnic (now the University of Central England).

Professor Gareth Rees is a Professor and Deputy Director in the Cardiff University School of Social Sciences. He has published widely in the areas of lifelong learning, the role of education in economic development and the governance of education policy. He is currently completing an ESRC-funded project on the impacts of devolution on vocational education and training and a study of 'learning regions' for the OECD. He has recently co-edited a collection on education policy and devolution, which will be published as *Education policy making in Wales: Studies in devolved governance* (University of Wales Press) in 2000.

Professor Sheila Riddell worked as Research Fellow in the Department of Education, University of Edinburgh following her PhD at the University of Bristol in 1988. From 1989 to 1996 she taught and researched at the University of Stirling and was promoted to a Personal Chair in 1995. After a period as Dean of Arts and Social Science at Napier University, Edinburgh, Sheila took up the post of Professor of Social Policy (Disability Studies) at Glasgow University where she is Director of the Strathclyde Centre for Disability Research. She has researched and written extensively in the areas of special educational needs/disability and gender and education.

Professor Tom Schuller is Dean of the Faculty of Continuing Education at Birkbeck College, London. He was previously Director of the Centre for Continuing Education at the University of Edinburgh, and has worked at the Universities of Glasgow and Warwick, and for four years at the OECD. He has published books on *Life after work* (with Michael Young), *Part-time higher education in Scotland* (with David Raffe and others, Jessica Kingsley Publishers), *Social capital: Critical perspectives* (edited with Stephen Baron and John Field, Oxford University Press, 2000: forthcoming), and *Lifelong learning: Policy and research* (edited with Albert Tuijnman, Portland Press, 1999). He is co-director of a new DfEE-funded research centre on the wider benefits of learning, based jointly at Birkbeck College and the Institute of Education; a governor of the Working Mens College; and a member of the Secretary of State for Education and Employment's National Advisory Group on Continuing Education and Lifelong Learning.

Professor Harold Silver is Visiting Professor in Higher Education, University of Plymouth, and co-directed the 'Innovations in Teaching and Learning in Higher Education' project. He was formerly Professor of Social History and Education, University of London, and Principal, Bulmershe College of Higher Education.

Alastair Wilson is Research Fellow in the Strathclyde Centre for Disability Research, University of Glasgow. After a period as a husky handler he graduated in History from the University of Glasgow where he also trained as an adult education worker. His research interests are in disability and learning difficulties, particularly the development of supported employment schemes.

This book is dedicated to the memory of
Mervyn Taylor

The three stages of lifelong learning: romance, evidence and implementation

Frank Coffield

Introduction

Is lifelong learning the big idea which will deliver economic prosperity and social justice, or will it prove to be yet another transient phenomenon like 'recurrent education' which came and went during the 1970s? The European Commission has chosen lifelong learning as the overarching concept which, it is hoped, will weld together in one policy both active citizenship and the knowledge economy. On the other hand, lifelong learning is so seriously under-theorised and under-researched that it seems a rather underdeveloped candidate to play the role of panacea for the economic and democratic problems of Europe.

It may be helpful to picture lifelong learning as currently making its way through three overlapping stages, namely, those of romance, evidence and implementation. For at least the last 20 years the concept has been stuck in the first pre-scientific phase, where, for example, 'vital, vibrant and vigorous' disciples listen to 'visionary' leaders who preach the new theology of lifelong learning at meetings which are no longer called conferences but 'festivals'[1] of learning (Longworth and Davies, 1996; Longworth, 1999). Self-styled 'learning philosophers' bring 'glad tidings of a feast' (Agenda for the First European Festival of the Learning City) and recite litanies of 'learning beatitudes', or learning platitudes as they should be called, to the faithful. The book by Norman Longworth and Keith Davies (1996) and the sequel by Norman Longworth (1999) include 17 of such beatitudes which are to be "emblazoned on the walls of every classroom, common room and workplace" (1996, p 24); some restraint will be shown in quoting only four of them, two from each book:

> Learning brings change – the Renaissance changed a civilisation. Today learning is transforming an empire in Eastern Europe. (1996, p 23)

> Learning pays … the education and training of [the] workforce is the single most important characteristic in determining economic performance. (1996, p 24)

> Learning empowers – it makes possible the realisation of our dreams. (1999, p 11)

> Learning nourishes – it gives vitality to our hunger to know and to wonder. (1999, p 11)

The faithful at such celebrations of learning can be imagined chanting the recommended mantras of "Learning is not teaching", "Education and training are dead" and, of course, "Learning can be fun". The two books consist of endless lists of, for example, the 10 principles of learning (eg "The learner is the customer and the customer's needs have first priority"); the 10 challenges to learning companies (eg "Staying alive in a competitive world"); the 10 skills for a lifelong learning age (eg "Learn to learn"); the 10 characteristics of a learning organisation (eg "A learning organisation shares its vision of tomorrow with its people"); the 10 challenges to Higher Education (eg "Quality of research, teaching and management"); the 10 characteristics of a lifelong learning school (eg "Expands lifelong learning in all its children and staff…"); the 10 essentials for successful partnerships (eg "Regular meetings of the partnership should be held…"); the 12 (why 12?) new skills of the teachers of tomorrow, renamed learning counsellors (eg "List all the needs of people in a database by carrying out audits in companies, the community and wherever people congregate"); and the 10-point charter for learning cities (eg *"Energise learning providers* to supply lifelong learning geared to the needs of each learner where, when, how and by whom it is required", original emphasis). Many of these lists are carefully arranged so that they spell out the key words *Learning* or *Learners*, presumably to enable them to be easily committed to memory.

If a new learning age could be created by issuing lists of instructions of a self-evident and patronising nature for other people to carry out, then this would be the way forward. But if progress is to be made, there has to be a radical break with this romantic tradition where learning – and learning on its own – magically solves the world's problems. All the *ex cathedra* statements above are made without reference to any evidence and without a scintilla of doubt. It is the safe, Panglossian, middle-class view of learning, which is removed from the clash of conflicting views and interests, and which is promulgated by those who appear never to have studied, never mind experienced, poverty, exclusion or unemployment. It is enough to turn even well motivated learners off learning for life.

Fortunately, lifelong leaning is now tentatively entering the second stage where research evidence will begin to challenge the vacuous rhetoric of the stage of romance. From now on it should no longer be sufficient for speakers at conferences on lifelong learning to mouth the received wisdoms of the day or to base their recommendations for policy on nothing more than their strongly-held beliefs. The trouble is, however, that after decades of under-funding of educational research, there is next to no hard evidence on which to construct policy or to guide practice.

The third stage of implementation still lies some way off, when theory, policy and practice will all be informed by valid and reliable evidence rather than political convictions or armchair musings; policy formation will also continue to be influenced by political priorities, and responses to some legitimate and some less legitimate pressures. But if lifelong learning in the next few years does not move steadily from stage one to stage three, it is likely to be discarded as a concept, just as the debate about 'learning organisations' is already moving on to a concern with 'high performance organisations'. To use a phrase of Tawney's (1924), "the lion in the path" of the future advancement of lifelong learning is at present not so much lack of resources as the dearth of evidence-based knowledge on the topic.

These reflections are the result of directing a research programme since 1994 on lifelong learning, and having to attend one evangelical and evidence-free conference after another. This book is dedicated to contributing to the task of ushering in the stage of evidence and is the second of two volumes which present the findings from the Economic and Social Research Council's (ESRC) programme of research into 'the learning society'. It is also the last joint publication from the programme, so it is appropriate that it should be devoted to drawing out some general themes and policy implications from all the research undertaken, as well as introducing the second set of overview chapters from six of the projects. The first volume contains chapters from seven of the projects, which set out the aims, methods, findings and policy implications emanating from their research. The same plan is followed here.

The introduction to the first volume offered a critical analysis of the concept of a learning society which presented 10 different models of such a society. These models were an attempt to distinguish particular features of the diffuse and contested concept of a learning society in the hope of imposing some order and clarity on a confusing literature. They also constitute a conceptual framework which was then used to evaluate current government policy on lifelong learning.

The introductions to the two volumes should be seen as complementary. Both are firmly based on the evidence from all the projects in the programme, and the first introduction used that evidence to interrogate the multiple and competing definitions of a learning society. This introduction draws on the same body of evidence to comment on specific policies and in doing so takes up David Blunkett's invitation to researchers "to have a real practical impact" on policy (2000, p 4). This second introduction also surveys the findings of the programme as a whole and, as a result, extracts a number of recurrent themes and policy recommendations from the detailed studies conducted by the projects – without once mentioning 'paradigm shifts', 'joined-up thinking', 'stakeholders', 'UK PLC', 'strategic partnerships' or 'government task forces'. As with the first volume, references will be made to, and examples will be drawn from, all the projects within the programme and not just from those whose findings are presented in the following six chapters. The findings from the programme will also be placed within a broad context of research on different types of learning societies and within policy debates on lifelong learning.

The Learning Society Programme

For those coming across *The Learning Society Programme* for the first time, a brief introduction is necessary, although fuller details are given in the first volume[2]. In 1994 the ESRC established a research programme with the title of *The learning society: Knowledge and skills for employment*. Fourteen projects[3] and a review of research on vocational education and training in the UK (Brown and Keep, 2000) were commissioned to investigate a variety of topics at a total cost of £2.5 million. The programme finished at the end of March 2000, and by that time it had published four joint reports on the themes of: learning at work[4]; studies of lifelong learning in Europe[5]; research and policy on lifelong learning[6]; and informal learning[7], all published by The Policy Press. Each of the 14 projects has also written, for the benefit of the general reader, a brief two-page summary of its objectives, achievements and outputs, and sets of these summaries are available free of charge[8].

Eight broad themes

What follows does not just repeat in different words what has been published previously in a variety of sources, but attempts to produce a new and challenging synthesis of the collective endeavours of the 14 projects by concentrating on their most significant findings, conclusions and policy implications. The following eight themes, which have been chosen for analysis, are all firmly grounded in the projects' findings:

* 'learn at work, if you can';
* participation and non-participation;
* an over-reliance on human capital theory;
* the shifting of responsibility to individuals;
* 'there's precious little society in The Learning Society';
* the centrality of learning for a learning society;
* new inequalities;
* lessons from elsewhere in Europe.

'Learn at work, if you can'

It is a cliché of the lifelong learning conference circuit that the workplace has become a more important channel for the acquisition of new skills than the formal education and training system. Findings from those projects within the programme which specialised in this topic can, however, take the public debate much further than that fashionable generality. For example, David Ashton, Alan Felstead and Francis Green (in Chapter Six of this volume) show how their large, nationally representative survey of the skills of British workers enables them to conclude that the policies and characteristics of employers have a remarkably strong association with workers acquiring new skills. In the organisations they term 'modern', because they have introduced such strategies as quality circles, consultation with employees and Investors in People, *all* types of employees increased their skills.

But here comes the rub: around two thirds of the British work force do *not* belong to such organisations. As the researchers themselves comment: "Given the right type of organisational environment even the unskilled can improve their abilities.... Public policy could help to extend the range of organisations which put effort into developing the skills of all their employees" (see Chapter Six, this volume). The significance of this finding needs to be underlined: new divisions are appearing in the labour market, which have serious implications for the distribution of new skills. It also means that employees need to understand that the type of firm they join (ie modern as opposed to traditional) will partly determine their access to new skills. Moreover, it is part-time workers (mainly women), those in non-standard jobs, those over 50 years of age and the self-employed who make up the largest groups missing out on upskilling.

The survey also indicated that in 1997, slightly more than 30% of jobs in Britain required no qualifications. This high figure suggests the burden that workplace learning is being asked to carry. Moreover, if the cliché about the significance of workplace learning is to enjoy continued circulation, then at least it must from now on be coupled with the caveat that, according to this survey, less than one third of British workers are employed by firms which use strategies to increase their skills. This would appear to be the biggest challenge facing the UK in creating a learning society; it is one which British society has known about for at least a generation, and which previous structural reforms (eg the establishment of the TECs) have conspicuously failed to solve. This finding is a timely reminder of the scale of the problem, and it is one that *employers*, aided by government, need to address.

This central finding from the national survey, funded by *The Learning Society Programme*, is supported by a case study of multi-skilling in three sectors (engineering, construction and care) in Wales and Germany. Phil Cooke and his colleagues reported in the first of these two volumes that, although workers developed a wide range of skills in all three sectors, "much of it is of an ad hoc nature, designed to cover immediate skill shortages rather than as part of long-term strategic planning" (Cooke et al, 2000). Perhaps this outcome is not too surprising, given the sectors which were studied, but it should caution against any easy talk about the steady growth of 'learning organisations' in the UK, especially given John Field and Tom Schuller's comment in Chapter Two of this volume that the commitment to Investors in People is weaker in both Scotland and Northern Ireland than in England.

The national survey directed by David Ashton et al also contains some heartening news, or at least so it appears at first. By repeating questions from previous surveys, the researchers were able to make comparisons over time, and as a result they conclude that work skills in Britain have increased since 1986. This success story, however, is qualified in two ways:

> First, there has not been any increase in the autonomy enjoyed by the average British worker. If anything, workers in 1997 were more constrained over the way they carry out their work, and more closely supervised, than in 1986. (see Chapter Six, this volume)

So much for the flexible worker, choosing which skills to acquire and which to deploy.

Second, their findings point to the deficient *demand* for, as well as the deficient *supply* of, intermediate skills, which supports the notion that the UK continues to suffer from a low skills equilibrium (Finegold and Soskice, 1991). If the UK is to break out of the trap "in which the majority of enterprises are staffed by poorly trained managers and workers produce low-quality goods and services" (Finegold and Soskice, 1991, p 215), then at the very least a deeper understanding of how knowledge and skills are developed at work will be needed. One of the many attractions of the theoretical framework of workplace learning developed by Michael Eraut and his team is that it contains clear practical implications. For example, in addition to personal factors such as confidence and capability, this project identified two key situational factors, the microculture of the workplace and how employees are managed:

> ... of all the mechanisms used at organisational level to promote learning the most significant is likely to be the appointment and development of its managers. However, while approaches to management development normally emphasise motivation, productivity and appraisal, comparatively little attention is given to supporting the learning of subordinates, allocating and organising work, and creating a climate which promotes informal learning. (Eraut et al, 2000, p 252)

The scale of the task facing British employers in developing the skills of all their workers has been stressed, but a range of creative new ideas have been advanced by Michael Eraut and also by David Hargreaves (1998) about how to manage the creation of knowledge at work.

Another important caveat comes from the work of Ken Roberts, who argues convincingly that a distinctive feature of the British approach to skill formation is that many skills are acquired informally: "Individuals can advance simply by demonstrating their capability. This particular feature of the British way ... gives labour markets and the entire occupational structure a distinctive flexibility", (2000, p 16), an approach which has served Britain well in science and engineering occupations since at least the 19th century, and which may serve her well again in the 21st. Moreover, if this analysis is accurate, the significance of all managers having a sophisticated understanding of informal learning becomes all the greater.

Participation and non-participation

In Chapter Three of this volume, Pat Davies and John Bynner enunciate a generalisation which captures the main features of participation in the traditional system: the more education and opportunities for training through employment that people have, the more likely they are to participate and progress further. Moreover, the Select Committee of the House of Commons on Education and Employment has neatly summarised the current state of play as follows: "there are persisting inequalities in participation despite great progress in recent years in expanding participation and encouraging the participation of under-represented groups" (House of Commons, Education and Employment Committee, 1999, para 27). But what is the scale of the problem we face? The National Adult Learning Survey interviewed a representative sample of 5,653 adults aged 16-69 in England and Wales in 1997, and concluded that 26% of those who had left full-time education had not taken part in any form of taught or non-taught learning[9] in the previous three years (Beinart and Smith, 1998).

Within the programme, Gareth Rees, Stephen Gorard, Ralph Fevre and John Furlong surveyed over 1,100 individuals in South Wales, and constructed their education and training histories. Those who could be described as 'lifelong learners' amounted to 32%, neatly balancing the 'non-participants' at 31%. Again, these two figures summarise the scale of the task: about a third of adults appear to be lifelong learners, but they are matched by an equally large minority who have not been involved in either education or training at work since leaving school. Rees et al point out one further trend which is significant for policy:

> ... the considerable growth in participation immediately after the completion of compulsory schooling has not been paralleled by the expansion of continuing participation through life ... it follows that priority should be given to the facilitation of lifelong progression routes, rather than focusing on *either* initial *or* continuing education and training. Certainly, the current 'front-loading' of public investment into initial schooling is called into question.... (Chapter Five, this volume; original emphasis)

That, in a nutshell, presents the 'learning divide' in the UK, as it has been called by Naomi Sargent (1997).

A number of projects have taken the public debate further by demonstrating the impossibility of detaching individual motives from the conditions in which individuals perceive opportunities and develop ambitions. Above all, current debates on lifelong learning need to move beyond naïve notions of motivation which seek to explain non-participation solely or mainly in terms of individual characteristics like self-esteem:

> ... the main argument of this paper is that those who lack motivation, feel excluded and appear disadvantaged ... are fundamentally lacking in self-esteem. This lack explains and causes all the others – demotivation, disbelief in one's potential, even lack of opportunity. How could it be otherwise? After all, our existing system offers everyone the opportunity of eleven years of free compulsory education and the entitlement to further education. (Ball, 1998, p 2)

The conclusion we are invited to draw is that all differences in outcome can be safely attributed to the self-esteem of individuals, because equality of opportunity has been achieved. The phrase 'lack of motivation' then becomes middle-class code for working-class behaviour that is not understood. Such a view is devoid of a sense of history, of place and of sharpening divisions in society. It chooses to ignore the polarisation between private and public education, and the growing polarisation within state education, between the most successful schools and colleges and the most stigmatised. The ignorance is culpable.

Instead of trying to cover all cases with a single explanation, Rees et al show how individual behaviour "is embedded in social relations which are shaped by social norms, interpersonal relationships, family and community structures ... the determinants of participation in lifelong learning vary systematically over time and from locality to locality" (Chapter Five this volume). A full explanation will require an understanding of at least four interacting levels:

• the patterns of historical change in the structure of learning opportunities (for instance, labour market conditions and educational provision are unlikely to remain the same in the West Midlands if the main Rover plants are finally closed);
• the interactions of social relations specific to particular places with historical patterns (for example, there may be continuity or discontinuity in social expectations – the learning opportunities of women being limited by 'forced altruism' with respect to family commitments);
• the ways in which access to opportunities is constrained by social, material and cultural resources (for instance, knowledge of, and attitudes towards, opportunities are likely to vary from family to family and individual to individual);
• the ways in which individual choices, life crises, biographies and 'learner identities' are shaped by all of the above.

In short, motivation is not a stable, individual personality trait which remains relatively uninfluenced by external factors, but a complex social construction; motivation is best examined at the intersections between history, geography and biography. If policy concentrates on improving the employability of individuals, it can only be partially effective, because "participation is structured profoundly by patterns of social disadvantage" (Rees et al, Chapter Five, this volume). The practical importance of this approach to the study of the social determinants of different patterns of participation is that it captures more of the rich complexity of people's lives and decision making. It also offers a corrective to catchy slogans like "If at first you don't succeed ... you don't succeed" (Kennedy, 1997, p 21). For example, Gareth Rees et al have shown that adults who left school with no qualifications are more likely to return to formal learning later in life than those who leave school with a poor clutch of GCSEs. This intriguing finding, which needs to be replicated, suggests that patterns of participation are more complicated than the generalisation quoted from Pat Davies and John Bynner's research at the start of this sub-section. The finding suggests that the determinants of later participation may well be different, reflecting changing access to learning opportunities or changing family circumstances.

The central task of policy in this area is not just to widen participation in post-compulsory learning, but to develop lifelong learning career routes. One project within the programme reports that credit-based learning, as practised by the London Open College Network, successfully opened up opportunities for participation and progression to previously under- represented groups. The majority of new learners were female, unemployed and from ethnic minorities. The researchers, Pat Davies and John Bynner, argue that what is now needed is a *national* credit framework "to bring the idea to fruition and fully exploit the possibilities offered, and in particular to underpin the status of qualifications acquired in this way" (Chapter Three, this volume). Another of their findings reinforces the conclusions arrived at in the previous section on learning at work: employers were still accounting for less than 1% of student registrations. In contrast, 7% were undertaking credits through trade unions.

Gareth Rees and his colleagues summarise this debate by claiming that the economic model "which currently underpins official versions of the learning society in Britain is not compatible with the realities of actual patterns of participation in lifelong learning and their determinants" (Chapter Five, this volume). This conclusion takes us neatly on to the next general theme.

An over-reliance on human capital theory

The election of the new Labour Government in 1997 has not broken the continuity in thinking with previous Conservative administrations on one matter of significance: official policy on education, training and employment has continued to find its justification in an over-simplified version of the theory of human capital. One quotation will have to suffice here, but similar claims can be found in each and every major policy paper issued by the Labour government in this area. The following quote comes from the first White Paper issued after the election:

> Investment in learning in the 21st century is the equivalent of investment in the machinery and technical innovation that was essential to the first great industrial revolution. Then it was physical capital; now it is human capital. (DfEE, 1997, p 15)

Consider for a moment that statement in relation to BMW's sudden dis- investment in the Rover Group. Arguably, it was the accumulation of chronic weaknesses, such as the repeated failures to invest in the most advanced machinery, in robotic technology and product innovation, rather than any lack of skills or flexibility on the part of the workforce, which precipitated the crisis. Indeed, in an earlier attempt to save jobs in 1997, workers accepted 'super flexible' working patterns. If the UK is to act as if it were trying to become a learning society, then official policy must move beyond simplistic nostrums which distort both industrial and educational policy and delay the advent of more comprehensive strategies (see Coffield, 1999 for a more detailed critique). The transformative potential of lifelong learning is in danger of degenerating into training to serve the interests of global capital.

One of the principal *leitmotivs* running through the chapters in these two volumes is that current policy texts are making a fundamental mistake in characterising all learners as if they were calculating human capitalists, intent on maximising personal benefits and minimising personal costs and risks via learning. Three examples from projects studying very different populations will reinforce this point.

Sheila Riddell, Stephen Baron and Alastair Wilson studied the meaning of the learning society for adults with learning difficulties and collected considerable evidence that "the veneration of human capital has deleterious consequences for people at the margins of society" (Chapter One, this volume). The government's stated aim of rebuilding the welfare state around work (DSS, 1998), by which is meant 'paid employment', has created a climate where learning is judged according to 'rates of return', and people are evaluated according to their employability and their capacity to deliver added value to the economy. One could be forgiven for inferring that the political objective is to create the *working* rather that the *learning* society. In such an atmosphere:

> ... people with learning difficulties appear a poor investment, limited in learning and less productive than non-impaired workers. Such reasoning lies behind the current, socially excluding, policy dichotomy of 'work for those who can; welfare for those who cannot'. (Riddell et al, Chapter One, this volume.)

In other words, a policy which was introduced to tackle social exclusion is, in practice, having exactly the opposite effect, as those on the borderline between work and welfare, and who wish to be employed, are pushed back into welfare. The researchers use strong language to depict this policy as "a powerful source of injustice in excluding people from the mainstream of contemporary society" (Riddell et al, Chapter One, this volume).

Further sharp criticism is added by Stephen Ball, Meg Maguire and Sheila Macrae, who studied one inner-city education and training market in London for 16-19 year olds and became concerned that:

> ... while the rhetoric of *The Learning Society* is inclusive in its aims and intentions, some young people would fall outside the range and scope of what was provided. Our findings have supported this concern. The policy texts of *The Learning Age* almost exclusively portray learners as an undifferentiated mass with the same kinds of capabilities, motivations and levels of support and encouragement, as if they were all equally ready and able to take the opportunity to upskill. The uneven distribution of relevant 'capitals' (eg social, economic, cultural, human) and differences in acquired learning identities are set aside. (Ball et al, Chapter One, Volume 1)

In similar vein, the findings of Jenny Hewison, Therese Dowswell and Bobbie Millar's study of the continuing education of nurses in the National Health Service (NHS) also failed to support human capital theory (see Chapter Five, Volume 1). In terms of the motivations of individuals, participation in continuing education seemed to be *less* to do with updating, or a desire to do their jobs better, or to earn more money; it had *more* to do with obtaining a qualification, because of feelings of personal inferiority as a result of the overall upgrading of qualifications in the NHS. This project also found that the individuals who respond to managerial pressures to upgrade their qualifications are then expected to 'pick up the tab', a finding which serves to introduce the next section. An important question remains unanswered, however: why does the theory of human capital continue to grip the political imagination and hold such widespread populist appeal? At one level, there is a kernel of truth in the notion. At a deeper level, the powerful everywhere have found in human capital a discourse which serves their purpose, namely, to shift the responsibility for, and the costs of, learning away from the state and employers and onto individuals.

The shifting of responsibility to individuals

Policy in both the UK and in the European Union has for some years given the pivotal role in constructing the learning society to individuals, and there are obvious financial incentives for governments to act in this way. Meanwhile, the Confederation of British Industry (CBI) continues its campaign to transfer some of the costs of training from employers to individuals, as can be seen from its latest publication on employability: the first recommendation reads "Help individuals take more responsibility for learning" (CBI, 1999, p 1).

This continuous pressure from employers and the state for individuals to assume greater responsibility has not been matched by any suggestion that they be accorded more rights. And yet, as Phillip Brown and colleagues have argued, lifelong education could be treated "as a citizenship right, like social security and pensions" (Brown et al, 1997, p 33). Interestingly, David Ashton and his colleagues point out in the final chapter of this volume that individuals *have* indeed responded over the last 20 years to public exhortations to take more responsibility, as reflected in sharply rising participation rates among 16 and 17 year olds and among university entrants. The onus is surely now on politicians and policy makers to accord European citizens an entitlement to a minimum level of attainment and not just an entitlement of so many years of initial education (see McIntosh and Steedman, 2000).

A predictable outcome of devolving to individuals the need to become and to remain employable by means of lifelong learning is an intensification of existing differences between individuals. Tony Edwards extends the point by arguing that such a policy is likely:

> ... to disadvantage those young people whose value to potential employers is low, and who are poorly positioned as buyers in an education-training market which is complex, competitive, hierarchical and offers providers few or no financial incentives to recruit young people likely to be hard to handle. (Edwards, 2000: forthcoming, p 8)

An appropriate response, he adds, would be to provide employers with financial incentives to train those considered to be of least worth in the training market.

The burden of the evidence collected by projects within the programme suggests that policies based on, and justified by, individualised notions of opportunities to learn, and responsibilities for seizing them, at times become over-simplified, deeply unfair and counterproductive. Over-simplified, because the major government initiatives in lifelong learning – Individual Learning Accounts, the University for Industry and the National Grid for Learning – are all targeted at individuals, without any consideration of the social determinants of participation, as discussed in a previous section. Deeply unfair and counterproductive, because the policy is likely to "systematically disadvantage certain sectors of the workforce previously targeted as training priorities: women and the less well qualified" (Hewison et al, Chapter Five, Volume 1). Within the NHS, training is increasingly offered to employees in their own time, who then 'choose' to take up or decline this 'opportunity'. Individual choice, however, is constrained because 'not taking the opportunity' is generally interpreted as a sign of lack of commitment to work. As the researchers comment:

> By these means, structural inequalities in access are turned into attributes of individuals. They cease to be problems and become useful selection devices in decisions relating to recruitment, promotion or availability of future training opportunities. (Hewison et al, Chapter Five, Volume 1)

One of the policy implications stemming from this project is that the *time* implications of current policies on lifelong learning must be re-examined. Individuals are being actively encouraged to take greater responsibility for their own learning with support from government and employers. However:

> Support is generally discussed in terms of financial support, as in the concept of individual learning accounts. Support in terms of time for learning has been relatively ignored in discussion to date … women in particular have very little spare time when they seek to combine paid work with bringing up a family. (Hewison et al, Chapter Five, Volume 1)

This concentration by the state and employers on the micro level of individuals may also result in the relative neglect of the meso level of civil society, of institutions, and of the beliefs and practices of those who work in them; this reflection moves the discussion on to our next theme.

There's precious little society in The Learning Society

Such is the emphasis on learners as sovereign individuals that it is at times easy to forget that politicians and policy makers aspire to create a learning *society*. In short, there is precious little about society in all the rhetoric about the learning society, and yet "contemporary change is as much social as it is economic in character" (Chisholm, 2000, p 3). It is important not to overstate the case. After all, determined efforts have been made to combat social exclusion by the new Labour government; unemployment, for instance, has been reduced by over a million in the last three years, youth unemployment has been reduced from over half a million in the 1980s to around 50,000 now, and the New Deal deserves some of the credit for the latest steep reductions. Moreover, 1.2 million children will have been lifted out of poverty by 2002, mainly as a result of the tax credit for working families. These are substantial achievements which will do much to foster social inclusion.

Three comments are apposite: first, the proposed measures will significantly reverse the trend set in the previous two decades, during which the numbers of those in poverty rose sharply to the highest levels in the European Union, but they will still leave a further two million children in poverty (Piachaud, 2000). Second, one only has to scratch the surface of policies on social exclusion for the strategy of rebuilding the welfare state around paid work to reappear. The recent merger of the 400 benefit agency offices and the 1,000 job centres is part of the same reform programme of welfare via work. Third, at a more fundamental level, the policy of integrating excluded people into society by altering their 'deficient' characteristics is flawed. The argument is forcibly put by David Byrne:

> ... exclusion is not a property of individuals or even of social spaces. Rather it is a necessary and inherent characteristic of an unequal post-industrial capitalism founded around a flexible labour market and with a systematic constraining of the organisational powers of workers as collective actors. (Byrne, 1999, p 128)

The corollary which Byrne draws immediately is that, if social exclusion is an inherent process of post-industrial capitalism, then policies directed only at the excluded will fail.

The irony, according to Zygmunt Bauman, is that current government policy is based on creating greater social cohesion by means of paid employment at the very time we are moving "from a society guided by the work ethic to one ruled by the aesthetic of consumption" (Bauman, 1998, p 2). His argument is that the poor who in the past played the role of the 'reserve army of labour' are today re-cast as 'flawed consumers'. The reserve army[10], however, shows no signs of disappearing, and serves to remind those in work that they are not irreplaceable. Moreover, the government's project of sharply dividing 'those who can work from those who cannot' is more reminiscent of 19th-century attempts to separate the 'deserving' from the 'undeserving' poor, because it suggests that finding paid employment is a task which is under the control of individuals.

It should therefore come as no surprise that two of the projects sought to explore the emergent theory of social capital, which stresses the embeddedness of education, training and employment in social networks. Another virtue of the social capital perspective is that it challenges the standard discourse which treats poor people and poor economies as 'deficits' and "allows theorists, policy makers and practitioners to take an approach based on 'assets'" (Woolcock, 1999, p 7).

For one research team the attraction of social capital was that it:

> ... has much greater potential for fostering the inclusion of people with learning difficulties than does the deficit model of human capital. People with learning difficulties can participate in networks of norms and trust and may also act as a catalyst for the formation of such. (Riddell et al, Chapter One, this volume)

Social capital versions of a learning society carry the potential for greater inclusion, but societies with strong networks may base their solidarity on the exclusion of vulnerable and feared groups, and so offer no guarantee of inclusivity. Most provision for people with learning difficulties, whatever its rhetoric, was found by Sheila Riddell and her colleagues to segregate and exclude. The more inclusive forms of provision (for example, supported employment) employ the rhetoric of both human and social capital to justify their existence, but were found to be somewhat marginalised and under-funded.

It is tempting to believe that stronger social networks and more inclusive practices are still to be found in rural areas, in some rustic idyll where local communities are more caring. Although a few examples of effective family and kinship networks were found in the rural area studied, some extremely old fashioned practices were also uncovered (for example, one man who had been chopping wood for 20 years had become so bored by the task that he did not notice there was no wood under his axe). The service in the city proved to be more progressive, and at least attempted to make contact with local communities, even if the attempt did not work out well in practice.

People with learning difficulties challenge the seriousness of our intentions to create an inclusive society. For instance, the researchers found, in sharp contrast to the inclusive rhetoric, adults with learning difficulties in "socially excluded groups, confined to segregated settings, undergoing mandatory and continuous training as a form of social warehousing" (Riddell et al, Chapter One, this volume). And, they add, as the category of special needs continues to expand, this tactic may be applied to more and more people – perhaps to those who cannot find paid employment no matter how hard they try. Ivan Turok and Nicola Edge have pointed out, for instance, the 'jobs gap' in Britain's cities, by which they mean the large-scale loss of full-time male, manual jobs (Turok and Edge, 1999). Endless retraining and upskilling will not create appropriate employment for such would-be workers.

For John Field and Tom Schuller the concept of social capital had a different use – it helped to explain the level and quality of continuing education and training in Northern Ireland and Scotland. They define social capital as the networks, norms and trust in a community and found, for instance, that it was strongly associated with a marked preference among adults for informal rather than formal learning:

> In Northern Ireland particularly, dense local ties shape patterns of lifelong learning in a number of ways. They work to secure a remarkably high level of initial education, but may have inhibited demand for formal adult education and training.... Particularly in a divided community, in which access to desirable resources such as employment and security are widely regarded as a zero-sum game, such conservatism is a way of managing the risks that are inherent in any process of change. (Field and Schuller, Chapter Two, this volume)

The important corrective being offered by this research is that levels of trust can be low, networks can be narrow and norms can be unambitious: "researchers and policy makers need to acknowledge the down side as well as the up side of social capital" (Field and Schuller, Chapter Two, this volume). This means that, in an audit of a local community's stocks of social capital, the liabilities must be assessed as well as the assets.

The ESRC programme has played its part in contributing to the current explosion of interest in social capital and its potential for reducing poverty and social exclusion. For example, Stephen Baron, John Field, Sheila Riddell and Tom Schuller have demonstrated the relevance of the work of American researchers like Robert Putnam and Mark Granovetter to debates on lifelong learning in this country. This trend is likely to intensify in the coming years when attempts are made to replicate in this country the intriguing notions of Michael Woolcock, who argues that what he considers to be the three basic dimensions of social capital – bonds, bridges and linkages – are all necessary for generating sustainable economic development. By 'bonds' he means the ties to immediate family members, close friends and professional colleagues; 'bridges' refer to making connections with more distant associates and acquaintances which may, for instance, provide information about job opportunities; and 'linkages' entail "forging alliances with sympathetic individuals in positions of power" (Woolcock, 1999, p 8). Woolcock claims that the poor have plenty of 'bonding' social capital, but meagre amounts of both 'bridging' and 'linking' social capital which are needed for success; these forms of capital can, however, be acquired. Such fruitful new theory has practical significance for the attempts of local Learning and Skills Councils and local Learning Partnerships to regenerate their communities in the UK.

The centrality of learning for a learning society

It has frequently been remarked that academics will, with great application, study everything under the sun apart from the processes under their own noses, namely, how they teach and how their students learn. One outcome is that we do not possess even the outlines of an adequate social theory (or theories) of lifelong learning, which is a necessary precondition for the creation of a learning society. This is by far the most significant gap in our present state of knowledge, and one which will plague the practice of lifelong learning until it is addressed. Such a social theory would minimally consist of the following two dimensions: first, an understanding of the kinds of information, resources, opportunities, activities, social conditions and participation in the social practices needed for learning; and second, an understanding of the historical production and transformation of different learner identities and of the ways in which communities of adults reproduce themselves (see, for instance, Lave and Wenger, 1991). It is to be hoped that the new ESRC research programme on Teaching and Learning sparks a renewed interest in the central concept

---

of learning among those professionals who should be acknowledged experts in these processes.

Two projects within the programme studied different features of higher education (HE), namely, innovations in teaching and learning, and the development of skills for employment. A few of their most important findings are quoted before any general conclusions are drawn.

Andrew Hannan, Harold Silver and Susan English, reflecting on the influential roles that graduates play in the world of work, point out that policy documents, for all their intense interest in all other aspects of HE, "showed no interest, however, in *how* people learn, and the implications of their passive or active learning for their future roles in society" (Chapter Four, this volume; original emphasis). Three overlapping phases or types of innovation were identified: *individual innovation* (enthusiasts pushing forward new ideas); *guided innovation* (supported by funds from national programmes); and *directed innovation* (driven by institutional imperatives). The issues uncovered by this project, however, go beyond the immediate processes of teaching and learning:

> Fundamental is the frequent realisation that, for one reason or many, in very many contexts the old ways are not working, and that what are needed are new ways to sustain motivated learners who are more autonomous and more able to take responsibility for their own continued learning. (Hannan et al, Chapter Four, this volume)

Notice that shifting the responsibility for coping with change onto individuals is not confined to government or industry. The transfer of the risks generated by economic restructuring to individuals appears to be a general quality of 'disorganised capitalism' (see Brown and Lauder, 1996). Anthony Giddens (1994) uses the term 'manufactured uncertainty' to describe the result of attempts to cope with modern dislocations between knowledge and control. Damage limitation in the face of new, manufactured uncertainties is fast becoming a way of life in British universities and further education (FE) colleges as, for instance, financial risks are transferred to staff on short-term contracts.

The second project examined how the kind of generic skills widely perceived as important for economic performance are being taught in higher education (HE) and in industry. Elisabeth Dunne, Neville Bennett and Clive Carré conclude as follows: "There is little evidence, even from university teachers committed to the development of these skills, that their espoused or actual theories of teaching are underpinned by understandings of learning theory, or that they intentionally teach for transfer" (Chapter Three, Volume 1). As a consequence, they call for a programme of professional development for all academics to ensure that they possess some theoretical and practical understanding of how students and graduate employees learn.

Two of the other projects – Stephen Ball's team in London and Gareth Rees' in Cardiff – independently developed from their data typologies of lifelong learners and the similarities in their classifications are quite striking, although there are also differences, as one would expect given the very different contexts. The London project, which was studying 16-19 year olds, identifies five crude and flexible categories: the embedded, notional and pragmatic acceptors, hangers-in and outsiders. The Welsh team constructed five lifelong learning trajectories from the education and training histories of a sample aged 15 to 64: lifelong, delayed, transitional, non-participant and immature (those still at school). The two categories at either end of the London continuum – the embedded and outsiders – closely resemble their Welsh counterparts, namely, 'lifelong learners' and 'non-participants'. The acceptors, both national and pragmatic, who view education purely as a means of getting a job, have much in common with the 'transitional learners', who continue with education and/or training only during the period immediately after leaving school. Hangers-in are described as low achievers on vocational courses with poor results from their GCSE exams: whether this group is similar to those on the 'delayed' trajectory who return to education and/or training after the age of 21 remains to be seen. These empirically derived typologies constitute a significant contribution to the concept of 'learner identities', and are an advance upon earlier categorisations.

New inequalities

The slow progress being made in the UK towards a Learning Age "simply exposes more sharply than ever the contradictions between our public discourses of democracy and social justice and the painful realities of precisely the reverse" (Chisholm, 2000, p 5).

The last 20 years, and especially the last 10, have witnessed substantial increases in the rates of participation in post-compulsory education and training. That solid success has had an unfortunate side-effect, which is well summarised by the House of Commons Select Committee on Education and Employment: "the substantial improvement in overall participation during the last two decades has widen[ed] the gap between the educational 'haves' and the 'have nots'" (1999, para 169). To quote Lynne Chisholm again, throughout Europe "the costs of being knowledge-poor are higher and more far-reaching" (2000, p 5), not only for gaining employment, but also for participating in the democratic process. It is this realisation that prompts the European Commission to talk of a "social rift" and of "several categories of the population being left by the wayside" (EC, 1995, p 62).

A number of projects reported the emergence of new divisions: for example, in the labour market, Ashton et al point out that "such a substantial section of the labour force as female part-timers [are] without access to the means of enhancing their skill levels" (Chapter Six, this volume); the polarisation being created by policy which separates those who can find work from those on welfare who cannot, so that adults with learning difficulties who in the past were ideal workers for certain types of jobs are now retained in endless 'circuits of training' (see Riddell et al, Chapter One, this volume); and changes in the pattern of further training at work which systematically disadvantages those adults with young children (Hewison et al, Chapter Five, Volume 1). In short, in a number of places projects have found evidence of the increasing polarisation among women in employment between those in full-time, high-skilled jobs and those confined to part-time or temporary work in the secondary labour market.

Phil Cooke and his team point specifically to the care sector in Britain, which is widely perceived as female, low-skilled and under-paid. In contrast to Germany "where the term *Beruf* (vocation) carries the image of an occupation for life that applies to all ranks in the hierarchy of occupations, from crafts to professions" (Heinz, 1999, p 8), and where care staff are fully qualified members of a profession, their counterparts in this country combine low status, poor pay and restricted career opportunities with low motivation for training (see their chapter in Volume 1 for a fuller account of this interacting set of inequalities which will prove very difficult to break into). Both Jenny Hewison et al's study in the NHS, and John Field and Tom Schuller's in Northern Ireland and Scotland, emphasise the higher structural barriers confronting women, some of which are long standing and some of which are new. The picture, as always, is blurred and confusing. For instance, Field and Schuller describe how gender and locale combine to generate very considerable variations in attainment with, for instance, more than double the percentage of girls in the Orkney Islands than boys in North Lanarkshire obtaining the highest academic grades.

Similarly, Pat Davies and John Bynner point out in Chapter Three of this volume that the London College system of credit-based learning was more successful than traditional forms of provision in attracting more women than men (by a ratio of 2:1), more unemployed than employed and more people from minority ethnic groups. However, the credits awarded to those learners are not generally valued as highly as the more traditional qualifications, and a *national* credit framework is required to underpin the status of such alternative forms of learning if we are to avoid exchanging old inequalities for new ones.

Stephen Ball, Meg Maguire and Sheila Macrae sum up the dialectic between old and new inequalities in this way:

> The expansions of further and higher education, and the economic upheavals and changes in the distribution and nature of work which they reflect, do change class relations and reproduction of social class in significant ways but not absolutely. The links between class, education and work are significantly re-worked – as they were at other moments of rapid economic restructuring – but not dissolved. They are reassembled differently, perhaps more loosely but it would be a mistake to see social class as somehow now irrelevant or contingent. What we are seeing *is* a break down of *some* of the stark and obvious class divisions of the past in post-16 education and employment but nonetheless some of these divisions obstinately remain and there is the emergence of a more fuzzy, more complex hierarchy with new markers of differentiation. (Chapter One, Volume 1; original emphasis)

Lessons from elsewhere in Europe

One of the main objectives of the programme was to develop a strong comparative dimension and, in particular, to learn from two types of comparison. First, the education and training systems in England, Northern Ireland, Scotland and Wales were interestingly different when this research programme began in 1994, and policies and debates on learning have since diverged even more. Second, some projects set out to assess the relative strengths and weaknesses of a particular system (eg adult guidance) within the UK against those of their European counterparts.

One project employed both types of comparison and developed a conceptual framework to enable it to compare different strategies for unifying academic and vocational learning in Britain with those in the rest of Europe (see Spours et al, ChapterTwo,Volume 1). Within the UK, the more evolutionary, consensual and consultative process in Scotland, compared with England, has resulted in a more "open version of a unified system, but its lack of an explicit vision may lay it open to strategy drift" (Spours et al, Chapter Two, Volume 1). This research project tested the intriguing hypothesis that policy making for a unified system may need to be a more top-down process, and so it proved in Scotland:

> ...it was a centrally-led, managed process, and the consultations, although genuine, were exercises in a form of 'democratic centralism' in which those who lacked the ability of centrally-based policy makers to take a view of the whole system found it hard to play a constructive role. (Spours et al, ChapterTwo,Volume 1)

When the unification strategies in England, Scotland and Wales were compared with similar European developments, some shared British characteristics became more apparent. First, British strategies are essentially qualification-driven, with qualifications acting as a proxy for quality. Second, workplace learning is more marginal to the strategies of all three British systems than in many European countries. The researchers stress the long-term significance of this neglect:

> No worthwhile vision of the learning society can ignore the enormous potential for learning provided by the workplace, especially if this is integrated with learning in other settings; yet even certified workbased learning remains marginal within the current unifying policies, let alone the less formal kinds of learning at work. (Spours et al, Chapter Two, Volume 1)

The comparative project directed by Will Bartlett and Teresa Rees was based on the belief that lifelong learning will require lifelong guidance, particularly when job mobility begins to affect more and more workers. They quote approvingly the criticism that "The citizen of Europe has better information when choosing a hotel or a restaurant than when choosing a type of training" (EC, 1995, p 34). Four English (and one Scottish) localities were chosen to study the impact of reforms on guidance services for adults; these were then compared with guidance systems in France, Germany, Italy and the Netherlands.

The international comparisons enabled the researchers to identify five alternative organisational and funding options, the first of which will be briefly mentioned here. Unlike the decidedly patchy and fragmented provision for adults in the UK, France organises well-resourced guidance services for adults, financed by an employer levy system. Since 1978, for instance, employees have had the right to take a leave of absence once every five years for a period of training and skills assessment. The implications for policy in this country are spelled out by the researchers:

> A possible route for the introduction of a variant of this system in the UK might be through the introduction of a guidance component for the Learning Accounts proposed by the Labour government. In the version promoted by the TUC these would be financed by both employer and employee contributions. (Bartlett and Rees, Chapter Four, Volume 1)

Elliot Stern, Kari Hadjivassiliou and Isabelle Darmon studied innovations in continuing vocational training (CVT) in the UK, France and Spain. The absence of a national, obligatory system in the UK for the planning and funding of CVT increased the importance of innovators – "internal champions of innovation who skilfully mobilise support and build coalitions across a company" (Stern et al, 1999, p 14). By contrast, in France, the concern was to check flexibility as well as to organise solidarity, with a levy on employers paying for the training of unemployed young people. In Spain, the contrast with the UK is even greater: a new regulatory framework for company training has been developed by the social partners and power has been decentralised to the regions and localities. Is it possible for the new Learning and Skills Council to learn from the experiences of Spain, which demonstrate both the complexity of issues which some policies in England over-simplify and that a wide range of political options exist?

A number of other projects also contained a strong comparative dimension. For example, Pat Davies' comparison of credit-based systems in London and Northern France drew attention to some key differences between the two. First, in France individuals have *rights*, and institutions (colleges, universities and employers) have *obligations* (Davies, 2000). These individual rights apply not only to guidance services but to the accreditation of prior learning and work-based learning, to a skills audit and to continuing education financed partly by employers. Moreover, the French system is tied to national qualifications, which confer status but constrain flexibility in the choice of subjects that can be studied, whereas the decentralised London system maximises the flexibility of subject choice, at the cost of the status of the qualification. These examples show that rather different and more democratic visions of the learning society are being developed elsewhere in Europe.

It is also not widely appreciated in the UK just how far other countries in Europe and beyond are outstripping our attempts to create a culture of lifelong learning. For instance, in comparison with paramedical staff in the NHS in the UK, who receive five days in-service training per year, in Denmark all employees are currently entitled to six weeks educational leave per year, which includes two weeks vocational training: "To avoid conflict between the employers and unions they agreed that both employees and employers were able to describe the skills they needed" (Ashton et al, 2000, p 8). Apart from the much greater investment in all workers, it is the model of reaching agreement among *social partners* that we so urgently need to reintroduce into this country.

Above all, researchers within the programme began to appreciate that lifelong learning is playing an increasingly central role in the policies of the EU, which aims to create a citizens' Europe. Lifelong learning has become the explicit overarching rationale for the new generation of EU policies on education, employment and culture. Certain words and phrases appear and re-appear throughout the policy documents of the European Commission and these are emphasised here by putting them in italics: *lifelong learning* has been identified as the main means of creating *active citizens* in a new *Europe of knowledge*. The explicit aim is to build human capital, but as a means to increased participation in social, cultural and political affairs as well as improving economic competitiveness; but just as in the UK the emphasis has been firmly on the latter, to the comparative neglect of the former. Whether EU policies on lifelong learning will lead to an attenuation or an exacerbation of social inequalities in life chances remains to be seen. What is already clear is that researchers in the UK need to monitor closely developments in European thinking and practice, which currently include drawing up a European Charter of Basic Skills and using the networks of civil society to create a European Area for lifelong learning.

So what is to be done?

Reviewing the work of the programme might have produced a dreary list of bullet points for future policy, but that approach was so roundly criticised by constructive colleagues that it was discarded. Instead, an approach more in keeping with the title of these two volumes – *Differing visions of a Learning Society* – will be attempted. Two options will be presented which will depict the probable and some possible (and perhaps preferable) futures for lifelong learning in the UK.

The first option, entitled *Full steam ahead, but where to?*, extrapolates existing trends, policies and practices into the next five to ten years. These projections are based as closely as possible on the findings from *The Learning Society Programme*, on the main tendencies identified by the projects, and on other cognate evidence from similar research projects, rather than on any wishful thinking or pessimistic predictions on the part of the present author. A detailed understanding of the present and of the past is one of the prerequisites for shaping the future.

The second option, called *Democracy instead of Technocracy*, draws its inspiration from reflecting on the combined set of policy implications, informed by evidence and suggested by the projects; it proposes different ways of thinking about a learning society than those currently on offer from all the political parties. It offers an alternative future, or rather, a kaleidoscopic array of options, the evidence for which readers can assess for themselves. Again, a self-denying ordinance has been imposed on the flights of fancy and hobby-horses of the author and the extrapolations find their source in the empirical work of the projects, other empirical studies of lifelong learning, and the literature in the field.

First option: *Full steam ahead, but where to?*

As this is being written, a radically new structure for post-16 learning is being prepared within the DfEE, which is simultaneously driving through a policy for primary and secondary schools of 'continuous improvement'. This latter notion comes from the Japanese industrial practice of *kaizen*, which in the manufacture of motor cars has been criticised as the technique whereby "worker know-how is continually being transferred to management" (Garrahan and Stewart, 1992, p 77). The new framework of continuous improvement, which, as the name suggests, repeatedly and deliberately both increases the challenges and tightens the means of accountability, has recorded considerable successes so far. For instance, the national literacy and numeracy strategies at primary level are steadily pushing up the percentages of pupils achieving national standards in English and Maths. The principles behind the notion of *kaizen* are now being applied to "the transformation of secondary education and the modernisation of the teaching profession" (Barber, 2000, p 23). The detailed and expensive proposals to strengthen leadership in schools and to provide teachers with greater support and professional development provide further evidence of a comprehensive and cohesive strategy which is likely to drive up standards still further in primary and secondary schools. The strategy, to use nautical metaphors, cannot be described as 'steady as she goes', but rather as 'full steam ahead'. Or, to change the metaphor, it is a 'ratchet model of change' to ensure that the reforms become "irreversible" (Barber, 2000, p 24).

It may appear churlish and ungrateful to question this determined bid to produce "a world class education service: one which matches the best anywhere on the planet" (Barber, 2000, p 24), especially when this ambitious project and the White Paper on *Learning to Succeed* (DfEE, 1999) are compared with the policy framework for lifetime learning produced by the previous Conservative administration in 1996 – a 30-page discussion of the main issues which was *devoid of any proposals for policy* (DfEE, 1996). However, such sweeping reforms as proposed by the present government deserve to be publicly debated (see Coffield, 2000, for a more detailed critique).

Some of the language used to introduce these plans prods the critical faculties awake; for example, one of the most important innovations, which apparently ensures both quality and cost-effectiveness, is described as "precision-targeting of professional development" (Barber, 2000, p 24). It should be remembered that the topic under discussion is not the precision engineering of the latest saloon to roll off the production line, but the continuing professional education of highly qualified professionals.

So the first question which needs to be asked of the national strategy is: 'Full speed ahead, but where to?' What is the destination? What kind of education system and what kind of society is it likely to create? The stated aim is the 'modernisation' of the teaching profession, a suitably flexible word for a flexible world, but is it possible that the profession will be 'modernised' by, for instance, linking pay and performance, without improving either the effectiveness of teachers or the quality of students' learning? In short, the national strategy is more likely to intensify the current slide into the *performative* society, where the maximisation of performance becomes the highest good, and where the transformative power of education is reduced to the increasingly rigorous measurement of inputs and outputs. The apotheosis of this approach is the claim of the High Reliability Schools project, which is co-directed by David Reynolds, a government advisor, to deliver failure-free schooling: "Schools get it right first time, every time. Pupils succeed every time" (*Project Newsletter*, Autumn 1998). Again, the parallel with modern motor manufacture is uncanny, as can be seen from Peter Wickens' account of Japanese management practices at the Nissan car plant in Sunderland, where "commitment to a zero defect product is absolute" (1987, p 61). Such an approach in education would certainly have its advantages because it would dispense with the need for inspectors, but is it seriously being suggested that creative, critical thinkers – lifelong learners – can be 'produced' in the same way as a Nissan Micra? Robert Graham who powerfully presents the case for the concept of the "good enough school" argues that:

> The essential mistake [in government thinking] lies in making the assumption that the outcomes of educational processes are measurable products, and in basing policy and practice on that assumption. (1998, p 175)

The panoply of measures which have been applied to primary and secondary schools are now being brought to bear on Further Education (FE) and higher education (HE). Ken Roberts has commented on the historic repetition in the UK of the pattern in vocational education and training of sustained critique followed by radical change: "We seem to lurch from reform to reform only to end up with much the same weaknesses as before" (Roberts, 2000, p 3).

The unrelenting focus on performance indicators, ever tougher targets, output-related funding and league tables – all the official trappings of a performative society – is certainly increasing the provision of education and training, but the attendant risk is that "the UK will veer towards the US model of higher participation rates but with much education and training being of dubious value" (Fevre, 1997, p 1). Indeed, Patrick Ainley argues that "rather than a learning society, the current direction of learning policy moves towards a certified society" (Ainley, 1999, p 3). Instead of implying that the over-examined society may need to be officially 'certified', it may be better to talk of the 'certificated society' or the 'credentialist society'. Whatever the term to be used, we are in danger of producing more and more students who are intent on increasing their credentials rather than their understanding, who have not internalised a love of learning, and who sit in serried rows listening to "unwanted answers to unasked questions" (Popper, 1976, p 40). It is Ralph Fevre's contention that such a utilitarian orientation towards education and training "gets in the way of economic success" (Fevre, 1997, p 24).

So there is likely to be an intensification of the present policy of *enforcing* change on the education and training system by means of legislation and regulation, while *encouraging* industry, and especially small and medium-sized enterprises (SMEs), politely but ineffectually, to invest more in training their workers. The long, dishonourable tradition of attributing economic weakness to educational failure is most likely to be maintained also. The choice of educational scapegoat becomes a matter of tactics and expediency, and is influenced by the constant need for new victims who can be blamed for Britain's low productivity: the FE sector is the next most obvious candidate for this role.

This deep contradiction in the differential treatment of education and industry at least has the merit of revealing that the government has no single, explicit and developed model of how change can be implemented – an unfortunate failing in a government so keen to 'modernise' large tranches of British society. Michael Barber, the head of the Standards and Effectiveness Unit at the DfEE, is alive to the criticism: "The sustained drive from central government is perceived as an entirely top-down reform with its associated pressures to conform, whereas all evidence suggests that successful reform requires a combination of top-down and bottom-up change" (Barber, 2000, p 24). Moreover, the Chief Inspector of Schools, Chris Woodhead, recently admitted: "We ignored [the teachers] in drawing up the National Curriculum and we must ensure that we don't repeat the mistake in our attempts to create the Learning Age" (Woodhead, 2000, p 3).

The key weakness in educational reform has been a marked absence of a feedback loop between practitioners and policy makers. Alan Brown and Ewart Keep, in a review of research on vocational education and training (VET) in the UK especially commissioned by *The Learning Society Programme*, describe this feature of the national policy scene which refers not just to VET but to all of education:

> The opinions of those who are required to implement and make work
> the policy initiatives have generally not been seen as valuable, particularly
> if they have been located within the education system. (Brown and
> Keep, 2000, p 15)

The same disregard for the implementors of 'top-down' policy is evident throughout government. Witness the proposal which would have required police officers to frog-march potential lager louts and football hooligans to cash machines to enable them to pay on-the-spot fines. The only problem was that those who would have had to enforce the policy considered it unworkable – the police.

The technocratic imposition of lifelong change is likely to have another serious impact on education; it may further sharpen the existing polarisation in attainment among students. Within the programme, Stephen Ball and his colleagues documented how "the A-level route continues to dominate and drive the post-16 system [which] now caters for many more people, including a broader, more diverse clientele [but] ... remains strongly segmented by the status of routes and the status of students" (Chapter One, Volume 1). Sheila Riddell and her colleagues also claimed that the government discourse of "work for those who can, welfare for those who cannot" is inherently polarising and a "powerful source of injustice", affecting all those who inhabit the debatable territory between the two policies (Chapter One, this volume). Similarly, Peter Robinson and Carey Oppenheim (1998) have convincingly demonstrated that the unintended outcome of providing teachers with incentives to concentrate on those pupils capable of obtaining five or more higher grade GCSEs (A*-C) has been the corresponding neglect of those students with few or no qualifications.

Or contrast the rhetoric of the Prime Minister with the reality found in one post-16 education market in London. At the Labour Party Conference in September 1999, Tony Blair made 'true equality' his goal for the UK, a term he defined as the creation of a society in which every individual is recognised as being of 'equal worth'. In an inner-city area, Stephen Ball and his colleagues describe an "economy of student worth", based on class, race and gender; for instance, some students (eg white, middle-class girls) were highly valued and competed for by educational institutions, but others (eg black, working-class boys) were less desirable and found their choices constrained (Chapter One, Volume 1).

The government is right to take credit for the significant drop in the percentage of students leaving school with no qualifications (now less than 6%). There are, however, schools, especially in the inner cities, where less than 20% of 16 year olds achieve five GCSEs (A*-C), while the private schools in the same cities are registering 96 and 98% success rates. Such extreme inequalities of outcome, repeated year after year, are the mark of a society which is becoming dangerously polarised. Even the most rigorous framework of continuous improvement in educational standards will fail the most disadvantaged students, unless it is integrated with an equally well-resourced and determined policy to combat poverty, unemployment, job insecurity and social exclusion; that is the unequivocal conclusion of those projects specialising in this area. The policy of publishing such league tables may yet prove to be of value, but *only if* it results in robust policies to tackle such unjustifiable, unacceptable but remediable inequality.

Other present trends are likely to continue, and may well intensify. The market principle is likely to be applied more rigorously, despite the evidence from, for example, Stephen Ball and his colleagues (in Chapter One, Volume 1) that in the post-16 sector, the former cooperation among institutions has disintegrated, competition has become cut-throat, and students have become secondary to the requirements of the market by being recruited to courses inappropriate to their needs. The language of the market has begun to corrupt the thinking of some educationalists, as can be gauged from the comment of one senior researcher who described the process of dissemination in education as "identifying target audiences, developing appropriate products and delivering the products to the targets" (name withheld to protect the guilty). The drive to widen participation is likely to continue to concentrate on removing structural barriers (eg costs, time and lack of childcare), despite the evidence from Gareth Rees and his colleagues that the removal of such barriers is a *necessary* but not a *sufficient* condition, because the social determinants of participation occur so early in the life course (see Chapter Five, this volume). Moreover, the criticisms from a number of projects about the official over-reliance on a simplistic version of human capital will most likely be ignored – after all, the powerful in all countries are all singing the same simple tune, so how could *they* be wrong? Finally, the economic imperative (competitiveness, global markets) will continue to lord it over the democratic imperative (social justice, citizenship), although many honeyed words will be used to pretend that both are being held in a 'dynamic equilibrium'. Jenny Hewison's study of the 'modernisation' of training in the NHS showed that the social and psychological costs to certain groups of staff (mainly women with young children) of managerial decisions need to be added to the economic calculus of such changes. To these women, lifelong learning had become a lifelong anxiety (Chapter Five, Volume 1).

Further negative trends could be identified and listed, but it is time to call a halt; after all, dystopia can become addictive and is almost certainly bad for the digestion. But one parting shot cannot be resisted. The technical rational approach, which lies at the heart of the government's project of wide-scale 'modernisation', assumes that there *is* a technical solution to the complex problems which beset us and that the future *can* be controlled. Michael Power's study of the 'audit society' concludes more humanely and more optimistically that:

> ... individuals are infinitely more complex and adaptable than normalising attempts to measure and control them; a substantive, messy rationality always reasserts itself over formal, technical rationality. (Power, 1997, p 120)

Second option: Democracy instead of Technocracy

The main aim in presenting an alternative set of possible futures is to show that the present clutch of policies are the consequences of particular political *choices* and not the result of immutable and inevitable laws of economics. In Pierre Bourdieu's words, the objective is to break "the appearance of unanimity which is the greater part of the symbolic force of the dominant discourse" (Bourdieu, 1998, p viii).

Let us begin with some principles, some minimum conditions for democracy. Basil Bernstein, who is the source of the following, argues for three democratic rights to provide everyone with a stake in society:

- the *individual* right to enhancement. Not simply the right to personal, intellectual, social and material advancement, but the right "to the means of critical understanding and to new possibilities" (Bernstein, 1996, pp 6-7);
- the *social* right to be "included, socially, intellectually, culturally and personally" (Bernstein, 1996) and to be different, to be separate, if desired;
- the *political* right to participate not just in discussions but in civic practice which has outcomes. "It is the right to participate in the construction, maintenance and transformation of order" (Bernstein, 1996).

The immediate attraction of this approach is that it lends itself to empirical enquiry. For instance, do *all* citizens receive and enjoy such rights? Is there an unequal distribution of these rights? The first task of the second option would be to embed these principles in all our institutions and in civil society more generally.

There is space here to develop only a small part of one of the above notions, namely, the need for 'critical understanding'. The debate over which knowledge, skills and attitudes will be required in the 21st century has recently become a battlefield, with some very curious interventions. For example, an influential commentator, Charles Leadbeater, has written a new book, *Living on thin air: The new economy* (1999), which, according to Peter Mandelson, "sets out the agenda for the next Blair revolution". Briefly, Leadbeater argues that the goal of a learning society "should be to maximise the production and distribution of knowledge", because "this process of creating, disseminating and exploiting new knowledge is the dynamo behind rising living standards and economic growth" (Leadbeater, 1999, p 222 and p 8). But what is the role of education, according to Leadbeater, in this new knowledge society? It would be logical to suppose that schools, colleges and universities become the central institutions in a knowledge-driven economy, introducing each new generation to the creation as well as the transmission of knowledge. Not a bit of it! Leadbeater believes that "the point of education should not be to inculcate a body of knowledge, but to develop capabilities" (Leadbeater, 1999, p 111). In other words, he proposes the modish but vacuous notion of a content-free curriculum, all capabilities and no subjects. If Leadbeater's advice were to be accepted, as it has been so often by New Labour in the past, knowledge, which in the economy has apparently become not just *a* resource but *the* resource, would become a *scarce* resource in education. This overt attack on subject knowledge is, irony of ironies, conducted in the interests of creating a knowledge-driven society: and such radical change is, again, advocated without reference to any hard evidence or research findings.

Luckily, there exists a body of research knowledge which enables us to turn 'learning to learn' from a fashionable phrase into a daily praxis. Guy Claxton (1999) reviewed the latest psychological research on learning and concluded that 'learning to learn' consists of three key components which are crudely summarised below:

- resilience – the ability for sustained engagement and for tolerating uncertainty;
- resourcefulness – employing a range of learning tools and strategies, for example, intellectual and practical skills, imagination and intuition;
- reflectiveness – standing back from learning and taking a synoptic, reflexive view.

These powers of learning are clearly and engagingly described, but one key ingredient is missing – critical understanding, or in the vernacular, the ability to detect bullshit and the moral courage to expose it. In addition to a solid grounding in the major disciplines, citizens of the 21st century will require a healthy scepticism, a critical faculty to enable them to insist on politicians, experts of all kinds, and teachers and researchers providing evidence and reasoned argument rather than promotional hype. In short, the literacy hour in primary schools needs to produce pupils who can criticise and go beyond the literacy hour. And 'a spiral curriculum' on the theory and practice of learning needs to run through our educational careers from primary to tertiary education and beyond like a message in a stick of rock.

In the second option, a broad and generous definition of lifelong learning will be adopted in practice which will, for instance, make some types of informal learning eligible for public funding and will not downgrade recreational or non-utilitarian adult learning (for example, the learning of foreign languages as a hobby). Such generosity will be extended to all kinds of learners, their abilities and their potential, so that instead of an over-concentration on academic ability, the capacity to apply knowledge, personal and social skills, motivation, commitment, courses of unified academic and vocational learning and critical understanding will all be celebrated (see Hargreaves, 1984; and Ken Spours et al, Chapter Two, Volume 1).

Other discontinuities and divisions will be removed: for instance, John Field and Tom Schuller found in Northern Ireland and Scotland, for all their relatively higher levels of attainment in *initial* education, a fixed and rather conservative view is taken of *adults*: "people are, educationally, what they have achieved by the time they leave school; change and development are neither expected nor desired" (Chapter Two, this volume). Similarly, Ken Spours and his colleagues argue that "the persistence of academic/vocational divisions reflects assumptions about the limited capacity to learn of those for whom vocational programmes are thought appropriate" (Chapter Two, Volume 1).

A variety of social theories of learning will be developed to provide school teachers, college lecturers and university tutors with a theoretical understanding of how they and their students learn, and of the social and cultural influences on that learning; and in this way the status of the teaching profession may slowly begin to rise, as its members become not only subject specialists, but experts in learning and pedagogy and their intimate connections with social control. Slowly, the tenacious hold of the old, ineffective system of transmission and assimilation as a model of teaching and learning begins to lose its grip. Independent, high quality lifelong guidance becomes available to all adults, no matter where they live and no matter whether they study in FE or HE. Indeed, the second option will seize the historic opportunity, missed by the Dearing Report on HE, to replace the divisive binary line between further and higher education with a tertiary system that celebrates diversity. Students in the near future will not only move from further to higher education, but from higher education back to further education for continuing professional and vocational development, thus improving the status of FE colleges.

The aim of policy becomes not just to widen participation in post-compulsory learning, but to develop clear lifelong learning routes which replace the discontinuities, deviations and dead-ends of the past. Commenting on the growing contrast between the well-defined pathways open to A level students and the indistinct routes available to those with few educational qualifications, Tony Edwards has summarised their relative prospects as follows:

> In short, those who might benefit most from clear structures are the least likely to find them, are most at risk of 'drifting' unaided, and are also forced to make potentially critical choices much earlier than contemporaries for whom extended full-time education provides a respectable 'waiting-room' in which they can delay decisions and look around. (Edwards, 2000: forthcoming, pp 4-5)

As Stephen Ball and his colleagues argued as a result of their findings (in Chapter One, Volume 1), a national strategy for lifelong learning needs to begin at three rather than sixteen and, in this regard, the government's Sure Start policy is most welcome but needs to become national in its remit and to be far more generously resourced. But in the DfEE, in the universities and in professional practice, education is dealt with in distinctive phases (from pre-school to adult education) and still more divisions are being created by the Learning and Skills Council which will establish two powerful committees, one for 16-19 year olds and the other for adults. A new cadre of professionals, committed to lifelong learning, needs to be established who can take a synoptic view of the variety of paths taken by learners and who can press for the removal of the major pitfalls, which at present occur at 11, 16 and 18.

In the second option, lifelong learning becomes a collective responsibility of the state, employers and individuals, rather than an individual obligation. Lifelong learning also becomes a right of citizenship, with all citizens accorded an entitlement, backed by sufficient resources and opportunities, to a minimum level of educational attainment, a level which rises steadily. Those who benefited least from initial education become the first beneficiaries of such a proposal: after all, those who leave school in the year 2000 without qualifications will be hoping to be part of the workforce until at least their sixtieth birthday in 2044.

The second option also harnesses the power of new theory: for instance, the potential of social capital, if sustained and enriched, to reduce poverty, while countering its tendency to operate against participation in education and training (see Field and Schuller, Chapter Two, this volume); and the potential of workplace learning, always remembering that David Ashton and his colleagues point out (in Chapter Six of this volume) that around two thirds of the British workforce do not belong to organisations which systematically increase the skills of their employees. In a separate study of workplace learning, David Ashton et al show how different countries (the Netherlands, Denmark, Singapore and the USA) provide a variety of national frameworks to support it and the clear conclusion to be drawn is that the UK is being left behind. Singapore, for instance, which transformed its low skills economy to a high skills one within one generation, has a long-term national training plan, integrated with a strategy for economic development, and agreed with all the social partners. One component of the training plan is a Skills Development Fund, which offers tax incentives to employers and individuals to engage in lifelong learning, but also imposes a training levy on low-skills employment to encourage employers to move towards higher value-added production (see Ashton et al, 2000).

The main challenge is *not* to create "a glorious revolution in the relations between the individual and education" (Wicks, 2000, p 8), but between the state, business and education. To ensure that the UK breaks out of the low skills equilibrium, the state slowly learns to stand up to not only large multi-nationals, but also to medium and small businesses (SMEs) in the interests of the country as a whole. We shall not, however, develop a culture of continuous learning where none exists by passing the financial burden to SMEs; instead of using the meretricious slogan 'learning pays', we, the taxpayers, will have to pay them to learn and to catch the habit of learning. The state introduces legislation, based on substantial financial incentives for SMEs to train and, in return, all companies are held responsible for the social consequences of their actions. Such timely intervention prevents another ESRC research programme in 2010 recording the failure of the latest structural reform – the Learning and Skills Council – to change the culture of learning in most British firms.

The government implements Will Hutton's call for the annual publication by firms of a social audit, which explains their policies towards the workforce, the community and the environment; and this publication becomes "a legal requirement for a company being listed on the stock exchange" (Hutton, 2000). The new Parliamentary Act, *Lifelong learning for all citizens,* begins by tackling the exclusion of the new categories who currently make up the 'knowledge poor': all those in non-standard jobs, part-time workers (mainly women), disabled people and those with poor basic skills in and out of employment.

The design and organisation of work, and the challenges it presents, come to be seen as equally significant in creating a high skill labour force as the provision and content of formal training. Organisations begin to take seriously the research finding that managers can impede as well as facilitate learning in the workplace, and courses in management change from an emphasis on appraisal and performance indicators to creating a micro-culture which supports the informal learning of subordinates (see Michael Eraut, Chapter Seven, Volume 1).

The second option offers new possibilities to individuals, companies, institutions and governments, but also to society itself. At one level, the concept of a learning society is used reflexively to enable the UK to learn about itself and to evaluate progress: valid, reliable and comparable data on lifelong learning is published annually, to evaluate and monitor policy and to benchmark progress against that of our trading partners. The Learning and Skills Council, both nationally and locally, becomes democratically representative and accountable, and concedes that its first conception of 'empowerment' as more power to the centre was mistaken. At an intermediate level, a test of whether English society is serious about becoming a learning society will be whether it shows itself willing to learn not just from Germany and Japan, but also from Scotland and Wales which have already introduced, for example, a *national* credit framework. At a still higher level, a learning society begins to remake communities through the values of citizenship, democracy and social justice. As Stewart Ranson and John Stewart put it, "For us, a learning society is one which has to learn to become a different form of society if it is to shape the transformation which it is experiencing" (1998, p 253).

So far, the first law of change has been scrupulously adhered to; change is essentially a matter for other people, who appear to find it tiresome. What will be required of researchers in education and the social sciences more generally? Many comparative and multi-disciplinary research projects operate in practice like some multi-cultural societies, where the separate ethnic groups all live side by side but walk past each other in the street[11]. It is easier for, say, psychologists to criticise the theories, methods and findings of economists and sociologists than to adjust their own theories and methods in the light of advances made by other disciplines. The experience of directing *The Learning Society Programme* also suggests that researchers funded by the public purse have an obligation to develop their policy recommendations more than at present in order to meet policy makers half way. Claiming, for instance, that a particular finding has 'implications for funding' is of little help to anyone. We researchers simply need to know far more about the whole messy processes of policy formation and implementation, with all their attendant struggles, compromises and revisions. Moreover, David Hargreaves (1998) has called for a fundamental reconstruction of the relationship between university-based researchers and the 'subjects' of their studies, arguing that if, for example, teaching and learning are being investigated, then more of the research agenda should be concerned with the problems encountered and identified by 'front-line' practitioners, who should also carry out more of the research. Amen.

Coda

In the UK we have a veritable cornucopia of differing visions of a learning society to choose from. Only the leading contenders are listed here: the Audit Society, the Certified Society, the Credentialist Society, the Democratic Society, the Educated Society, the Flexible Society, the Flexploitative Society (a new French coinage), the Full Employment Society, the Information Society, the Knowledge Society, the Learning Society, the Market-led Society, the Networked Society, the Performative Society, the Post Industrial Society, the Post-Modern Society, the Privatised Society, the Socially Controlled Society, the Socially Just Society, the Virtual Society and the Working Society. Richard Sennett devotes the last chapter of his book *The corrosion of character* (Sennett, 1998) to the dangerous pronoun 'we'; it has prompted me to think that whatever vision or combination of visions of a learning society we end up with will depend not so much on Tony Blair, William Hague or Charles Kennedy as on you and me, on us[12].

Notes

[1] All the quotations in these paragraphs are taken from the book by Norman Longworth and W. Keith Davies (1996) and the sequel by Norman Longworth (1999), or from the publicity material issued by Norman Longworth for the 'First European Festival of the Learning City'.

[2] The first volume, also entitled *Differing visions of a Learning Society: Research findings*, was published by The Policy Press in July 2000 and contained the following articles: 'A critical analysis of the concept of a learning society' by Frank Coffield; 'Worlds apart – education markets in the post-16 sector of one urban locale 1995-98' by Stephen J. Ball, Meg Maguire and Sheila Macrae; 'Unifying academic and vocational learning in England, Wales and Scotland' by Ken Spours, Michael Young, Cathy Howieson and David Raffe; 'Skill development in higher education and employment' by Elisabeth Dunne, Neville Bennett and Clive Carré; 'The variable contribution of guidance services in different types of learning societies' by Will Bartlett and Teresa Rees; 'Changing patterns of training provision in the National Health Service' by Jenny Hewison, Therese Dowswell and Bobbie Millar; 'Working and learning in Wales and Germany: findings of a regional study' by Phil Cooke, Antje Cockrill, Peter Scott, John Fitz and Brian Davies; and 'Development of knowledge and skills at work' by Michael Eraut, Jane Alderton, Gerald Cole and Peter Senker.

[3] Readers may find it useful to see a complete list of all the 14 projects within the programme in case they wish to contact them directly:

(1) 'Education markets in the post-16 sector in one urban locale'
     Professor Stephen Ball, King's College, University of London
(2) 'Adult guidance and the learning society'
     Dr Will Bartlett and Professor Teresa Rees, University of Bristol
(3) 'Developing skills in higher education and employment'
     Professor Neville Bennett and Elisabeth Dunne, University of Exeter
(4) 'Training for multi-skilling: a comparison of British and German experience'
     Professor Philip Cooke, University of Wales, Cardiff
(5) 'The impact of credit-based systems of learning on learning cultures'
     Dr Pat Davies, City University and Professor John Bynner, Institute of Education, London
(6) 'Learning in the workplace'
     Professor Michael Eraut, University of Sussex

(7) 'Divergence between initial and continuing education in Scotland and Northern Ireland'
Professor John Field, University of Warwick and Professor Tom Schuller, Birkbeck College, London

(8) 'Learning, skills and economic rewards'
Professor Francis Green, University of Kent and Professor David Ashton, University of Leicester

(9) 'Changing patterns of training provision: implications for access and equity'
Dr Jenny Hewison, University of Leeds

(10) 'Unified learning project'
Professor David Raffe, University of Edinburgh and Professor Michael Young, Institute of Education, London

(11) 'Participation in post-compulsory education and training: a regional study'
Professor Gareth Rees, University of Wales, Cardiff

(12) 'The meaning of the learning society for adults with learning difficulties'
Professor Sheila Riddell and Stephen Baron, University of Glasgow

(13) 'Innovations in teaching and learning in higher education'
Professor Harold Silver, University of Plymouth and Dr Andrew Hannan, University of Plymouth

(14) 'Innovations in continuing and vocational training: a comparative perspective'
Mr Elliot Stern, The Tavistock Institute

[4] The first publication in the series, entitled *Learning at work* and published by The Policy Press, contains articles by Michael Eraut et al (on learning from other people at work); Davis Ashton (on learning in organisations); Peter Scott and Antje Cockrill (on training in the construction industry in Wales and Germany); Reiner Seibert (on jobrotation); Kari Hadjivassiliou et al (on Continuous Vocational Training); and Stephen Baron et al (on what the learning society means for adults with learning difficulties).

[5] The second report, entitled *Why's the beer always stronger up North? Studies of lifelong learning in Europe*, contains some cross-national observations on lifelong learning by Walter Heinz (Bremen); an article on adult guidance services in Europe by Teresa Rees and Will Bartlett; a chapter on different models of Continuous Vocational Training in the UK, France and Spain by Isabelle Darmon and colleagues; a comparison of credit-based systems of learning in London and

Northern France by Pat Davies; a study of the links between initial and continuing education in Scotland, Northern Ireland and England by Tom Schuller and Andrew Burns; a comparison of policy strategies to reduce the divisions between academic and vocational learning in England and Scotland by David Raffe and colleagues; and reflections on devising and conducting cross-national studies in the social sciences by Antje Cockrill and colleagues.

[6] The third report, entitled *Speaking truth to power: Research and policy on lifelong learning*, contains two overview articles on the impact of research on policy (by Frank Coffield and Maurice Kogan); a chapter on the impact of the manager on learning in the workplace (by Michael Eraut, Jane Alderton, Gerald Cole and Peter Senker); a study of a post-compulsory education and training market in one urban locale in London (by Stephen Ball, Sheila Macrae and Meg Maguire); an examination of the policy implications of changes in training of NHS staff (by Therese Dowswell, Bobbie Millar and Jenny Hewison); the first findings from a major new survey of the skills of a representative sample of British workers (by Alan Felstead, David Ashton, Brendan Burchell and Francis Green); and, finally, a paper on the provision of adult guidance services in England (by Will Bartlett and Teresa Rees).

[7] The fourth report argues for a fundamental reassessment of the significance of informal learning. Under the title of *The necessity of informal learning*, it consists of five articles as follows: a seminal, theoretical piece by Michael Eraut on non-formal learning, implicit learning and tacit knowledge in professional work; an essay on informal learning and social capital, by John Field and Lynda Spence, drawing on their empirical research in Northern Ireland; a study of implicit knowledge in the training of people with learning difficulties by Stephen Baron, Alastair Wilson and Sheila Riddell; a report on the impact of accreditation on formalising learning by Pat Davies; and an historical and sociological analysis of necessary and unnecessary learning in the acquisition of knowledge and skills in and outside employment in South Wales in the 20th century by Ralph Fevre, Stephen Gorard and Gareth Rees.

[8] These brief summaries from *The Learning Society Programme* are available in two forms. A set of summaries in hard copy is available, free of charge while stocks last, from Frank Coffield, Department of Education, University of Newcastle, St Thomas' Street, Newcastle upon Tyne, NE1 7RU. The same summaries are also available from the programme's website, whose address is: http://www.ncl.ac.uk/learning.society. The website provides more detailed information on publications by individual projects, as well as by the programme as a whole.

———

[9] The researchers used a definition of learning which was not restricted to education and training as conventionally understood. Their definition was broken down into six types of 'taught' learning (eg courses leading to qualifications or skills, evening classes etc) and four types of 'non-taught' learning (eg studying for qualifications on one's own, supervised training at work, or keeping up to date by reading books etc).

[10] Pierre Bourdieu pushes the argument further, " … the term 'army' is inappropriate, because unemployment isolates, atomises, individualises, demobilises and strips away solidarity" (Bourdieu, 1998, p 98).

[11] A good example of inter-disciplinary work can be found within the programme, where the strengths of the different approaches to the analysis of skills at work taken by economics, sociology and occupational psychology were combined in a new methodology for the Skills Survey (1997). See Chapter Six, this volume.

[12] I am grateful to John Bynner, Bruce Carrington, Pat Davies, Kathryn Ecclestone, Tony Edwards, Francis Green, Andy Hannan, David Raffe, Gareth Rees, Sheila Riddell, Tom Schuller, Harold Silver and Geoff Whitty for their helpful comments on an earlier draft of this introduction. As this is the final joint publication from the programme, I would like to record my thanks to the ESRC and in particular to Geoff Whitty, Oliver Fulton and all members of the Steering Committee, and to the ESRC officers, Ros Rouse and Alex Monckton. Three secretaries have worked for me at various times since 1994 and I would like to thank them all – Dorothy Smith, Jane White and Jill Hughes. My main intellectual debt is to the projects, from which I learned a great deal. It is a privilege to have one's work commented upon by so many good minds; it is also the best way to learn. At the start of the programme these researchers were either professional colleagues or quite unknown to me; they have since become personal friends. The building of social capital in this way should be considered one of the positive outcomes of the programme.

References

Ainley, P. (1999) *Learning policy: Towards the certified society*, Basingstoke: Macmillan.

Ashton, D., Powell, M. and Sung, J. (2000) *National frameworks for workplace learning*, London: Institute of Personnel and Development.

Ball, C. (1998) *Motivating the excluded*, London: Campaign for Learning.

Barber, M. (2000) 'High expectations and standards for all – no matter what', *Times Educational Supplement*, 7 July, pp 22-4.

Bauman, Z. (1998) *Work, consumerism and the new poor*, Buckingham: Open University Press.

Beinart, S. and Smith, P. (1998) *National adult learning survey, 1997*, London: DfEE.

Bernstein, B. (1996) *Pedagogy, symbolic control and identity*, London: Taylor and Francis.

Blunkett, D. (2000) 'Influence or irrelevance: can social science improve government', Secretary of State's ESRC lecture, 2 February, London: DfEE.

Bourdieu, P. (1998) *Acts of resistance: Against the new myths of our time*, Cambridge: Polity Press.

Brown, A. and Keep, E. (2000) *Review of vocational education and training research in the United Kingdom*, EUR 19243, Luxembourg: Office for Official Publications of the European Communities.

Brown, P. and Lauder, H. (1996) 'Education, globalization and economic development', *Journal of Education Policy*, vol 11, no 1, pp 1-25.

Brown, P., Halsey, A.H., Lauder, H. and Wells, A.S. (1997) 'The transformation of education and society: an introduction', in A.H. Halsey, H. Lauder, P. Brown and A.S. Wells (eds) *Education: Culture, economy and society*, Oxford: Oxford University Press, pp 1-44.

Byrne, D. (1999) *Social exclusion*, Buckingham: Open University Press.

CBI (Confederation of British Industry) (1999) *Making employability work: An agenda for action*, London: CBI.

Chisholm, L. (2000) *The educational and social implications of the transition to knowledge societies*, (forthcoming).

Claxton, G. (1999) *Wise up: The challenge of lifelong learning*, London: Bloomsbury.

Coffield, F. (1999) 'Breaking the consensus: lifelong learning as social control', *British Educational Research Journal*, vol 25, no 4, pp 479-99.

Coffield, F. (2000) 'Lifelong learning as a lever on structural change? Evaluation of White Paper: Learning to Suceed: A new framework for post-16 learning', *Journal of Education Policy*, vol 15, no 2, pp 237-46.

Cooke, P., Cockrill, A., Scott, P., Fitz, J. and Davies, B. (2000) 'Working and learning in Britain and Germany: findings of a regional study', in F. Coffield (ed) *Differing visions of a learning society: Research Findings*, Volume 1, Bristol: The Policy Press, pp 199-229.

Davies, P. (2000) 'Rights and rites of passage: crossing boundaries in France', *International Journal of Lifelong Education*, vol 19, no 3, pp 215-24.

DfEE (Department for Education and Employment) (1996) *Lifetime learning: A policy framework*, London: DfEE.

DfEE (1997) *Excellence in schools*, Cm 3861, London: The Stationery Office.

DfEE (1999) *Learning to Succeed: A new framework for post-16 learning*, Cm 4392, London: The Stationery Office.

DSS (Department for Social Security) (1998) *A new contract for welfare: New ambitions for our country*, Cm 3805, London: The Stationery Office.

Edwards, T. (2000: forthcoming) *Transitions, trajectories and rational choices*, Working Paper for ESRC project 'Routes: Youth transitions in the North East', Newcastle: School of Education, University of Newcastle.

EC (European Commission) (1995) *Teaching and learning: Towards the learning society*, White Paper on Education and Training, Luxembourg: Office for Official Publications of the EC.

Eraut, M., Alderton, J., Cole, G. and Senker, P. (2000) 'Development of knowledge and skills at work', in F. Coffield (ed) *Differing visions of a Learning Society: Research Findings, Volume 1*, Bristol: The Policy Press, pp 231-59.

Fevre, R. (1997) *Some sociological alternatives to human capital theory and their implications for research on post-compulsory education and training*, Patterns of Participation in Adult Education and Training Working Paper no 3, Cardiff: School of Education, Cardiff University.

Field, J., Baron, S. and Schuller, T. (2000) 'Social capital and human capital revisited', in S. Baron, J. Field and T. Schuller (eds) *Social capital: Critical perspectives*, Oxford: Oxford University Press (forthcoming).

Finegold, D. and Soskice, D. (1991) 'The failure of training in Britain: analysis and prescription', in G. Esland (ed) *Education, training and employment*, vol 1, Wokingham: Addison-Wesley for Open University, pp 214-61.

Garrahan, P. and Stewart, P. (1992) *The Nissan enigma: Flexibility at work in a local economy*, London: Mansell.

Giddens, A. (1994) *Beyond left and right: The future of radical politics*, Cambridge: Polity Press.

Graham, R. (1998) *Taking each other seriously: Experiences in learning and teaching*, Durham: University of Durham, School of Education/ Fieldhouse Press.

Hargreaves, D.H. (1984) *Improving secondary schools*, London: Inner London Education Authority.

Hargreaves, D.H. (1998) *Creative professionalism: The role of teachers in the knowledge society*, London: Demos.

Heinz, W.R. (1999) 'Transitions to employment in a cross-national perspective', in W.R. Heinz (ed) *From education to work: Cross-national perspectives*, Cambridge: Cambridge University Press, pp 1-21.

House of Commons, Education and Employment Committee (1999) *Access for all? A survey of post-16 participation, vol 1: Report and proceedings of the committee*, London: The Stationery Office.

Hutton, W. (2000) 'It's time to rein in business, Mr Blair', *The Observer*, 9 April.

Kennedy, H. (1997) *Learning works: Widening participation in further education*, Coventry: The Further Education Funding Council.

Lave, J. and Wenger, E. (1991) *Situated learning: Legitimate peripheral participation*, Cambridge: Cambridge University Press.

Leadbeater, C. (1999) *Living on thin air: The new economy*, London: Viking.

Longworth, N. (1999) *Making lifelong learning work: Learning cities for a learning century*, London: Kogan Page.

Longworth, N. and Davies, W.K. (1996) *Lifelong learning*, London: Kogan Page.

McIntosh, S. and Steedman, H. (2000) *Low skills: A problem for Europe*, London: Centre for Economic Performance, London School of Economics.

Piachaud, D. (2000) 'Sickly youth', *The Guardian*, 29 March.

Popper, K. (1976) *Unended quest: An intellectual autobiography*, Glasgow: Fontana/Collins.

Power, M. (1997) *The audit society: Rituals of verification*, Oxford: Oxford University Press.

Ranson, S. and Stewart, J. (1998) 'The learning democracy', in S. Ranson (ed) *Inside the learning society*, London: Cassell, pp 253-70.

Roberts, K. (2000) 'Skill formation among young people: are we winning? The impact of successive waves of reform of vocational education and training in Britain', Lecture at Newcastle University, 30 March.

Robinson, P. and Oppenheim, C. (1998) *Social exclusion indicators*, London: IPPR.

Sargant, N. (1997) *The learning divide*, Leicester: NIACE.

Schuller, T. and Bamford, C. (2000) 'A social capital approach to the analysis of continuing education: evidence from the UK Learning Society research programme', *Oxford Review of Education*, vol 26, no 1, pp 5-19.

Sennett, R. (1998) *The corrosion of character: The personal consequences of work in the new capitalism*, NY: W.W. Norton

Stern, E., Hadjivassiliou, K. and Darmon, I. (1999) *End of award report*, Swindon: ESRC.

Tawney, R.H. (1924) *Secondary education for all: A policy for Labour*, London: The Labour Party.

Turok, I. and Edge, N. (1999) *The jobs gap in Britain's cities: Employment loss and labour market consequences*, Bristol/York: The Policy Press/Joseph Rowntree Foundation.

Wickens, P. (1987) *The road to Nissan: Flexibility, quality and teamwork*, Basingstoke: Macmillan.

Wicks, M. (2000) 'Lifelong learning', *Adults Learning*, February, pp 8-9.

Woodhead, C. (2000) 'Is lifelong learning a utopian ideal?', Annual Lecture, 29 February, London: OFSTED.

Woolcock, M. (1999) 'Managing risks, shocks and opportunity in developing economies: The role of social capital', World Bank Group, website: http://www.worldbank.org/poverty/scapital/library/woolcock.htm

The meaning of the Learning Society for adults with learning difficulties: bold rhetoric and limited opportunities

Sheila Riddell, Stephen Baron and Alastair Wilson

Background

In the ESRC's *Learning Society Programme* specification, the key concept of the learning society is defined as one "in which all citizens acquire a high quality general education, appropriate vocational training and a job (or series of jobs) worthy of a human being while continuing to participate in education and training throughout their lives" (Coffield, 1994). People with learning difficulties are particularly likely to experience social marginalisation and difficulty in accessing the labour market. It is therefore important to consider what opportunities the Learning Society is likely to hold for them, and to consider what can be learnt from their experiences which may be applicable to wider social groups. This was the central concern of our research. The structure of this chapter is as follows. We begin by outlining developments in a range of public policy arenas which all play a part in shaping the nature of the Learning Society for people with learning difficulties. Subsequently, we discuss findings from our interview survey which mapped lifelong learning services for people with learning difficulties in Scotland and their underpinning discourses. Finally, we discuss ethnographic case studies to explore the way in which dominant visions of the Learning Society shape the identities and lived experiences of people with learning difficulties.

Definition of learning difficulties employed in the study

Clinical definitions of learning difficulty identify approximately 4% of the population as falling into this category. The present study did not employ a medical, but rather adopted an operational definition, so that people were defined as having learning difficulties if they had been labelled in this way by service providers. Accordingly, learning difficulties included those with a background of a Record of Needs and/or special schooling, a small proportion of whom had little or no speech and had spent a significant proportion of their lives in long-stay institutions. In addition, the category included adults who had difficulty with coping skills, oracy, functional literacy and numeracy, estimated by professionals as up to one third of people in areas of social disadvantage (Riddell et al, 1998a). Young people from disadvantaged backgrounds who had missed a lot of school due to accident or illness were also categorised as having learning difficulties. It is suggested that the number of people with learning difficulties in the UK is increasing. From a medical perspective, it is suggested that the increase is due to the greater survival rates of very premature babies, many of whom have complex difficulties in later life. From a sociological perspective, it is argued that the increasing use of the category 'learning difficulties', and 'disability' more widely, is due to high levels of structural unemployment in the Western world. Describing young men as having learning difficulties both explains and justifies the exclusion of many from the labour market (Tomlinson, 1982). Stone (1984) points out that within societies which distribute money largely on the basis of earned income, disability offers an acceptable justification for the distribution of some resources on the basis of need. This results in the expansion of the category of disability, followed by government efforts to tighten definitions so that it does not become an unmanageable drain on resources.

Objectives

The main objectives of the project were:

- to explore the concept of the Learning Society and its expression in the policy and practice of a range of agencies including education, social work, Local Enterprise Companies and voluntary and user organisations;
- to map services provided by these agencies throughout Scotland;
- to assess the experiences of adults with learning difficulties at different points in their life cycle in relation to education, training and employment opportunities;

- to develop key theoretical debates about choice, barriers to full social participation and the attainment of adult status by people with learning difficulties;
- to develop ways of involving adults with learning difficulties in the research process in order to contribute to thinking about the development of policy and practice in the field of learning difficulties.

Methods

The research was carried out in two main phases. Phase one was a study of education, training and employment opportunities for people with learning difficulties in Scotland. Documentary analysis of policy texts was carried out and key informant interviews conducted with representatives of a range of agencies (see Riddell et al, 1997a, for a report of this phase of the work).

The interviews were carried out, mainly by telephone, in late 1996 and early 1997, hard on the heels of regional reorganisation in Scotland which created 32 unitary authorities, each with education and social work functions, in place of the 12 regional authorities. Eight authorities were reluctant to be interviewed because they felt that their policies were still in a state of flux. In addition, six of the 22 Local Enterprise Companies declined to be interviewed because they felt that their policies in relation to people with learning difficulties were insufficiently developed. Interviews were also carried out with informants from further education (FE), the Employment Service, Careers Service and the Scottish Office (inspectors of social work and education). Interviews with 10 user and voluntary organisations were also conducted. These organisations were selected to reflect a range of service provision and practice with regard to service planning. In particular, People First Scotland is an organisation of disabled people and AccessAbility describes itself as 'disability-led'. The aim here was to understand the perspective of user organisations rather than that of professionals.

In all, 80 semi-structured interviews were conducted, each organised into five domains: the nature and characteristics of services provided by agencies, the groups of people with learning difficulties for which services were intended, the underlying service ethos and the conceptualisation of the target population, the extent to which people with learning difficulties were offered choice and personal progression and the existence of competition with other services within a social market. These domains also formed the basis of the analysis which involved summarising responses under domain headings and thematising responses.

The second phase of the study, lasting over 18 months, consisted of case studies of 30 adults with learning difficulties in two authorities in Scotland (one urban and one rural), drawn from three age groups: the post-statutory education phase (age 16–23), the post-transition phase (age 28–35) and the middle to older age phase (age 40+). The case studies were selected to reflect the varied nature of the population in relation to gender, ethnicity, nature of impairment and level of contact with services and Table 1(a) and (b) summarise their key characteristics, the conduct of the fieldwork and the major life issues facing the individual.

Data gathered in relation to each case study consisted of both observation and interviews. At least 10 visits were made to each case study individual. The timing of each visit was carefully arranged to sample varied aspects of the person's life. For instance, the first visit might be to a person's morning placement in a Further Education College and the second visit to a person's social club in the evening. In most cases significant others in the person's life (eg parents, partners or keyworker) were also studied. Field methods ranged from participant observation (eg mountain biking and muffin making) through semi-structured interviews to the innovative use of visual techniques. The latter included one person making a video about her discharge from a long-stay hospital. Several people were given disposable cameras and were asked to photograph what was important in their lives. The photographs were used in later discussion. Symbol cards were used to explore the evaluations of a FE class by non-speaking young adults. The data from each case study were analysed in terms of the theoretical concerns of the project (prior and emergent) and each case was written up into a long pen portrait of some 10–15,000 words. These provided the basic material for subsequent writing for publication.

A particular feature of this research was its commitment actively to include people with learning difficulties in the research process. In addition to the methods outlined above, a formal research group of people with learning difficulties was convened to identify and explore issues relevant to their experience of the Learning Society and to disseminate findings through their networks. While useful in deepening the researchers' understandings of emerging themes, this process did not fulfil entirely the requirements of 'emancipatory research' and became, effectively, a 'focus group'. The lessons of this process are analysed in Riddell et al (1998b).

Table I (a): Case studies from urban area

Pseudonym	Age	Gender	Nature of impairment	Domestic circumstances	Primary responsible organisation	Main daytime placement	Primary context studied	Interviews conducted with significant others	Major issues
Fred	17	M	Communication disabilities	Home: mother	FE	FE College	FE class	Mother – course tutor – keyworker – observation of FE class	Mother withdrew permission for case study to continue. Whole FE class researched while studying Open University module 'Equal People'
Roger	17	M	Heart complaint and non-specific mild learning difficulties	Home: mother – partner and brother	Local voluntary organisation specialist training provider	LEC Skillseekers specialist training provider	Work placement	Voluntary organisation training manager – placement employer	Health problems and difficulties finding employment
Dean	17	M	Autistic spectrum	Home: parents – brother	FE	FE class	FE class – outdoor activities class	College tutors – parents	Need to find niche in which to use considerable IT skills
Regie	18	M	Non-specific learning difficulties – scarring as a result of an accident	Home – mother and three siblings	Local voluntary organisation specialist training provider	LEC Skillseekers specialist training provider	Work placement	Voluntary organisation training manager – placement employer	Continual training – difficulties in finding employment – viewed as suitable for marginal employment only

Table I(a): continued

Pseudonym	Age	Gender	Nature of impairment	Domestic circumstances	Primary responsible organisation	Main daytime placement	Primary context studied	Interviews conducted with significant others	Major issues
Kelly	19	F	Muscular dystrophy – non-specific mild learning difficulties	Home: mother – brother and sister	FE	FE class	Home – FE class	Mother – father – course tutor	Serious debilitating health problems – limit engagement with education and work
Martin	23	M	Down's syndrome – moderate learning difficulties	Home: parents and sister	Social work and FE	Adult resource centre/classes at college	FE class – adult resource centre	Mother – keyworker	Difficulties in becoming independent from home and day care
Mick	33	M	Down's syndrome – moderate learning difficulties	Home: elderly mother	Social work	Adult resource centre	Adult resource centre – FE class – dance class	Mother – keyworker	Over full timetable with only 2 hours work – benefits problems
Bobby	39	M	Non-specific moderate learning difficulties	Supported in own home by housing association	Social work and housing association	Adult resource centre and part-time work – via supported employment with job coaching	Adult resource centre – home – work	Keyworker – employer – voluntary organisation manager	Benefits difficulties permitting only 2 hours work per week and supported living difficulties – problems surrounding development of intimate relationships

Table I(a): continued

Pseudonym	Age	Gender	Nature of impairment	Domestic circumstances	Primary responsible organisation	Main daytime placement	Primary context studied	Interviews conducted with significant others	Major issues
Clare	43	F	Down's syndrome – moderate learning difficulties	Supported in own home by housing association	Social work	Adult resource centre with part-time work at weekends	Adult resource centre – home – FE classes – dance class – camera class	Social worker – keyworker – home support worker	Issues around legal status of Incapax preventing increased independence and work – value of employment to increasing social contacts
Ronald	44	M	Non-specific mild learning difficulties	Home: elderly mother	Employment Service	Supported employment – ES wage subsidy scheme	Work	Employer – union representative – manager of specialist voluntary organisation providing ES supported employment place	Rationalisation by employer leading to threat of disciplinary action and certification as disabled with ES intervention
Liam	47	M	Non-specific moderate learning difficulties	Home: brother and brother's family	Social work and voluntary organisation	Adult resource centre/voluntary organisation specialist training provider work programme	Work – adult resource centre – FE class – voluntary organisation recreation club	Keyworker – brother – voluntary organisation training manager	Failure of specialist training provider to cope with challenging behaviour

Table 1(a): continued

Pseudonym	Age	Gender	Nature of impairment	Domestic circumstances	Primary responsible organisation	Main daytime placement	Primary context studied	Interviews conducted with significant others	Major issues
Fiona	49	F	Non-specific moderate learning difficulties	Supported in her own flat (weekly visit)	Social work and voluntary organisation provided supported living	Adult resource centre/looking for employment with assistance of voluntary organisation	Adult resource centre – home – FE class	Social worker – support worker	Previously worked full-time now restricted by benefits problems to part-time – social life structured around activities of now deceased mother, need for new social opportunities
Basil	50	M	Non-specific moderate learning difficulties	Home: elderly parents	Voluntary organisation providing supported employment	Part-time work via supported employment through specialist training provider	Work – pub – voluntary organisation disco	Manager voluntary cafe – supported employment provider – employer	Social life organisation restrictions – benefits issues preventing increased hours of work
Bryce	55	M	Non-specific mild learning difficulties	Bed & Breakfast: social work registered	Social work	Adult resource centre	Adult resource centre – swimming – voluntary organisation recreational activities	Keyworker – landlady	Loneliness – difficulties of living arrangements – cycles of training

Abbreviations: Employment Service – ES, Further Education – FE, Department of Social Security – DSS.

Table I (b): Case studies from rural area

Pseudonym	Age	Gender	Nature of impairment	Domestic circumstances	Primary responsible organisation	Main daytime placement	Primary context studied	Interviews conducted with significant others	Significant analytical issues
Chris	18	M	Down's Syndrome – non-specific moderate learning difficulties	Home: parents	FE classes	FE	Home – FE classes – work placement	Mother – father – FE course tutor – placement employer	Benefits of FE – limited options post FE – subsequent return to day services
Maureen	20	F	Non-specific severe learning difficulties – severe mobility problems	Home: parents	Social work	Adult resource centre	Adult resource centre	Parents – manager adult resource centre	Ongoing serious health difficulties – problems of diagnosis – day services provision
Jack	21	M	Non-specific moderate learning difficulties	Home then supported accommodation	Social work	Adult resource centre	Adult resource centre	Keyworker at adult resource centre	Allegations of abusive within family resulting move to supported accommodation – death of parent ended case study prematurely
Lois	21	F	Non-specific mild learning difficulties	Home: with mother	LEC specialist training provider	Training for Work programme placement – then unemployed	Home – work – voluntary organisation specialist training provider	Mother – employer – manager voluntary organisation specialist training provider	Cycles of training – failure to gain employment – abusive relationships

Table I (b): continued

Pseudonym	Age	Gender	Nature of impairment	Domestic circumstances	Primary responsible organisation	Main daytime placement	Primary context studied	Interviews conducted with significant others	Significant analytical issues
Sally	21	F	Non-specific mild learning difficulties	Home: mother, father and brother	LEC specialist training provider	Skillseeker/ Training for Work/ ES supported employment – then unemployed	Work – home – jobcentre	Father – employer – manager voluntary organisation specialist training provider	Cycles of training – sporadic training and support – abusive relationships
Greg	26	M	Serious eczema – non-specific mild learning difficulties	Home: mother and sister	LEC specialist training provider	Full-time work – ES supported employment	Work	Father – supervisor at work – manager of voluntary organisation specialist training provider	Successful full-time employment – adaptive employer – benefits of ES supported employment
Imran	27	M	Down's Syndrome – non-specific moderate learning difficulties	Residential group home	Social work and voluntary organisation providing residential and day care	Adult resource centre/voluntary work – one morning per week	Adult resource centre – home – voluntary organisation recreational activities	Best friend – keyworker – mother	Dissatisfaction with day services/ difficulties in finding alternatives – depression
Mavis	27	F	Cerebral palsy – non-specific severe learning difficulties	Home: parents and siblings	Social work	Adult resource centre	Home – adult resource centre	Mother – keyworker at adult resource centre – social worker	Allegations of abusive by family – inadequacy of day services provision

Table 1(b): continued

Pseudonym	Age	Gender	Nature of impairment	Domestic circumstances	Primary responsible organisation	Main daytime placement	Primary context studied	Interviews conducted with significant others	Significant analytical issues
Lisa	27	F	Non-specific mild learning difficulties	Home: mother and father	Social work then voluntary organisation specialist training provider	Day services/ES work placement/ part-time voluntary work	Home – work placement – voluntary work placement	Parents – keyworker – 2 employers – voluntary organisation (employment support) manager	Withdrawal from inadequate day services – difficulties encountered in accessing ES/voluntary organisation work programmes
Kirsty	28	F	Non-specific moderate learning difficulties	Home: parents and sister	Social work	Adult resource centre	Adult resource centre – home – FE class	Parents – adult resource centre keyworker – course tutor	Increasing independence – lack of differentiated services preventing progression
Doris	33	F	Non-specific mild learning difficulties	Supported in own home by housing association	Social work	Adult resource centre – community education class – voluntary work	Home – adult resource centre – community education class	Boyfriend – community education worker – keyworker – home support worker	Lack of differentiated provision beyond day services to enable increased independence
Isa	41	F	Non-specific mild learning difficulties	Home: parents and brother	Community Education	Part-time work	Work – community education class	Community education class coordinator and course tutor – employer	Increasing independence

Table 1(b): continued

Pseudonym	Age	Gender	Nature of impairment	Domestic circumstances	Primary responsible organisation	Main daytime placement	Primary context studied	Interviews conducted with significant others	Significant analytical issues
Ewan	46	M	Non-specific mild learning difficulties	Residential group home	Social work and voluntary organisation providing residential and day care	Day services – part-time work	Home – adult resource centre	Keyworker – employer – adult resource centre staff	Restrictions on independence/ employment opportunities imposed by DSS/ social work/ voluntary organisation funding
Kate	47	F	Non-specific moderate learning difficulties	Home: shares with husband	Social work and specialist housing association	Adult resource centre/looking for part-time employment	Adult resource centre – home	Husband – keyworker	Supported in long-standing marriage and own home
Maud	56	F	Non-specific moderate learning difficulties	Group home: shares with three others	Social work	Adult resource centre	Adult resource centre	Keyworker at adult resource centre – home support keyworker	Lifetime in training
Ruth	67	F	Mild depression – non-specific moderate learning difficulties	Residential group home	Social work and voluntary organisation providing residential and day care	Day services/FE	Home – FE College – adult resource centre	Keyworker – FE College tutor	Difficulties adjusting to group home following 20 years in institutional setting – long-term treatment for depression – restrictive nature of residential care preventing increase in social networks formed at FE

The policy context

Lifelong learning opportunities for people with learning difficulties were delivered by a bewildering array of agencies including the Employment Service, Further Education, Adult and Continuing Education, Local Enterprise Companies, social work departments, NHS Primary Care Trusts and voluntary organisations. Other agencies, such as the European Social Fund, were not involved in delivery but played a major role in funding innovations. In addition to the education, training and employment policy arena, the experiences of people with learning difficulties were shaped by health, social security, social work and community regeneration strategies. All agencies expressed commitment to 'normalisation' of people with learning difficulties (O'Brien, 1987) through participation in mainstream activities. However, tensions within and between agencies, fuelled by contradictory elements within the notion of a learning society (Coffield, 2000) frustrated this goal. In this section, we describe the broad thrust of policy emanating from a number of key agencies and then consider their degree of congruence or disjunction.

Lifelong learning policy

The theme of lifelong learning has become increasingly prominent in government policy, signalled in the publication of a number of policy texts (Scottish Office, 1998; DfEE, 1998, 1999). Lifelong learning is portrayed in these texts as the key to individual and national economic prosperity, and, of secondary importance, as the means of nurturing social networks, fostering social cohesion and improving the quality of life for all. The document *The Learning Age: A renaissance for a new Britain* (DfEE, 1998), for example, begins by setting out the rationale for a human capital version of the Learning Society:

> Learning is the key to prosperity – for each of us as individuals, as well as for the nation as a whole. Investment in human capital will be the foundation of success in the knowledge-based economy of the twenty-first century. This is why the Government has put learning at the heart of its ambition. (DfEE, 1998, p 7)

This thinking is informed by Becker's (1975) human capital theory, subsequently developed by Coleman (1988), Putnam (1995) and Fukuyama

(1995). Human capital theory suggests that individuals are rational beings motivated by economic self-interest which leads them to participate in lifelong learning and justifies state expenditure in this area. The reductionist view has been criticised on the grounds that investment in education and training may be necessary, but is certainly not sufficient, to produce economic growth (Edwards et al, 1993; Maguire et al, 1993; McNabb and Whitfield, 1994; NIACE, 1994) and that people participate in education and training for a range of reasons including the desire to acquire qualifications and because of intellectual curiosity, not just financial self-interest (Fevre, 1996). The Learning Society is seen by some critics as an ideological concept, designed to blame those who have been deprived of education, training and employment (Hughes and Tight, 1995; Coffield, 1999). Tett (2000), for instance, argues that the Learning Society is a gender-blind concept which fails to take account of the systematic exclusion of some groups of women from training and work-based learning.

Alternative readings of a learning society suggest that the generation of social capital, the network of reciprocal social relations which leads to social cohesion, should be seen as a worthy end in itself. *The Learning Age: A renaissance for a new Britain*, for example, states:

> As well as securing our economic future, learning has a wider contribution. It helps make ours a civilised society, develops the spiritual side of our lives and promotes active citizenship. Learning enables people to play a full part in their community. It strengthens the family, the neighbourhood and consequently the nation. It helps us fulfil our potential and opens doors to a love of music, art and literature. That is why we value learning for its own sake, as well as for the equality of opportunity it can bring. (DfEE, 1998, p 7)

Societies high in social capital may not be idyllic places for all and indeed may base their cohesion on the exclusion of feared and despised social groups (Durkheim, 1938; Wolfensberger, 1972; Riddell et al, 1999b). However, there is much evidence that the veneration of human capital has deleterious consequences for people at the margins of society. Whereas it might be argued from a social capital perspective that disadvantaged groups need additional support to compensate for previous exclusion and injustice, a human capital perspective would suggest that there should be only minimal investment in such individuals because of their limited power to compete in the market place. This minimal investment approach can be traced through a range of official reports on 'the problem' of disabled people. The Egerton Commission, for instance, commented:

> It is better for the state to expend its funds on the elementary education of the blind, than to have to support them through a life of idleness.
> (Egerton Commission, 1889, cited in Tomlinson, 1982, p 13)

To summarise thus far, lifelong learning policy in the UK is informed predominantly by human capital theories, portraying individuals as driven by economic rationalism. Learning society discourse tends to assume that learning is open to all and that all learners are alike, thus ignoring historical patterns of exclusion. Social capital theories of a learning society occur as a substratum within lifelong learning policy. Acting as a counterforce to human capital theory, social capital theory suggests that expenditure on education, training and employment does not require an economic justification, but rather is essential to the nurturing of cohesive social relationships. As we shall see below, both human and social capital versions of the Learning Society influence the nature of education and training services delivered to people with learning difficulties.

Community care policy

Within community care policy, there is a strong commitment to provision for people with learning difficulties in 'homely settings within the community' and to the provision of services reflecting 'normal life principles'. There is also an ambition to empower consumers by providing a 'mixed economy of care' (Secretaries of State for Health, Social Security, Wales and Scotland, 1989), with a range of services provided by the public, private and voluntary sectors. Inter-agency working is regarded as of paramount importance in providing services and in facilitating choice. The shift from segregated to mainstream services is underlined strongly in recent policy documents such as the Scottish Executive's review of services for people with learning disabilities (Scottish Executive, 2000) and Glasgow City Council's strategy for people with learning disabilities (Glasgow City Council, 2000). The latter document states:

> Substantial investment in a range of providers to develop employment opportunities for people with learning disability in Glasgow will take place. A target of creating 500 jobs for people with learning disability

will be set over the next three years. Such opportunities should be available for all, regardless of level of disability or complexity of need. (Glasgow City Council, 2000, p 31)

Although official policy documents lead us to expect a considerable degree of overlap between lifelong learning and community care policy, our key informant interviews suggested that in practice services delivered by social work insulated people with learning difficulties from mainstream services (see below).

Health policy

The emphasis on normalisation[1] and inter-agency working has meant that new agencies have become involved in the formulation of policies on education, training and employment. For instance, the NHS generally made provision for people with significant learning difficulties in long-stay hospitals. With the closure of such institutions, health boards have had to consider how they can best meet the health needs of people with learning difficulties in the community (Barnes, 1997; Espie et al, 1999). In line with wider health policy (Scottish Office Department of Health, 1999), which construes health in terms of general wellbeing and not just the absence of sickness, health agencies have been forced to consider the types of services likely to promote or compromise health. Since employment is regarded as having largely positive effects on people's mental and physical wellbeing, health agencies have entered into collaboration with social work, housing and voluntary sector organisations. For example, a Glasgow City strategy, endorsed by health and social work, expresses commitment to the expansion of employment opportunities for people with learning difficulties regardless of "level of difficulty or complexity of need" (Glasgow City Council, 2000, p 31). There is an ongoing tension between health service providers and advocates of community care. While (almost) everyone is happy to see the demise of long-stay hospitals (Stalker and Hunter, 1999), there is a fear that people with learning difficulties will not be treated well in mainstream services, where, for example, some GPs allocate four minutes per surgery consultation. The argument is made that there is still a need for some specialist primary care services targeted at people with learning difficulties (Espie et al, 1999).

Social security policy

The operation of community care policy is closely linked to the benefits system, which in turn connects with employment policy. The Green Paper *New ambitions for our country: A new contract for welfare* (DSS, 1998) expressed a commitment to tackling worklessness and removing barriers to employment arising from the benefits system. Disabled people and those with a long-term illness were identified as being one of the principal beneficiaries of "rebuilding welfare around the work ethic" (DSS, 1998, p 3). In order to encourage these developments, the Department of Social Security (DSS) introduced Personal Adviser schemes in pilot areas to advise and assist disabled people in obtaining employment. A number of new work incentive measures were also introduced to counter existing disincentives. A study conducted by some of the authors as part of the National Disability Development Initiative (Wilson et al, 2000) suggested that disabled people were suspicious of any change which might alter their benefits status, and were particularly concerned at having to 'retake' the All Work Test, which determines whether an individual is fit to work or not. One of the DSS's work incentive measures, referred to as the '52 week linking rule', was designed to ensure that individuals who entered jobs but left them during the course of a year could return to their original benefits status. Our study of Employment Service programmes (Wilson et al, 2000) suggested that people with learning difficulties and their families simply did not believe that the 52 week rule would be applied fairly and believed that entering employment was tantamount to giving up entitlement to benefits.

Another work incentive measure having a particular impact on people with learning difficulties concerned 'therapeutic earnings'. This rule states that individuals on Income Support with severe disablement allowance are allowed to work for 16 hours a week without losing benefit. Any additional work undertaken may have devastating financial consequences and may threaten the individual's status as permanently disabled. In this way, what is billed as a work incentive measure may act as a powerful disincentive to greater economic activity (see Simons, 1998 for further discussion of the complexities of the benefits system for people with learning difficulties). In a later section, we discuss in more detail the way in which individuals' benefits packages influence their willingness to participate in lifelong learning.

Employment and training policy

Employment and training policy in the UK has a somewhat cumbersome structure. The Employment Service, an agency of the DfEE, has responsibility for employment programmes whereas responsibility for training rests with Local Enterprise Companies (LECs) in Scotland and Training and Enterprise Councils (TECs) in England. Since the advent of the Scottish Parliament in 1999, the situation has become even more complex. Employment is a 'reserved' area of policy, with Westminster policy mediated through the Office for Scotland in Edinburgh, while Lifelong Learning and Enterprise is controlled by the Holyrood Parliament. There is some unease among MSPs about the division between enterprise and employment and the extent to which Westminster and Holyrood policies are aligned.

The Employment Service (ES) has a remit to assist disabled people, including those with learning difficulties, to access the labour market. Disability employment advisers, based in disability service teams at job centres, assess the training needs of their disabled clients and place them on appropriate programmes, usually delivered by the voluntary sector and private training agencies. Such programmes include the New Deal for Disabled People, Access to Work, Job Introduction Schemes, Supported Employment (formerly known as wage subsidy) and Work Preparation (formerly known as job rehabilitation). Demand for such programmes is growing as more disabled people seek inclusion and support in the labour market. Annual expenditure on ES programmes is rising (eg government funding for Work Preparation was £8.7 million in 1998/99. For the year 1999/2000, £10.2 million was allocated). However, demand for support, for example through Access to Work, outstrips funding. The ES is forced by the Treasury to report on the effectiveness of its programmes in moving disabled people into sustainable employment. Statistics on programme outcomes do not always support an economic case for expansion. For example, in Scotland between 1997 and 1999, only 20% of individuals participating in the Work Preparation programme were working 13 weeks after the end of their placement (Wilson et al, 2000).

Many ES programmes were not developed with people with learning difficulties in mind and may not offer enough support and flexibility to meet their needs. For example, job rehabilitation, now known as Work Preparation, arose out of a recommendation of the 1944 Tomlinson Report and formed part of the 1945 Employment Act. It was designed to meet the needs of disabled servicemen returning from the Second World War, offering a period of intensive training in Employment Rehabilitation Units. Although Work Preparation now tends to take place in workplace settings, it still only allows an individual 6-8 weeks training and is evaluated in relation to successful outcomes. Because of the lack of support available both during the training period and in subsequent employment, relatively few people with learning difficulties are included in Work Preparation programmes.

The New Deal for Disabled People (NDDP) outlined in the DSS White Paper (DSS, 1998) was allocated £195 million. Targeted initially at people on Incapacity Benefit (IB), its aim was to move long-term IB claimants back into the labour market. The DSS's work incentive measures, described above, were intended to lubricate the process. Letters were sent to IB claimants encouraging them to contact personal advisers at job centres to receive advice on the Single Gateway to Employment (now referred to as One). Although the letters emphasised that participation in the NDDP was voluntary, response by IB claimants was very low at 3.3% (Riddell and Wilson, 1999). Further, despite the promises of novelty, people were directed towards existing and rather inflexible training programmes such as Work Preparation. Evaluation of the NDDP (Arthur et al, 1999) suggests that relatively low numbers of disabled people, particularly people with learning difficulties, have moved into jobs as a result of the programme and, viewed through Treasury eyes, it is regarded as less cost-effective than New Deal programmes aimed at lone parents and 18-24 year olds.

Training for disabled people is also provided by Local Enterprise Companies (LECs) through Skillseekers and Training for Work Programmes. The principal task of LECs is to promote local economic development. Given this *raison d'être*, investment in people with learning difficulties may be contentious given that they may be, in perception or reality, less effective workers than their peers. There has been no planned development of LEC and ES training programmes and as a result there is overlap in provision for people with less significant impairments, while very little provision is targeted at people with higher support needs.

The brief outline of the policy framework above indicates areas of tension and overlap between the wide range of policy arenas relevant to a learning society. As in the rest of the public sector (Deakin, 1994), quasi-markets have been established within all service areas, but there is potential for power to remain with service purchasers (care managers) and providers rather than service users, particularly when this group is likely to be poor, inarticulate and lacking powerful advocates. While community care and lifelong learning policies recognise the contribution to be made by a range of service providers, competition among services for control of a particular area may render such cooperation potentially difficult. All agencies emphasise the importance of participation in mainstream society, but most offer segregated rather than inclusive services. While gesturing towards equal access, resource allocation policies tend to reflect the belief that investment in individuals' education and training must be in relation to their future ability to deliver added value to the economy.

In the following section, we summarise findings from key informant interviews in relation to overlapping theoretical concerns. These were the operation of quasi-markets in learning society policy arenas; the nature of adult status and citizenship for people with learning difficulties and the barriers encountered in attaining full citizenship; the salience of human and social capital versions of the Learning Society for people with learning difficulties; and the negotiation of risk and the construction of identity for people with learning difficulties.

Findings from key informant interviews: mapping Scottish lifelong learning services

Education services

To maintain their employability, individuals are called upon to update continually their knowledge, skills and credentials, choosing from a range of competing education and training services. Such policies are problematic in a number of ways for people with learning difficulties. For example, the policy assumes that lifelong learning will have broadly positive effects, but Coffield (1999) and others have pointed out that constant pressure to upgrade qualifications may have significant negative effects. Nurses, for instance, may have to devote time to study in the evenings and at weekends, as studied by Hewison and colleagues (Dowswell et al, 1998) in another project within *The Learning Society Programme*. This is likely to intensify the conflicting demands of work and family. In such situations, rather than acting as personal liberation, education comes to be regarded instrumentally as a necessary evil or a threat. People with learning difficulties may also be victims of dystopic elements within the Learning Society. Reduction in the demand for unskilled workers in the labour market over the last two decades has meant that they have experienced perpetual cycles of training with little prospect of employment (Riddell et al, 1998a). Resource scarcity may restrict job opportunities to relatively more able individuals.

Further Education (FE) has a statutory responsibility to 'have regard' to the needs of disabled students under the terms of the 1992 Further and Higher Education (Scotland) Act, and premium funding is made available from the Scottish Executive for this. Colleges as independent incorporated bodies appeared to interpret this duty differently with individual colleges sometimes specialising in one aspect of disability. Almost all students who attend post-school extension courses in FE are independent travellers and young people with significant learning difficulties are generally not catered for in college. Little choice is available for post-16 students with learning difficulties. Because of a shortage of provision, colleges select students rather than vice versa. In the urban study area, the three FE colleges worked closely together, allocating students to each college. There was thus no competition among service providers within FE, although there was fierce competition between FE and Community Education (see below). Courses for older people were generally short-term and covered a range of leisure and life skills topics. Here, the supply of courses was not able to keep pace with demand. In FE there was tension between the ethics of personal development and training for work. The perceived low level of 'employability' of people with learning difficulties sat uneasily with the general mission of FE to meet the needs of employers. People with learning difficulties were almost always taught separately from mainstream students and often used separate rooms and facilities when studying subjects such as home economics or horticulture.

Whereas patterns of resource allocation in FE reflected human capital understandings, in Community Education services there was comparatively little emphasis on skills directly related to employment, but more on personal and social skills. Community Education felt that it was an under-funded service and had lost out to FE, whose mission of meeting the requirements of the labour market did not fit comfortably with the provision of quality services for people with learning difficulties. This view of FE from the perspective of Community Education is illustrated below:

> "I think there's a competitive market with the colleges because they're fighting for their lives since incorporation. I'm sure you'll be aware of the colleges, every corner you come to in City B you'll find an FE college. And there's a tremendous amount of in-fighting among

themselves ... and they're very protective of what they do.... It means that around the table everyone is not quite open and up front about what they're doing.... They think they can do everything and when they're driven by performance indicators that are all about money they say:'Oh, we can deliver on that', but we know they can't. They've got a tremendous role to play but they haven't got the staff on the ground working with the people on a daily basis.... We've got to be working in the community, doing the confidence building bits, the essential skills bits which colleges can't." (Community Education respondent)

It should be noted that the city referred to by this Community Education respondent was not the urban area in which our case studies were conducted. Whereas in our study area FE colleges operated a cartel, in City B they appeared to compete with each other for special needs clients. This intensification of competition might reflect the greater number of FE colleges in City B and the precarious financial position of many.

There are interesting points of comparison with the work of Stephen Ball, Meg Maguire and Sheila Macrae within *The Learning Society Programme* (Ball et al, 2000). In the urban area studied by Ball and colleagues, schools and FE colleges were seeking to attract young people in the post-16 age group. FE colleges were attempting to colonise the academic niche previously monopolised by schools, and schools were seeking to attract some young people into vocational courses. In addition, schools themselves were increasingly competing with each other for post-16 customers, as those which had previously catered for young people in the 11-16 age range applied to open sixth forms. According to Ball and colleagues, 'cut-throat' competition was generated by the proximity of multiple providers, the entry of new players and the FE funding regime itself. While this competition might result in greater choice for consumers, it also appeared to lead to a deterioration in quality, as providers relied on glossy presentation to attract customers, arranged courses at short notice to plug any perceived holes in the market and strayed increasingly into areas where they lacked expertise. Ball et al describe the young consumers of post-16 education provision as "complex, struggling, diverse and uncertain". This description might equally be applied to adults with learning difficulties in the post-16 education market.

Training services

Local Enterprise Companies (LECs) provided training with a particular focus on work-related skills and confidence building for young people in normal workplaces, in special workshops and in FE colleges (Skillseekers). For older people, Training for Work programmes were provided. The dominant ethos in the LECs was that of 'employability' – the acquisition of skills, attitudinal and technical, which would make the person an attractive employee. Within this ethos the person with learning difficulties could appear as a poor investment, being more expensive to train and potentially less able to adapt to changing work practices. Many training programmes, including Skillseekers and Training for Work, which claimed to cater for people with special needs, were targeted at the socially disadvantaged and specifically excluded people with learning difficulties, who were seen as the responsibility of social services. The funding regime established by LECs, linking payment to the attainment of vocational qualifications, made this an unattractive area for most private training agencies. A minority of LECs attempted to include people with learning difficulties in their programmes, but often had difficulties in finding a training placement for them. The following training manager explained the basic principle informing LEC activity:

> "Generally speaking, it would be unusual to assist people in sheltered employment because they are the responsibility of the social work department. It's aimed at people who can be economically active. It doesn't need to be full-time, but you have to be able to take up employment outside a sheltered environment." (LEC training manager)

Careers Services have a statutory responsibility to work with young people with special needs after they leave school. Contact was normally initiated at the Future Needs Assessment, about 18 months before the statutory school-leaving age. Careers Services 'endorse' young people as having special needs for the purpose of participation in FE and Skillseekers programmes. A sifting mechanism operated, whereby some young people were channelled towards programmes leading to the open labour market (mainstream or special needs Skillseekers), while others, regarded as marginal workers, were channelled into FE extension programmes. People with the most significant difficulties moved directly from school into adult resource centres. Young people with learning difficulties had little choice of route or service due to shortage of placements.

Employment services

Key informant interviews with the ES and voluntary organisations running supported employment services illustrated the gulf between the mission of each.

Employment Service programmes are described earlier and included the Wage Subsidy Supported Employment programme and Work Preparation. Like the LEC programmes, they were based on strict economic principles so that investment in an individual had to be commensurate with national economic development. Programmes, therefore, were geared at people who, with some initial support, were able to hold their own in the labour market. The ES offered no programmes for those with more significant difficulties, whose only contact with the labour market was through the supported employment programmes run by voluntary organisations.

Voluntary organisations operated supported employment programmes, funded from a range of sources including the European Social Fund and social work. Supporting people in a real job was seen as the best means of achieving social inclusion and enhancing social networks. It was also seen as contributing to better health, access to normal living arrangements and opportunities to develop a range of social relationships. However, proponents of supported employment felt that the market was rigged against them so that there were far too few opportunities available to accommodate the number of people expressing a preference for paid employment. This view is encapsulated below:

> "Most people with learning difficulties tell me they would rather be working than in an Adult Training Centre. The usual primary objective is to get a job. And a lot of the more able people with learning difficulties are voting with their feet – they just refuse to go.... Every one of our supported employment schemes has a unit cost less than an Adult Training Centre placement.... The irony for me is that if there was a proper market we would be inundated with work." (Chief executive, voluntary organisation)

Community care services

Much provision for people with learning difficulties is funded and delivered by social work departments. Key informant interviews revealed a mismatch between stated goals and existing services. Most day services took the form of traditional adult resource centres, each providing a menu of activities geared towards leisure and recreation and often offered in segregated settings. For people with the most significant difficulties, the emphasis was on meeting both social care and health needs, with no attempt to develop work-related skills. More progressive adult resource centres attempted to implement principles of person-centred planning and offered supported employment opportunities. Managers who had experience of successful supported employment programmes were glowing in their endorsement:

> "People are seeing how, if you give people with learning difficulties a job, they do it to the letter and they've been so reliable. We had one lad working in Macdonald's and he was incredible. The best burgers they had ever seen – the burger in the middle of the bun, the relish in the middle of the burger. He accepts nothing less, nothing sloppy about it. One woman is a cleaner and she is meticulous, keeps the place much cleaner than any of the other cleaners they've got there." (Social work manager)

Another social work manager spoke of the difficulty in effecting real change. Some projects, established to provide real work opportunities, ended up reverting to their underlying warehousing purpose:

> "[The project] is supposed to provide horticultural opportunities for employment but it has become a big day centre with plants – people don't get paid and they don't move on." (Social work manager)

Shortage of placements and restrictions imposed by social security rules meant that supported employment opportunities were too few and time-restricted to meet demand. In the urban study area, adult resource centres tended to specialise in particular types of impairment, some catering for people with more significant difficulties. All adult resource centres had waiting lists, and carers often opposed greater involvement of people with learning difficulties in training and employment for fear of losing a placement. The social care model of provision described by most social work managers is a logical outcome of the dominance of the human capital version of the Learning Society. Those who cannot compete economically are considered to have little social value and, while given the basic means of sustaining life, are provided with few opportunities for personal growth and development. Although no longer held in long-stay institutions, they are segregated within mainstream communities.

To summarise findings from key informant interviews across services, the following conclusions may be drawn:

- Open labour market employment was seen as the ultimate goal of much provision but the segregated nature of training inhibited this.
- Supported employment schemes, not common and catering for only a few people each, were seen as more likely to result in open labour market employment.
- The potential for 'circuits of training' with little progression to an end goal of a job was presented as a key weakness of existing service provision.
- There was little competition between providers or choice for service users. Budgetary pressures were felt to limit definitions of needs to those which could be met by existing services and choice of services was particularly difficult to maintain in sparsely populated areas. Choice for service users was reported to be at the 'micro' level of certain details within existing services rather than at the level of the nature of services.
- Evaluation of many services, particularly in the field of training, consisted of evaluative questionnaires. While this was in accordance with the Scottish Quality Management Scheme, it did not provide opportunities for qualitative evaluation and did not appear to feed into changes in the programmes on offer.
- The planning of education services for this group of learners appeared haphazard, ranging from formal development plans agreed between agencies on a long time horizon to planning being the responsibility of individual tutors at local level.
- Adult guidance services and impartial advocates were felt to be of increasing importance in helping people determine their own course through the complex web of provision. The need for an impartial guidance agency to inform people with learning difficulties and carers of the range of services on offer was necessary for there to be any possibility of choice for service users.

Findings from ethnographic case studies

Our 30 ethnographic case studies were designed to give insight into the material conditions and lived experiences of the informants and how these enabled or disabled full participation in contemporary Scottish society. Here, we briefly summarise findings in relation to three key domains of people's lives which are of critical importance in terms of their relationship to the Learning Society. These interconnected domains are domesticity, work and social networks. Finally, we consider findings from the case studies in relation to central theoretical questions concerning the negotiation of risk and identity within a learning society.

Domesticity

Among our case studies, homes of origin provided the most common domestic location from birth until early middle age with only 5 of the 30 having recognisably their own home. Parental illness or death, or allegations of abuse, were the usual triggers for a move from the parental home into one form of residential care or another. Such moves appeared to be ad hoc responses to events rather than part of a planned progression for the individual concerned.

Supported accommodation or residential group care settings provided for more independent living but this potential was limited by the ad hoc transfer system and by the relative late age of such independence. There was evidence that the interaction of benefit regimes and social work systems for contracting 'blocks' of services from external agencies could act to lock people into inappropriate accommodation and hinder progression. Independent living was the least common domestic arrangement and appeared to depend on significant determination on the part of the case study individual and the availability of specific, and scarce, physical, social and professional infrastructures.

Intimate personal relations were an expressed aspiration of many of the case study individuals but were not commonly established: one person was married, another had a steady partner. For many of the others in our case study sample having a boyfriend/girlfriend was a matter of staff banter and/or personal fantasy. The fantasy relationship with 'stars', usually associated with the early teens, characterised the lives of several of our adult sample, with the Spice Girls or women wrestlers as the very public objects of desire. Attempts to move beyond such fantasy were hindered by lack of initiation into the rituals of courtship with, for example, one person buying an engagement ring for the sibling of a casual social acquaintance. There was little evidence of parents and staff offering structured support in the necessary process of learning such rituals and there was substantial evidence of their limiting relationships to the fantastic because of fears that individuals with learning difficulties would be unable to develop and sustain intimate relationships and that, even with support, they would be unable to parent effectively. Some of the people with learning difficulties were engaged in various stages of courtship, but having been deprived of some of the social experiences of adolescence and lacking transport and private space, had difficulties in negotiating such relationships. Some expressed a hard material view that, without access to work and a wage, it was not possible to sustain a relationship.

Work

Work was widely perceived by the case study individuals as the key to progression and identity. For some people, work was not an actively pursued option, it being deemed beyond their capacity by professionals and parents/carers. For others, work was seen as a possibility, but they were caught in webs of benefit regulations and service agreements which acted to discourage or prohibit engagement with work. The 'therapeutic earnings' rule allows limited work while drawing benefit at the cost of a formal declaration of disability, while engagement with work beyond this limit would lead to the withdrawal of benefit packages far in excess of what could be earned. One person, for example, had to give up full-time work in favour of such 'therapeutic' work because the funding of their residential accommodation depended on their being deemed unfit for work.

'Training' in a variety of settings provided the main daytime activity for the case study individuals. Such training was nominally directed towards work, particularly in the light manufacturing, service and horticulture sectors. Such training was, however, poorly linked to opportunities to put the training into practice in open contexts and rounds of training, perhaps for life, appeared to be the norm. One person was about to 'retire' from a lifetime of training for work, on which the youngest of the sample were about to embark. Leisure classes organised by adult resource centres, often in segregated classes in community settings, provided a counter-point to training sessions. In the absence of work, such 'leisure' tended to be just another slot in the timetable rather than a self-initiated process of development (Baron et al, 1998a).

Those who had a limited engagement with work saw it as central to their lives, with for example, one person making disproportionate efforts to travel home to change clothes, ready to travel for two hours office work. Supported employment schemes with job coaching or similar support were difficult to find for us to study, despite the high profile which they have been given in the literature in recent years. Run by voluntary organisations, those identified provided not only meaningful work and income for our case study individuals but also engagement with new social networks and with the public (Riddell et al, 1999b).

The wage subsidy scheme of supported employment run by the ES presented a less happy picture in our sample: the one person working under this scheme had held a full-time job as a cleaner in a public utility for 18 years on the same terms and conditions as other cleaners. When the service was prepared for privatisation, he was asked to choose between disciplinary action for lack of productivity and an assessment interview with the doctor. This resulted in a declaration of 50% disability and a matching wage subsidy to the employer.

Such an active construing of people as being disabled and inefficient workers was complemented in our data by a minority discourse of the person with learning disabilities as the paradigm worker: hardworking, obedient and uncomplaining (Baron et al, 1998b).

Social networks

There was little evidence that people with learning difficulties were being enabled to form social networks independent of parental home or service setting. Networks based on the parental home provided a major social context for many of our case study individuals and, in one case, offered essential and ongoing support after the death of the parent. Special provision either in segregated settings, or in special sessions in community settings, dominated services, contrary to the ethic of 'normalisation' which most services espoused. Inherited professional service structures and limited resources were the main barriers to better social integration (Stalker et al, 1999).

The friendship networks of our case study individuals thus tended to be limited to those based around daytime service settings and their living accommodation. The formal social events attended were mainly 'special' leisure activities organised for people with learning difficulties (Baron et al, 1998a). More informal activities were based mainly on the residential group and it was sometimes difficult for people to maintain networks formed outwith these settings due to transport and escort staffing difficulties. Where activities did take place in non-segregated settings the level of encounter with the wider public was low: for example, the weekly outing of three people from the same bed and breakfast accommodation for tea and scones at the café of a local multiple store was an essentially self-contained activity with little or no contact with the public.

The consequences of such limiting of the social networks of people with learning difficulties became increasingly apparent to us as the research progressed, particularly as the social benefits of engaging with work were highlighted by those in our sample who were in employment. At a personal level, the oft-noted limitations of people with learning difficulties as social partners may substantially be traced to such restrictions in their networks. The possibilities for them to form and pursue personal friendships outwith the 'special' circle were severely limited. Restricted to 'special' networks, and those of their family of origin, the people with learning difficulties in our sample had significantly reduced opportunities to build their participation in Scottish society and, crucially as we suggest in the Conclusions, to challenge some of its assumptions by their presence.

Identity or biography: issues of structure and agency for people with learning difficulties in a learning society

The question of 'identity' has become a central concern of social theory in recent years and it grew in importance as our research proceeded. Up to the last decade, social theory was largely concerned with an agenda centred on class, and latterly gender and race, as the main determinants of social action and social being. In the last decade, as globalisation and the development of flexible forms of production have increased, arguments about 'late modernity', 'risk society' and 'postmodernity' have all highlighted negotiating and adopting different identities as one of the key strategies available to individuals in a time of substantial social change (Beck, 1992, 1994, 1999). The thrust of these arguments is away from conceptualising subjectivity as unitary, passive and determined by social location. Rather, individuals are seen as active players, choosing identities and re-forming themselves as desired (Baron et al, 1999). To what extent was 'learning difficulty' an identity which our informants chose, negotiated or used actively to manage their lives?

As we noted earlier, learning difficulties as a category was not pre-defined by the research team, as we sought to understand how the term was used in practice and what were the consequences of this usage. Our case studies show that the label is a subject of struggle, contested by the various groups involved. Those so classified rarely used the term in talking about themselves, more often ignoring or rejecting it or, when using it, placing it 'outside' their core identity. A group discussion with the 'Extension Class' of 16-18 year olds in a FE College, for example, produced complex explanations of their classification and segregation, in which their various 'difficulties' were seen as exacerbated (occasionally caused) by bullying peers, uncomprehending teachers and an unsympathetic community.

Parents used the category actively to make sense of their ongoing experience of caring. It is not surprising that such parental perspectives, rooted in the daily material reality of community care, were often in tension with those of professionals seeking to implement community care policies of an 'ordinary life' for their clients with limited support for independent living and for work placements. The use of the term by professionals thus reflected an unresolved tension in current thinking about 'learning difficulties' between such 'ordinary life' principles and the perceived need for extraordinary services to achieve these (Stalker et al, 1999).

The nature of impairment was predominantly conceptualised by professionals in terms of medical or quasi-medical categories, such as 'Down's Syndrome', 'Autistic Spectrum Disorder' or 'Non-Specific, Mild Learning Difficulties', combined with functional assessments of 'life skills'. Multidimensional constructions of abilities and impairments were only present in a minority of cases. These tended to challenge the structure of service provision, especially, for example, the complex mixture of abilities and impairments of 'Asperger's Syndrome' which posed considerable difficulties for teachers and lecturers involved. Cases tended to be arrayed along a one dimensional continuum of ability, with choices of services diminished with severity of impairment (Stalker et al, 1999). Those who had learning difficulties as a result of a lack of learning opportunities (poverty, accident or illness) tended to occupy a marginal position in the labour market, undertaking, or heading towards, low skilled and insecure work in the grey or black economy. People with mild or moderate learning difficulties were usually based in adult resource centres. Some had limited contact with the labour market through supported employment schemes. Those with the most severe learning difficulties spent all their time in adult resource centres with no contact with the labour market (Riddell et al, 1999a).

Overall, the category of learning difficulty was dominant in terms of describing people's characteristics and justifying their allocation to particular services. Irrespective of the severity of impairment, the negative status of being a person with learning difficulties appeared to override many benefits which might follow from other social characteristics such as social class. A comparison of the lived experiences of people in our study aged 27, 37 and 47 suggested that full adult status, characterised by access to independent income, living space, relationships and basic civil rights, was routinely denied to people with learning difficulties (Baron et al, 1999). Despite the operation of learning difficulties as a master category, gender and social class had a significant impact on life chances and experiences and these are discussed below.

Gender was a significant component in the construction of the identities of the case studies. While sexuality was an issue for the participants of all our case studies this, reflecting wider gender roles, was particularly pertinent for the female cases, where pregnancy and the need for medical and social protective measures featured significantly in parental and professional talk. One woman had been sterilised without consent, being deemed incapable of giving informed consent. There was evidence, in some cases, that female gender roles, particularly those of 'domesticity', provided a resource which could be utilised to negotiate the demands of a learning disabled identity. In the employment market the availability of waitressing work enabled one person to work at the weekends, thus defining herself as independent from the round of leisure classes of the adult resource centre and from the lawyer who controlled her main finances. There was some evidence that women were more able to establish and maintain independent living arrangements by drawing on the gendered repertoire of domesticity. Conversely some of the men in our case studies were inhibited from moving towards independent living by not having developed the necessary skills due to the receipt of high levels of service at home from female relatives (Baron et al, 1999).

We sought to include members of ethnic minorities in our case studies but ethnicity was the significantly absent dimension of the sampling frame. With the exception of one case (American Indian/Scottish) no individuals from ethnic minorities could be identified by the service providers in either urban or rural contexts. This was thought to be typical by the staff when asked to review their contacts with members of ethnic minorities over recent years. Although, in comparison with the UK, there is a relatively low minority ethnic population in Scotland (about 2%), it is unlikely that the absence of minority ethnic people from services over the years is simply a product of sampling. Rather, it suggests that ethnic minorities do not seek services by way of the category 'learning difficulties'. It was not possible to pursue this striking phenomenon within the terms of the current research.

Social class was not used in the sample design as people with learning difficulties are among the poorest in the population (Booth and Booth, 1994). The circumstances of the case study individuals ranged from poverty to significant inherited wealth, with the former being most prevalent. In these cases the welfare benefits of the person with learning difficulties could play a significant role in household finances, acting as a serious material disincentive to independent living. Where there was significant wealth, the lives of the case study individuals were tangibly different, enabling, for example, supported living in the inherited family home. However, the social advantage of inherited wealth might be over-ridden by the negative status of having 'learning difficulties'. One of our female case studies, for example, was designated an incapable adult as a result of the terms of the parental will. (See McKay and Patrick, 1995, for a useful overview of the legal position of people with learning difficulties in Scotland[2].) Overall, while class position clearly impacted on the lives of the case study individuals, it tended to mediate, rather than negate, learning disabled identities (Baron et al, 1999).

The attempts by such people to form their own identity, and thus to move between different social settings, foundered due to the power of the global, ascribed identity 'learning difficulty'. This suggests that parts of postmodern and late-modern theorising have overstated the decline of the social determination of identity and this is the focus of a forthcoming book reporting the research (Riddell et al, 2000: forthcoming).

Conclusions

In this chapter we have already presented the main substantive conclusions to which we have been drawn by our data, the more detailed arguments for which are available in the papers listed in the References. To conclude, we want to reflect on two theoretical concerns which structured the design of our research (choice in welfare quasi-markets and the applicability of the social model of disability to people with learning difficulties); on two theoretical issues which emerged during the course of the research (human and social capital theories and the re-professionalisation of the field of learning difficulties); finally, on the significance of studying 'learning difficulties' for analysing the idea of a 'learning society'.

The welfare quasi-market

'Choice' has been a leitmotif of social policy for a decade as the idea of a welfare quasi-market has increased in popularity (Stalker, 1995). For many people with learning difficulties, the regime of the long-stay hospital, or parallel provision in the community, had severely restricted choice about both daily and long-term life issues. In services avowing a normalisation ethos, encouraging and enabling choices is a central tenet to combat such institutionalisation. In the research we therefore wished to explore the place of choice in service provision, both in theory and in practice.

Our data suggest that the preconditions for a welfare quasi-market existed in the urban case study area. There was a variety of providers of different forms of service for people with learning difficulties, the public transport system was efficient and accessible, the local authority was committed to enabling choice between these services, and there was a group of carers who were politically active in seeking to improve provision. This urban context was, arguably, the best in Scotland for the development and operation of a welfare quasi-market. There was, however, little evidence of an active market, with either cooperation between nominally competing providers or with purchaser and contractor agreeing an effective monopoly. The experience of the urban case study individuals suggests that choosing between fundamentally different types of service ('macro-choice') was severely limited, with choice effectively limited to details of the service being provided ('micro-choice') (Riddell et al, 1999c).

Outside the conurbation, the preconditions for the quasi-market in services for people with learning difficulties did not exist. The rural case study area was characterised by sparse service provision with the consequences of little or no possibility of choice between services and of little differentiation of provision within services. The local authority placed a 'block' contract with one major provider, the terms of which inhibited flexibility of provision. Those with relatively high dependency were provided for on the same basis as those whose needs for support were both less and different. Arguably, the needs of neither group were being met as fully as they might have been given a more flexible funding regime.

The social model of disability

Understandings of disability have been transformed in the past decade by the 'social model of disability'. Rather than locating disability in the impairment of the individual, the social model attributes disability to the socially constructed barriers which prevent impaired people from participating fully in contemporary society. Such barriers range from the explicit (such as inaccessible public transport or overt discrimination) to the deeply implicit (especially assumptions about normality). The social model has been developed almost exclusively in terms of physical impairments, mobility difficulties being the classic site of contestation. In this research we were anxious to apply this model to people with learning difficulties, particularly as the polarising discourse of 'work for those who can, welfare for those who cannot' developed. Does the impairment of 'having a learning difficulty' intrinsically prevent people from full participation in Scottish society or a learning society? We sought to illuminate this issue rather than answer it.

Our research reinforced the view that the term 'learning difficulties' is highly flexible. Some of our case study individuals were severely impaired both physically and cognitively, requiring the constant attention of others. Contrary to one reading of the social model, such impairment itself constituted a barrier to full participation; while barriers may be removed, impairments cannot be wished away. The situation of those with severe impairments challenges the nature of 'full participation'. In seeking to dismantle barriers for (largely) physically impaired people, the social model of disability has tended to assume one model of normal social participation (work, family, leisure etc) which, in itself, excludes some of those with learning difficulties. If inclusion is to become a reality, then definitions of 'normality' will have to change (Wilson et al, forthcoming)

At the other end of the range of impairments, the term 'learning difficulty' or its close correlates such as 'special needs', appeared to be expanding to include a much wider population than previously. In particular, the terms were including those who employers and/or training agencies deem hard to place in work. The Local Enterprise Companies were classifying around 15% of the young 'Skillseekers' as having 'Special Training Needs', with special programmes and reduced expectations to match. Some areas of multiple deprivation were thought to have 30% or more of the population having 'special needs'. We explore below the implications of this widening of the definition of such terms in a 'learning society'.

The majority of our case study individuals fell in between these two positions, being classified as having moderate learning difficulties. Here, barriers to full citizenship range from the *social structural* (especially the recomposition of the labour force which has destroyed many of the employment niches previously available to people with learning difficulties), through the *institutional* (especially the continued collection of people with learning difficulties into segregated settings), through the *family* (especially the drive of parents to protect their offspring), to the *personal* (especially poor social skills, largely resulting from the action of the other barriers). It was the interaction of these different barriers which, for most of our case study individuals, served to maintain them in marginal positions.

Emergent theoretical issues

In researching people with learning difficulties in a 'learning society', we necessarily explored issues which challenge fundamental tenets about the nature of such a society. One of these is the dominance of 'human capital' explanations of the role of education in technologically advanced economies (we consider other challenges in the final section of this chapter). Human capital explanations of education have dominated the policy research field since the 1960s and provide the theoretical underpinning of most 'learning society' arguments (Riddell et al, 1997b). In this framework, education is conceptualised as an investment made both by society and the individual in order to maximise future gains through enhancing the international competitiveness of the national economy and the labour market position of the individual. From this theoretical perspective, with 'rates of return' routinely being calculated on educational expenditure, people with learning difficulties appear a poor investment, limited in learning and less productive than non-impaired workers. Such reasoning lies behind the current, socially excluding, policy dichotomy of 'work for those who can; welfare for those who cannot'.

Theories of 'social capital' emerged as a central concern of a group of projects in *The Learning Society Programme* and offer a complementary, if not competing, conceptualisation to that of human capital. The term social capital refers to the productive potential which inheres in the social relationships between people rather than in machinery, money or individual skills (physical, financial and human capitals respectively)[3]. Central to ideas of social capital are networks of norms and trust which enable people to cooperate effectively. The idea has variously been used to explain the 'over-achieving' of pupils in Catholic schools in the USA, the reproduction of elites and the relative success of different regions or countries. A social capital perspective has much greater potential for fostering the inclusion of people with learning difficulties than does the deficit model of human capital. People with learning difficulties can participate in networks of norms and trust and may also act as a catalyst for the formation of such (Riddell et al, 1999b). We develop this in the final section of this chapter.

A second theoretical concern which emerged during the research was the nature of professionalism and learning difficulties. The move out of long-stay hospitals in the past decade has seen the role of the medical profession with those with learning difficulties come under increasing attack from those espousing 'ordinary life principles' and the social model of disability. What became increasingly apparent during the research was that the discourse of ordinary life, normalisation, choice and rights was itself subjugating those with learning difficulties to a new form of professional power based in social work and, increasingly, in the 'consultancy' activities of voluntary organisations. How far current versions of 'empowerment' enable people with learning difficulties to maximise self-determination and self-development are issues which we are currently pursuing (Baron and Dumbleton, 2000: forthcoming).

Test criteria from The Learning Society *Programme's working definition*

The working definition of a 'learning society', which informed the programme and which was quoted in the first sentence of this chapter, can be seen to contain six test criteria by which the existence of a 'learning society' in Britain might be gauged. Applying these to the experience of our 30 case study individuals, whom we might expect to be among the last to be included in a 'learning society', gives us a measure of whether the idea is nearing fruition in contemporary Scotland:

- Access to excellent services was limited by the geographical location of services and by the dominance of segregating services.
- Developmental progression of the individual was notable by its absence. Services did not provide the framework by which the transition to adulthood could be made fully and a process of lifelong development undertaken.
- Contribution to the social and economic whole was limited by the scarcity of suitable work, by inappropriate support services and by benefits regimes which pivoted on the dichotomy between those who

'could' work and those who 'could not'. Lack of work severely restricted personal development and opportunities for wider social engagement.

- Social integration was limited by the dominance of special social networks and the paucity of work opportunities.
- Participative citizenship was limited by the relatively closed nature of the social networks and by segregated provision.
- Equity for people with learning difficulties in terms of the programme may best be defined as the combination of the previous five test criteria which, in their delineation of exclusion from mainstream social, economic and personal life-chances, suggest inequity.

Learning difficulties in a learning society

Is this not to be expected? Is it not reasonable to expect that people with cognitive impairments will be marginal to a society increasingly characterised by a 'knowledge economy'? Why should we research learning difficulties in a learning society? Such challenges to our research were presented at the first coordinating meeting of the programme by the mandatory industrialist present (Peter Wickens, sometime Personnel Director of Nissan UK) and we have met them in full elsewhere (Baron et al, 1998c). At the conclusion of the programme we offer arguments about the significance of understanding learning difficulties in a learning society at three progressively demanding levels:

- Social justice and learning difficulties. Current policy thinking, reflecting existing social attitudes, envisages social justice as being appropriate welfare provision for those who are unable to work. The experience of the 30 case studies suggests that such a conception of social justice is not adequate for three principal reasons: provision is scarce and liable to further restriction as the proportion of GDP devoted to state expenditure is reduced; the nature of provision tends to lock people into dependent and non-developmental roles; the dichotomy between those who 'can' and those who 'cannot' work on which current welfare provision is predicated is, in itself, a powerful source of injustice in excluding people from the mainstream of contemporary society.
- People with learning difficulties as pioneers of a learning society. The learning society literature, and the majority of projects in the programme, are characterised by enthusiasm for the idea of lifelong learning. Few voices have been raised to question what lifelong learning is as a social

practice, and whether it is always and everywhere desirable. The attraction of the concept, or more likely the implausibility of arguing for lifelong ignorance, has dulled the critical faculties of the educational research community. People with learning difficulties have followed the path of lifelong learning for decades, raising a nightmare vision of the Learning Society – socially excluded groups, confined to segregated settings, undergoing mandatory and continuous training as a form of social warehousing. The current expansion of the category of 'special needs' noted above suggests that this tactic is of growing importance.

• People with learning difficulties as catalysts for a more broadly conceived vision of a learning society. As campaigns by people with mobility difficulties have helped access to public facilities for all and have challenged many assumptions about disability and normality, so may including people with learning difficulties in a learning society improve access to learning for all and pose challenging questions about the social purposes of learning. Clarity of vision, understanding and purpose, combined with supportive social networks, are especially important for enabling people with learning difficulties to learn and to participate. The conscious development of these can provide one foundation for the development of a learning society more critical and more inclusive than can the tired repertoire of knowledge-skills-employment-competitiveness.

Notes

[1] 'Normalisation' refers to the social policy advocated by Wolfensberger (1972) and O'Brien (1987). Developed in the US and subsequently adopted in the UK, normalisation suggests that the role of services should be to assist people with learning difficulties to 'pass' in mainstream society. Critics of normalisation (eg Brown and Smith, 1992) suggest that it is conservative in its orientation, maintaining that disabled people must adapt to society rather than vice versa.

[2] Scots law relating to people with learning difficulties deemed 'incapable adults' dates back to the 14th century and derives from Roman law. A number of different types of guardian may be appointed by different agencies with a range of powers. For instance, the *statutory guardian* has an interventionist role, with powers limited to deciding place of residence; ensuring that medical care, training and so on is provided. The *tutor dative* is appointed by order of the Court of Session and normally has power to deal with personal decisions (eg medical consent) but can

also be given financial powers. The *curator bonis*, appointed by Sheriff Court or Court of Session, has power to deal with all financial affairs. The DSS may appoint a person, usually a relative or carer, to claim, collect and spend welfare benefits. For residents of learning disability hospitals, the hospital manager may administer a person's funds. The law is extremely complex and the Incapable Adults Bill, debated in the Scottish Parliament at the time of writing, is intended to simplify matters.

[3] Social capital theories in relation to education and training are being explored further in a forthcoming publication produced as a result of collaboration with another project within *The Learning Society Programme* (Baron et al, forthcoming).

References

Arthur, S., Corden, A., Green, A., Lewis, J., Loumidis, J., Sainsbury, R., Stafford, B., Thornton, P. and Walker, R. (1999) *New deal for disabled people: Early implementation*, London: DSS.

Ball, S.J., Maguire, M. and Macrae, S. (2000) '"Worlds apart" – Education markets in the post-16 sector of one urban locale 1995-98', in F. Coffield (ed) *Differing visions of a Learning Society: Research findings,Volume 1*, Bristol: The Policy Press, pp 39-70.

Barnes, M. (1997) *Care, communities and citizens*, London: Longman.

Baron S. and Dumbleton P. (2000: forthcoming) *The politics of learning disability*, Basingstoke: Macmillan.

Baron, S., Riddell, S. and Wilkinson, H. (1998a) 'After karaoke: adult education, learning difficulties and social renewal', *Scottish Journal of Adult and Continuing Education*, vol 4, no 2, pp 19-45.

Baron, S., Riddell, S. and Wilkinson, H (1998b) 'The best burgers? The person with learning difficulties as worker', in T. Shakespeare (ed) *The -disability reader*, London: Cassell.

Baron, S., Stalker, K., Wilkinson, H. and Riddell, S. (1998c) 'The learning society: the highest stage of human capitalism?', in F. Coffield (ed) *Learning at work*, Bristol: The Policy Press, pp 49-61.

Baron, S., Riddell, S. and Wilson, A. (1999) 'The secret of eternal youth: identity, risk and learning difficulties', *British Journal of Sociology of Education*, special edition on Youth and Social Change, vol 20, no 4, pp 483-99.

Baron, S., Field, J. and Schuller, T. (eds) (forthcoming) *Social capital: Critical perspectives*, Oxford: Oxford University Press.

Baron, S., Wilson, A. and Riddell, S. (2000) 'Implicit knowledge, phenomenology and learning difficulties', in F. Coffield (ed) *The necessity of informal learning*, Bristol: The Policy Press, pp 43-53.

Beck, U. (1992) *The risk society*, London: Sage Publications.

Beck, U. (1994) *Ecological politics in the age of risk*, Cambridge: Polity Press.

Beck, U. (1999) *Democracy without enemies*, Cambridge: Polity Press.

Becker, G.S. (1975) *Human capital: A theoretical and empirical analysis*, Chicago, IL: University of Chicago Press.

Booth, T. and Booth W. (1984) *Parenting under pressure: Mothers and fathers with learning difficulties*, Buckingham: Open University Press.

Brown, H. and Smith, H. (eds) (1992) *Normalisation: A reader for the nineties*, London: Routledge.

Coffield, F. (1994) *Research specification for the ESRC Learning Society Programme: Knowledge and skills for employment*, Swindon: ESRC.

Coffield, F. (1999) 'Breaking the consensus: lifelong learning as social control', *British Educational Research Journal*, vol 25, no 4, pp 479-501.

Coffield, F (2000) 'Introduction: A critical analysis of the concept of a learning society', in F. Coffield (ed) *Differing visions of a learning society: Research findings, Volume 1*, Bristol: The Policy Press, pp 1-38.

Coleman, J. (1988) 'Social capital in the creation of human capital', *American Journal of Sociology*, vol 94, supplement S, pp 95-120.

Deakin, N. (1994) *The politics of welfare: Continuities and change*, London: Harvester Wheatsheaf.

DfEE (Department for Education and Employment) (1998) *The Learning Age: A renaissance for a new Britain*, Cm 3790, London: The Stationery Office.

DfEE (1999) *Learning to succeed: A new framework for post-16 learning*, Cm 4392, London: The Stationery Office.

Dowswell, T., Hewison, J. and Millar, B. (1998) 'Joining the Learning Society and working in the NHS: some issues', *Journal of Education Policy*, vol 12, no 6, pp 539-51.

DSS (Department of Social Security) (1998) *New ambitions for our country: A new contract for welfare*, Cm 3805, London: The Stationery Office.

Durkheim, E. (1938) *The rules of sociological method*, New York, NY: The Free Press.

Edwards, R., Sieminski, S. and Zeldin, D. (eds) (1993) *Adult learners, education and training*, London: Routledge.

Espie, C., Curtice, L., Morrison, J., Dunnigan, M., Knill-Jones, R. and Long, L. (1999) *The role of the NHS in meeting the health needs of people with learning disabilities*, Report to the Scottish Executive Learning Disabilities Review, Glasgow: University of Glasgow.

Fevre, R. (1996) 'Some sociological alternatives to human capital theory and their implications for research on post-compulsory education and training', Paper presented to the European Conference on Educational Research, University of Seville, 25-28 September.

Fukuyama, F. (1995) *Trust: The social virtues and the creation of prosperity*, London: Hamish Hamilton.

Glasgow City Council (2000) *Achieving partnership: Services for people with a learning disability in Glasgow City*, Glasgow: Glasgow City Council.

Hughes, C. and Tight, M. (1995) 'The myth of the learning society', *British Journal of Educational Studies*, vol 43, no 3, pp 290-304.

McKay, C. and Patrick, H. (1995) *The care maze: The law and your rights to community care in Scotland*, Glasgow: Enable and the Scottish Association for Mental Health.

McNabb, R. and Whitfield, K. (1994) *The market for training*, Aldershot: Avebury.

Maguire, M., Maguire, S. and Felstead, A. (1993) *Factors influencing individual commitment to lifetime learning: A literature review*, London: Employment Department.

NIACE (National Institute of Adult and Continuing Education) (1994) *Widening participation: Routes to a learning society*, NIACE policy discussion paper, Leicester: NIACE.

O'Brien, J. (1987) 'A guide to lifestyle planning: using the activities catalogue to integrate services and natural support systems', in B.W. Wilcox and G.T. Bellamy (eds) *The activities catalogue: An alternative curriculum for youth and adults with severe disabilities*, MD: Brookes, pp 175-89.

Putnam, R. (1995) 'Tuning in, tuning out: the strange disappearance of social capital in America', *Political Science and Politics*, vol 28, no 4, pp 664-83.

Report of the Royal Commission on the Blind, the Deaf, the Dumb and Others of the United Kingdom (The Egerton Commission) (1889), 4 vols, London: HMSO.

Riddell, S. and Wilson, A. (1999) 'Disabled people, employment and the New Deal', Paper presented to the Social Policy Association Conference, Roehampton Institute, London, 20-22 July.

Riddell, S., Baron, S. and Wilkinson, H. (1998a) 'Training from cradle to grave? Local Enterprise Companies, the marketisation of training and young people with learning difficulties', *Journal of Education Policy Special Issue on Social Justice in Education*, vol 13, no 4, pp 531-44.

Riddell, S., Baron, S. and Wilson, A. (1999a) 'Supported employment in Scotland: theory and practice' *Journal of Vocational Rehabilitation*, special issue: European perspective on employment and disability, vol 12, no 3, pp 181-95.

Riddell, S., Baron, S. and Wilson, A. (1999b) 'Social capital and people with learning difficulties', *Studies in the Education of Adults*, special edition on the Learning Society, vol 31, no 1, pp 49-66.

Riddell, S., Baron, S. and Wilson, A. (2001: forthcoming) *Learning difficulties in a learning society*, Bristol: The Policy Press.

Riddell, S., Wilkinson, H. and Baron, S. (1998b) 'From emancipatory research to focus group: people with learning difficulties and the research process', in P. Clough and L. Barton (eds) *Articulating with difficulty: Research voices in inclusive education*, London: Paul Chapman, pp 78-96.

Riddell, S., Wilson, A. and Baron, S. (1999c) 'Captured customers: people with learning difficulties in the social market', *British Educational Research Journal*, vol 25, no 4, pp 445-61.

Riddell, S., Baron, S., Stalker, K. and Wilkinson, H. (1997b) 'The concept of the learning society for adults with learning difficulties: human and social capital perspectives', *Journal of Education Policy*, vol 12, no 6, pp 473-83.

Riddell, S., Wilkinson, H., Stalker, K. and Baron, S. (1997a) *The meaning of the learning society for adults with learning difficulties: Report of phase 1 of the study*, Glasgow: University of Glasgow.

Scottish Executive (2000) *The same as you: From care to inclusion, review of Learning Disability Service*, Edinburgh: Scottish Executive.

Scottish Office (1998) *Opportunity Scotland: A paper on lifelong learning*, Cm 4048, Edinburgh: The Scottish Office.

Scottish Office Department of Health (1999) *Towards a healthier Scotland*, Cm 4269, Edinburgh: The Scottish Office.

Secretaries of State for Health, Social Security, Wales and Scotland (1989) *Caring for people: Community care in the next decade and beyond*, London: HMSO.

Simons, K. (1998) *Home, work and inclusion: The social policy implications of supported living and employment for people with learning disabilities*, York: Joseph Rowntree Foundation.

Stalker, K. (1995) 'The antinomies of choice in community care', in S. Baldwin and P. Barton (eds) *The international handbook of community care*, London: Routledge.

Stalker, K. and Hunter, S. (1999) *Resettlement of people with learning disabilities from Scottish hospitals*, Edinburgh: Scottish Executive.

Stalker, K., Baron, S., Riddell, S. and Wilkinson, H. (1999) 'Models of disability: the relationship between theory and practice in non-statutory organisations', *Critical Social Policy*, vol 19, no 1, pp 5-31.

Stone, D. (1984) *The disabled state*, Basingstoke: Macmillan.

Tett, L. (2000) 'Gender equality, the "learning society" policies and community education', in J. Salisbury and S. Riddell (eds) *Gender, policy and educational change: Shifting agendas in the UK and Europe*, London: Routledge, pp 245-57.

Wilson, A., Lightbody, P. and Riddell, S. (2000) *A flexible gateway to employment? An evaluation of Enable Services' traditional and innovative forms of work preparation*, Report to the Employment Service, Glasgow: Strathclyde Centre for Disability Research.

Wilson A., Riddell, S. and Baron, S. (forthcoming), 'Welfare for those who can? The impact of the quasi-market on the lives of people with learning difficulties', *Critical Social Policy*.

Tomlinson, S. (1982) *A sociology of special education*, London: Routledge.

Wolfensberger, W. (1972) *Normalization: The principle of normalization on human service*, Toronto, Canada: National Institute on Mental Retardation.

TWO

Networks, norms and trust: explaining patterns of lifelong learning in Scotland and Northern Ireland

John Field and Tom Schuller

Background

If we accept the notion of a learning society, it seems logical to conclude that some social arrangements promote learning more than others. It also follows that different social arrangements are likely to promote different types of learning. Most attempts to explore the Learning Society, and identify the different factors which promote lifelong learning, have focused on either the prospects facing individuals (particularly 'access factors' associated with entry into learning programmes or the barriers which prevent entry) or on the fate of nations and other large organisations (here, the focus tends to be on policy issues or the impact of external change factors). Our work within the ESRC *Learning Society Programme*[1], while accepting the importance of both individual and macro levels, focused on what might be called the meso-level of institutional environments and the belief systems of those who inhabit and shape them. In particular, our work was concerned to find out whether patterns of participation and achievement in organised learning were associated with those intermediate relationships, shared values and habits known to some sociologists as 'social capital' (Bourdieu, 1985; Putnam, 1993; Coleman, 1994; Riddell et al, 1999).

This paper draws on a detailed empirical study of schools attainment and adult learning in Northern Ireland and Scotland. At the outset, in 1995, we asked whether there was less adult learning in Scotland and

Northern Ireland than elsewhere in the United Kingdom (Field and Schuller, 1995). We noted that there seemed to be strong evidence in both societies of an apparent divergence between very high rates of attainment in initial education on the one hand, and reports of relatively low levels of participation by adults on the other. In what was then the largest UK-wide survey of participation in organised learning, 38% of Scots and 28% in Northern Ireland reported that they had done so in the last three years, compared with 42% in England. There were similar differences in respect of future learning aspirations: 54% in England described themselves as 'very' or 'fairly' unlikely to take part in the future, compared with 61% in Scotland and 64% in Northern Ireland – these last two being higher than any other parts of the UK (Sargant et al, 1997[2]). We also drew on published official statistics, including the Labour Force Survey, which suggested that participation in continuing vocational education was lower in Scotland and Northern Ireland than elsewhere, while the proportion of employees lacking qualifications was higher (Field and Schuller, 1995). These figures were surprising because – at least in conventional wisdom – Scotland and Northern Ireland outperform England in initial education. Certainly so far as academic qualifications are concerned, both societies lived up to the stereotype. Proportionately more young people gained GCSEs and A levels/Highers, and the age participation rate for higher education remains significantly above English and Welsh levels.

If accurate, this evidence would run counter to most published survey evidence, which for Britain, as for other OECD nations generally, demonstrates a strong association between level of school attainment and the propensity to take part in organised learning as an adult (McGivney, 1991; O'Connell, 1997; Beinart and Smith, 1998). Our findings were also at odds with established theories of adult participation in learning, which tend to identify prior educational success as a critical factor in explaining participation later in life (Cross, 1981; Courtney, 1992). In neither case are we aware of any work that identifies precisely which aspects of schooling are most likely to be associated with participation later in life; but at the general level, a straightforward 'reproduction' model appears to be broadly accepted. Admittedly, both surveys and theoretical approaches had tended to concentrate on the association at individual level, but even so the extent of the consensus on this relationship meant that our data – showing instead an apparent divergence – were puzzling. Given the importance now widely attached to lifelong learning both by policy makers and researchers, the apparent divergence was in need of more detailed treatment.

This chapter reports on our attempts at a more careful and thorough analysis of this issue. Empirically, our findings led us to conclude that the relationship between initial and continuing education in Scotland is far more complex and ambiguous than first appeared, but that there is persuasive evidence of a marked divergence between the two in Northern Ireland. We offer a number of possible explanations for these patterns, and consider in particular the role of social institutions and norms in shaping patterns of lifelong learning. In particular, the concept of social capital appears to offer a productive framework for analysing the ways in which new information, ideas and methods can be disseminated with varying degrees of reliability and speed.

Methods

The objectives of the study were to:

- explore the nature, extent and patterns of any statistical divergence between performance in initial education and continuing education in Scotland and Northern Ireland;
- identify possible reasons for the divergence;
- gather views from a range of stakeholders on the significance of the divergence;
- compile recommendations on action to be taken;
- contribute data and analysis for comparison with the rest of the UK as part of the overall *Learning Society Programme* of research.

In turn, this involved a deliberately eclectic methodological approach. As well as a re-examination of official statistics and other quantitative data, we undertook fieldwork using a combination of focus group interviews and individual interviews, largely but not exclusively focused on a limited number of sectors of economic activity (Sims and Godden, 1998). These primary data were supplemented by and checked against a careful analysis of documentary material, including a large volume of published reports and internal documents from key providers of education and training, as well as the major public agencies and government departments.

Statistical compilation and analysis

Our first aim was to check the survey data against other quantitative evidence. This analysis covered various educational statistics, including those found in the Labour Force Survey, Family Expenditure Survey and General Household Survey/Continuous Household Survey. Extracting a coherent and robust set of data over time was both difficult and problematic, even in relation to formal education and training. It was virtually impossible in respect of informal learning. One key recommendation that followed was for an annual 'state of the nation' report on learning, to improve the level of information supplied on a consistent basis. A learning society must have access to a wider range of information if it is to live up to that title by learning reflexively from its own experience.

Fieldwork

Our fieldwork rested on two main methods. Focus groups, the first, were intended to generate a high level of qualitative data from stakeholders, drawing out their experiences and perceptions of education and training issues. We viewed focus groups not solely as a means of identifying issues that could be pursued subsequently by other means, but also as significant sources of evidence in their own right (Morgan, 1997). We conducted a total of 20 focus groups, 10 in Scotland and 10 in Northern Ireland (NI). Recruited from among those with training and development responsibilities in the sector concerned, the aim was to attract between 6 and 12 participants to each group. These covered the following industrial sectors:

Agriculture (2 in Scotland, 2 in NI)
Electronics (1 in Scotland, 2 in NI)
Tourism (1 in NI only)
Healthcare (2 in Scotland, 2 in NI)
Financial services (1 in Scotland, I in NI),

and the following areas:

Education/training providers (3 in Scotland[3], 1 in NI)
Voluntary and community sector (1 in NI[4])
Gender-related concerns (1 in Scotland).

Numbers in the focus groups varied, with the Scottish groups generally smaller than those in Northern Ireland. The groups were facilitated by one member of the research team, and recorded by another. Discussion was preceded by a short introduction, and then structured around identical questions in both countries (see Field, 2000). The discussions were recorded and transcribed. A manual analysis was undertaken to identify themes and patterns that might subsequently be explored in the individual interviews[5].

Participants in the focus groups were selected in order to achieve a blend of expertise. Typically within each sectoral group, we recruited a range of people involved in the industry's training as human resources managers, training managers, training providers or analysts; and within the other areas were people who were well placed to make informed comment on the issues raised. In recruiting interviewees, we paid attention to such matters as geographical distribution (the rural/urban division is a significant one in both societies), and in each group we sought as broad a gender balance as was reasonable in the sectoral context (this meant a majority of women in healthcare, for example). In Northern Ireland, we tried to secure a broad balance between the two main communities, and to hold the meetings in neutral spaces.

We carried out 56 individual interviews, 31 in Scotland and 25 in Northern Ireland. These were primarily designed to explore in greater depth the issues raised in the focus groups. The interviews followed a semi-structured format; some of the questions were common to both Scottish and Northern Irish interviews, but not all since the outcomes of the focus groups led to different emphases. The interviews were recorded but not transcribed in full, and then analysed manually. The interviewees were selected for various reasons. A minority had already participated in a focus group, and had offered what we saw as particularly informative messages. The majority were selected because the focus groups pointed towards them as key sources of further information.

Results

Statistical summary

Is there really less adult learning in Northern Ireland and Scotland? How far does the apparent divergence hold up when a wider range of statistics are examined in more detail? The key results may be summarised succinctly.

In Northern Ireland, analysis confirms the divergence, with consistent evidence of very high achievement in initial education compared to the rest of the UK, combined with low participation in adult education and training. In Scotland, the picture is far more nuanced: it is one of convergence over time between English and Scottish performance in initial education – a feature which challenges some Scottish myths of educational superiority – and of less difference than at first appeared in adult participation. At the time of writing it remains to be seen how such patterns will be affected by the existence of a new Scottish Parliament and Northern Ireland Executive, both of which exercise devolved powers for education and training policy.

'Performance' is not a simple concept to measure at the education system level. High achievements at the top end may accompany poor achievements in the middle or lower ranges. We have therefore covered a number of different angles. Moreover, in any analysis of this kind, it is crucial but extremely difficult to trace trends over time. By using the notion of trajectory we are able to see how the relationship has changed, especially in the Scottish context, so that 'advantages' which existed in the 1970s may now have disappeared (see Bamford and Schuller, 1999). Nevertheless, there may be a widespread belief both within the education/ training system and outside it in distinctive features despite their erosion over time, and these perceptions can in turn be significant in shaping behaviour.

School education

Historically, both Scotland and Northern Ireland have had more polarised patterns of achievement than England. Despite convergence in recent years the legacy will persist for some time. Thus, adult literacy and numeracy levels among older adults in Northern Ireland, and particularly among those from Catholic families, are lower than in Britain, as a consequence of past inequalities in the schools systems of the 1940s, 1950s and 1960s (Sweeney and Morgan, 1998). There is a widespread belief that the schooling system in Scotland and Northern Ireland is of a higher standard than elsewhere in the UK; this is not entirely without foundation, but the evidence suggests a much patchier pattern of attainment overall, combined again with a degree of convergence between the four parts of the UK.

In Scotland, through the 1960s, 1970s and much of the 1980s, more young people gained qualifications adequate for university entrance, but more also left school early with no or almost no qualifications. By the mid-1990s, this polarisation had been reduced: school leavers in England had made substantial advances at higher levels of achievement, while Scotland had reduced the numbers leaving with no graded results. Likewise, Northern Ireland's long 'tail' of unqualified school leavers was dramatically reduced in the 1970s and 1980s, partly as a result of the importance of credentialism to middle-class and then subsequently working-class Catholics (McKeown, 1996). But these historical patterns, and the higher percentages leaving with no graded results some one to three decades ago, will leave their legacy for another 30 years. Demographic profiles accentuate the issue: in Scotland, for example, the population aged 40-59/64 is expected to increase by 266,000 by 2011, compared with a drop of 295,000 for those aged 20-39. The picture is slightly different in Northern Ireland, whose population remains comparatively youthful.

Gender differences are significant

In Northern Ireland, in 1997/98, 71.5% of boys were still in full-time education, compared with 91.4% of girls; boys outnumber girls by about 4:1 on Jobskills courses. The gap between boys and girls leaving with no qualifications is greatest in Northern Ireland. The trend in girls outperforming boys at school in Scotland goes back to the mid and late 1970s. By 1996/97, the gap between girls and boys in attaining three or more Highers stood at 7%. More boys leave school with no recognised qualifications, and they have been slightly more likely to do so in Scotland than elsewhere. While the percentages have dropped dramatically, boys are still a little more likely to have no qualifications than are girls.

Gender and locale combine to generate wide variation within each of the countries; for example, in relation to the Advisory Scottish Council on Education and Training Targets (ASCETT) target 1 on the academic route (five or more standard grades at grades 1-3 by age 16), the highest achievers were girls living in the Orkney Islands (73.4% in 1996/97), while the lowest were boys in North Lanarkshire (34.5%).

Staying on

Since the school leaving age was raised in 1972/73, more 16 year olds have stayed on in school in Scotland than in England[6]. However, Scotland's advantage is largely offset by other countries' greater participation in non-school provision, and for full-time education Scotland loses its lead beyond age 16. By age 17 plus, 44% of young people in Scotland, compared with 52% in England, were at school, further or higher education, and by 18 plus, the percentages were 35% in Scotland, and 39% in England (Raffe et al, 1998). But in Northern Ireland the relative advantage is as strong for 17 year olds. In 1996/97, 76.7% of 16 and 17 year olds were still in full-time education, as against 63.2% in England. In the 'Status Zero' studies of 16 and 17 year olds who were not in training, employment or education, it appeared that this group was proportionately much smaller in Northern Ireland, making up some 6% of the age group in comparison with around 20% in South Glamorgan (Armstrong, 1997).

Initial higher education

Scotland and Northern Ireland both lead England in the proportions of young people moving into higher education. However, in Scotland the margin is rather smaller than is usually believed. The Dearing Report's figures, covering 1989-93, showed Scotland to have the highest Age Participation Index (API), at 35%, followed by Northern Ireland at 33%, with England on 28%. Both countries are therefore ahead of England, but the rate of increase is slower in Scotland. In Northern Ireland, moreover, entry is normally after two rather than one year of post-GCSE study, and undergraduate study follows the English three-year model. In Scotland, the headline API is inflated by the fact that first degrees involve four years of full-time study (Osborne, 1999).

A wider range of qualifications are used to achieve admission to first degree courses in England: 55% of students in Wales, 63% in England, almost 66% in Northern Ireland and 70% in Scotland entered first year degree courses with conventional academic qualifications – Highers and GCE A levels. For entry to part-time first degrees, academic qualifications were again more dominant in Scotland than elsewhere (Parry, 1997).

Northern Ireland's schools have been particularly effective in widening access to higher education (HE). In Northern Ireland, increased participation has been accompanied by an increase in the proportion of students coming from manual and white collar working-class families (Field, 1997). This is in marked contrast with England, where expansion has not benefited the working class more than any other groups. One result is that the University of Ulster has the largest proportion of undergraduates from working-class backgrounds of any UK university. The Garrick figures for Scotland have been disputed in some quarters, with one recent study suggesting that, despite its reputation, Scotland is actually less socially inclusive in its recruitment than England (Osborne, 1999).

Higher education in Northern Ireland (especially) and in Scotland is more frontloaded than in England. In 1995/96, in Northern Ireland under 24% of undergraduates were aged over 25, compared with 37.4% in the UK as a whole. Higher education students in Scotland are also younger on average than their counterparts in England: 48% of undergraduates in Scotland were under 21, compared with 40% in England (HESA, 1997). There is evidence of 'crowding out' by younger people; Northern Ireland universities admit a lower proportion of access students than English institutions (Field, 1997).

Scotland has more higher education provision in FE colleges, and a higher percentage of students taking non-degree courses, in particular higher national diplomas (HNDs). But this difference appears to be shifting, with Scotland moving closer to England in the proportions of students taking undergraduate degrees and HNDs (Schuller et al, 1999).

Qualifications and training in the workforce

Qualification levels are higher in the Scottish workforce on average, but are rising more slowly. In 1998, 49% of the employed workforce in Scotland was qualified to level III; this compared with 43% in the UK and England, 42% in Wales and 41% in Northern Ireland. Compared with a UK average of 24%[7], 27% had reached level IV. However, Scotland has recently made relatively little progress, so the other countries are catching up (ASCETT, 1998).

In neither Scotland nor Northern Ireland have National/Scottish Vocational Qualifications (N/SVQs) attracted the same degree of interest as in England and Wales. A Scottish 'penetration rate' of 2.09% and one of 3.3% in Northern Ireland compares with 5.96% in England and Wales. While numbers taking SVQs have risen in Scotland, the numbers taking other vocational qualifications have fallen, especially at level III (Canning,

1999). In Scotland, it is possible that demand for National Certificate modules may have depressed the uptake of SVQs. In both countries there appears to be a significant esteem problem in relation to vocational qualifications.

UK-wide, women are underachieving in vocational qualifications. Vocational qualifications are more sharply gendered than school ones. The gender gap is biggest in Scotland, where, on 1994 figures, almost 10% more men had vocational qualifications at level III or above. In his analysis of regional data for the UK, Alan Felstead has concluded that women are less likely to undergo certification for work-related skills than men, making qualifications an even less reliable guide to relative ability for women (Felstead, 1996). Moreover, these figures may underestimate the extent of gender inequality in vocational qualifications as the ASCETT/NACETT targets only include those in employment, and qualifications are distributed more unequally among women and men if everyone of working age is included.

In both countries, commitment to Investors in People (IiP) appears relatively weak. By March 1998, 9% of Scottish organisations employing 50-199 people, and 22% of Scottish organisations employing over 200 people, were recognised as IiP. This compares with 12% for smaller organisations and 29% for larger ones in the UK (ASCETT, 1998). In Northern Ireland the Training and Employment Agency has consistently failed to meet its local targets for IiP; in 1997/98, for example, 37 employers achieved IiP status, against a target of 50 (TEA, 1998).

Recorded participation in training is weak, but in Scotland this may be a function of social attitudes to what counts as a learning episode. In Northern Ireland, under 5% of manual workers received training in the four weeks reported to the Labour Force Survey in Spring 1996, compared with 9% for the UK; for non-manuals the figures were 12% and 18%. Labour Force Survey figures consistently show a slightly lower percentage of employees and self-employed people receive job-related training in Scotland than in the UK as a whole. In 1996, 14% of people in employment in Great Britain received job-related training compared with 12% in Scotland, and the gap is bigger for women. However, in Scotland, the training which people report lasts for longer, both in hours per week and in length overall. Of those receiving training in spring 1996, it lasted an average of 16.1 hours per week in England and 25 hours in Scotland for manual workers, and 13 and 16.1 respectively for non-manuals (13.8 for Northern Ireland, where no figures were available for manuals). In spring 1998, for 23% of people in employment in Scotland reporting training, their training lasted for three years or more, compared with a UK average of 17%.

Adult education

Our whole investigation was prompted by figures suggesting lower adult participation in both general adult education and continuing vocational training in both countries. There was also some evidence suggesting that both populations of adults had, relative to England, lower aspirations to learn. However, statistics on adult participation are extremely patchy, and even reported local authority spending figures for adult education may not cover the same fields exactly. For what it is worth, official data suggest that in 1994/95, adult education accounted for 9.8% of local authority spending in Northern Ireland, 13% in Wales and almost 16% in England. Any further comparison is made more difficult because of different interpretations of adult education. For example 'community education' is used as the label for Scotland's local authority provision; this refers to a broader set of activities than adult education in England, and this in turn may partly account for lower reported rates of participation or indeed apparently higher rates of public funding. On the one hand, the balance of provision may be more towards the informal, and on the other Scots are less likely to think of themselves as 'learning' outwith formal courses. The Scottish Office has estimated that, in an average week, 130,000 youths, and 260,000 adults participate in community education in Scotland (Scottish Office, 1997). Figures for continuing education in universities, by contrast, do not suggest any significant difference in participation either way.

Libraries and museums

Finally, we sought to identify adequate proxy measures for participation in self-directed learning. Self-directed learning (that is, learning undertaken by individuals under their own steam, in non-educational settings) is a potentially vast area, and measuring its incidence is fraught with difficulty (Eraut, 2000). Attendance figures for museums and library usage rates are not entirely satisfactory as indicators, since it is by no means certain that they are being used for self-directed learning, but they can be taken as providing a very rough proxy.

Scotland has the highest and Northern Ireland the lowest level of borrowing of books and audio visual materials from libraries. In 1997, the average numbers of books borrowed per head of population in Scotland was 8.51, but only 5.86 in Northern Ireland. This compares with a UK average of 8.18. Glasgow has the lowest level of borrowing – 6.39 books per head. In all other areas of Scotland, levels of borrowing are 9 or more books per head – well ahead of the UK average, and one of the highest levels of borrowing in Western Europe. It is estimated that about twice as many people use libraries as borrow books[8]. Scotland has the highest and Northern Ireland the lowest level of per capita library expenditure; however, Scotland's libraries have lost £8 million since 1996. A higher percentage of people in Scotland, and a lower percentage in Northern Ireland, than in the UK as a whole visit museums. These data are broadly consistent with our other findings, and support the view that while there is a marked degree of divergence in Northern Ireland, the Scottish picture is somewhat more blurred.

We have cast our net widely, and attempted to give a sense of trajectories over time. This has exposed some rather worrying gaps in our knowledge – hence our recommendation for a regular and systematic overview. However, we have demonstrated two strikingly different outcomes. In Northern Ireland the original supposition was broadly confirmed, with a marked contrast between high levels of attainment in initial education (IE) and subsequent low levels of participation in continuing education (CE). Even here, however, we point to the weakness of the data in respect of adult learning, especially the less formal types. In Scotland, the divergence disappeared on closer inspection, with higher IE achievement dwindling and the appearance of lower CE participation resulting from different reporting habits – itself an interesting cultural feature. We now turn to the question of how these patterns might be explained.

Explaining the patterns

Any divergence is likely, we think, to arise from combinations of factors. In particular, it is likely that significant features of social and economic patterns are at work, including the following: industrial structure, labour force composition, migration, gender, cultural characteristics and a variety of supply side factors. Moreover, the issues of gender, culture and the quality of provision are prominent in the findings from our fieldwork in both societies.

Industrial structure is particularly relevant in Northern Ireland, with industries where training is weak, such as farming, comparatively strongly represented. The concentration of long-term unemployment is particularly severe, due to factors such as extreme urban segregation and the perceived and actual risks of geographical mobility in a divided society. The labour market is dominated to an unusual extent by small firms; over half the workforce is in firms with fewer than 50 employees, and 20% work in firms with fewer than five. Northern Ireland is the only UK region where firms of 500+ employees have a smaller share of turnover than they do of the workforce.

None of this applies to anything like the same extent in Scotland, although here too there is a higher proportion of the workforce (35.3%) employed in small (1-49 employee) firms than in the UK (31.3%)[9]. Slightly fewer people are self-employed, a category which is particularly associated with low levels of recorded training (Sims and Godden, 1998). While Scottish unemployment rates are slightly higher than the UK average, there is a lower proportion of long-term claimants.

One common factor which can be seen to play a major part is migration. In both Scotland and Northern Ireland emigration rates are particularly high among those qualified at graduate level and above. It is well established in the literature that the most highly educated are most likely to participate in adult learning. An analysis of those from Northern Ireland who graduated in 1996-97 – at a time when the local economy was relatively buoyant – showed that 36% of those who took a first degree went to a position outside Northern Ireland, almost invariably elsewhere in the UK (DENI, 1998, Table 1b).

While Scotland provides more higher education places relative to its share of the population, the proportion of graduates in the population is broadly in line with the UK average. Most migration is from North to South, so that while Scotland provides 11.4% of higher education places, around 9% of all employed UK graduates are located in Scotland. The net outflow of graduates from Scotland has moved from 14% in 1983, to 21% in 1989, to 10% in 1992, reflecting changes in job opportunities. HESA figures for 1995/96 show that a quarter of Scottish domiciled graduates leave Scotland for their first job. It is higher in Northern Ireland, where the figure is 32%, and in Wales, where it is 46% (MacEachan et al, 1995).

Networks, norms and trust: the importance of informal learning

The central theme of our fieldwork analysis is the importance of social capital – that is, norms, networks and trust – in shaping the level and quality of continuing education and training. The concept has been applied in sociology to explain educational attainment (Coleman, 1994), in political science to explain civic participation and stability (Putnam, 1993), and in economics to explain the prosperity of small open economies (Maskell et al, 1998). It has also been applied elsewhere within the *Learning Society Programme*, particularly in the Glasgow-based study of people with learning difficulties (Riddell et al, 1999). How might this concept be applied to the analysis of lifelong learning (Schuller and Field, 1998)?

One way of visualising the relationships is the loose network shown in Figure 1. At its simplest, it means that any given society will approximate more closely to the ideal of a learning society if these relationships are supportive of lifelong learning.

Figure 1: Sources of social capital

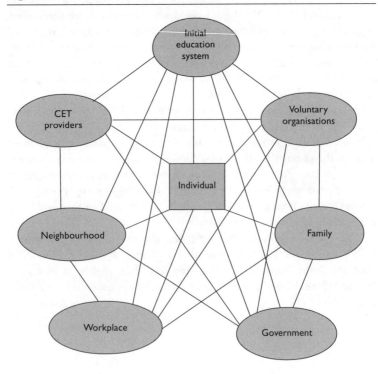

This network is simplified, but still generates a large number of possible relationships. Moreover, for Coleman and Granovetter, the significance of any possible bilateral linkage is not simply whether it exists, but how strong it is, and how far it is interwoven with other linkages, creating what Coleman calls a relatively high degree of closure (Coleman, 1994; Granovetter, 1974). Our interviews therefore explored, in addition to the factors identified in the introduction to this sub-section, the significance of these relationships, their strengths and weaknesses, and their implications for adult learning.

A summary and selective account of the empirical findings of the study follows. In each case, we have indicated where the finding applies to Scotland (S), to N Ireland (NI) or to both.

The relationship between IE and CE is a complex and evolving one. Given the legacy we pointed to earlier, the attitudes which schooling has engendered in adults are likely to endure for some while. These include a highly conservative view of education and what it is expected to deliver (NI); and a strong sense of the education system as something to which responsibility for educational achievement is 'contracted out' (S).

The impact of extending initial education, notably through the rapid rise in undergraduate numbers, is still unclear. But there is some evidence that its impact on motivation to learn throughout life is at best ambiguous, and possibly negative (both, but especially S).

Trust levels between employers and CE providers were not consistent. Employers may choose to rely on informal networks rather than qualifications for recruitment, sending a distinct message about the relative value of learning (NI). They may stress qualifications, but exhibit a lack of trust in the providers of CE to assure their quality, at least as they see it (both). Conversely, providers see employers as having exaggerated and narrow expectations of a 'product' from them (S).

Internal staff training is often shaped by change in the nature of the employment contract; on the one hand, a greater use of subcontracting and temporary labour (both), and on the other, the emergence of CE as a feature of a recast relationship between employer and employee (S). Generational relationships impact on learning, especially in sectors where technological change may have left older senior management stranded (S). Parallel patterns were noted, incidentally, in another *Learning Society Programme* study in respect of professional staff in the National Health Service (Dowswell et al, 1999).

Supply side concerns varied between sectors. FE colleges are still perceived as youth-oriented (both). The introduction of markets has

enhanced responsiveness, but also driven up costs and narrowed the range
(S). In some sectors, for example financial services and electronics,
companies are becoming providers of training beyond their own staff (S).
Perceptions of further education tended to be out of date, with public
understanding lagging behind the rapid changes in the sector in recent
years (NI). Diversity of providers was more apparent in Northern Ireland
than in Scotland, with the 'third sector' of community-based and voluntary
sector provision being strong but volatile and highly disparate.
Geographical factors may in part account for the large variations in
attainment, with performance in IE and CE interrelated.

Cultural influences are most strongly seen in family and peer influences
on learning (see also Gorard et al, 1999). This includes the decisive
influence exercised by the family, and particularly mothers, on the
educational and vocational behaviour of both young people and adults,
which can sustain commitment to education but also inhibit career risks
(NI); the difficulty of extracting men from a peer culture which does not
value organised learning unless it has a visible material reward (S); and
the strong sense that women are more able to realise the joy of learning,
even though there may be higher structural barriers confronting them
(both). Even where learning is implicitly valued, it may be more or less
taboo to give voice to this (S).

There is a relationship between learning, motivation, and occupational
or social cultures, for example where a strong can-do mentality prevails.
Thus a passionate advocate of self-build housing, interviewed within the
agricultural sector, saw self-build as the key to a learning society, because
of the mix of skills and responsibility which it involved (S).

The state has a major role in shaping the context within which these
relationships are formed. This is not so much as provider of CE, but as
campaigner and framework-provider, for instance for coherent
qualifications (both), and as the guarantor of independent information in
an increasingly confusing context of multiple providers.

Legal requirements, for example on health and safety in agriculture or
on regulatory standards in financial services, can raise the volume of
training, but not necessarily the overall standard or breadth of learning
(both).

Finally, social capital was strongly associated with a marked preference
among adults for informal rather than formal learning. Strong claims on
behalf of the voluntary and community sector – particularly in relation
to women learners – went largely unchallenged in the focus groups (NI).
In Northern Ireland particularly, dense local ties shape patterns of lifelong

learning in a number of ways. They work to secure a remarkably high level of IE, but may have inhibited demand for formal adult education and training. At one level, this can be seen as an adherence to a relatively fixed and conservative view of the adult: people are, educationally, what they have achieved by the time they leave school; change and development are neither expected nor desired. Particularly in a divided community, in which access to desirable resources such as employment and security are widely regarded as a zero-sum game, such conservatism is a way of managing the risks that are inherent in any process of change.

Scotland is not a divided community in the same way. There is a stronger commitment to meritocratic patterns promoted by education. On the other hand, Scottish people also exhibit tendencies to regard their paths as set once initial education is completed, at whatever stage that may be. Attachment to locality – an advantage when it comes to access to a local university – is a drawback when it inhibits mobility and adaptability (except for the highly qualified – see above, under migration).

Social capital offers abundant opportunities for informal and incidental learning, but it also has a clear down side: it is inherently narrowing, in that it gives access only to the limited range of resources that happen to be available in any given locale, and familial forms of social capital can be particularly limiting and inward-looking, making it more difficult to build 'bridging ties' (Pahl and Spencer, 1997, p 102).

Our deployment of social capital as a central concept has led to tentative rather than to any firm conclusions. We do not offer our conclusions in any abstract or mechanistic manner. "The social world is accumulated history", as Bourdieu has put it (Bourdieu, 1985, p 241), and it is not only circumstances that alter cases, but also their baggage of inherited beliefs, structures and memories. We are suspicious, for example, of the kinds of analysis which relate trust levels directly to economic performance (eg Knack and Keefer, 1997). However, we would argue strongly that its use opens up lines of argument and reflection which have been largely neglected in the debate on the relationship between education, economy and society, which has for too long been overshadowed by the dominance of models derived from human capital approaches.

Recommendations and research priorities

As well as contributing to an understanding of the social context of adult learning, our analysis also led us to make a number of recommendations.

It appears appropriate in a programme of research into the Learning Society to identify implications for further reflection or action. While the bulk of these are addressed to policy makers, particularly within Northern Ireland and Scotland, others concern the wider field of those involved in managing and delivering learning programmes.

First, we conclude that the annual publication of a 'state of the nation' report on lifelong learning, bringing together achievements in the different fields, relating to all age groups and including indices of informal learning and acknowledging existing weaknesses, is a highly desirable precondition of the Learning Society. This is a general conclusion, applicable to a wide range of societies as well as those involved in this particular study. Similarly, it is not only in Scotland and Northern Ireland that serious attention should be given to the lasting legacy of highly polarised schooling systems, especially in basic skills among older adults (40+). Higher education is still focused on the initial phase of learning, especially in Northern Ireland. The impact of expansion on motivation for CE should be assessed. Further expansion should directly seek to favour lifelong learning. Effective demand for skills and qualifications varies widely within countries and economic sectors. Supply side measures need to be matched by effective, and perhaps localised, demand side initiatives, with attention paid to the variable impact of new technologies on skill levels. Partnerships are a key component of a lifelong learning strategy, as well as other aspects of economic development. Successful partnerships require new skills, in the sharing of information and understanding different values. Finally, in a more turbulent and crowded learning market, educational guidance has an increasingly important function, with the proliferation of providers and the prospect of Individual Learning Accounts.

We believe that the research implications of this project are potentially enormous (see Field and Schuller, 1999). Four main areas will have to suffice at this stage:

- As with a number of projects in the ESRC programme, we were led to pay more attention to informal learning than we had expected. Informal learning has attracted some attention in the past, and is likely to receive more as policy makers and researchers increasingly focus on the distribution and application of tacit as well as codified knowledge, and on learning that is situated in workplace and community settings, particularly as they affect economic performance and social inclusion (Coffield, 2000). Yet this remains something of a black box, with few reliable indicators beyond the anecdotal. Appropriate accountancy tools are needed to measure investment and returns to learning on an appropriately broad basis, embracing if possible informal learning as well as more structured and formal participation.

- Our findings suggest that policies geared to the prolongation of initial education may have contradictory effects (Alheit, 1999). One area for investigation is the impact of expanded HE on motivations and attitudes among graduates. The impact of schooling – and particularly of recent curriculum reforms in a number of Western European nations – on attitudes towards and aptitudes for learning later throughout the adult life span is also an important area for inquiry.

- We have already alluded to the relationship between information about learning on the one hand, and the process of policy making for lifelong learning on the other. Using interactive methods such as focus group interviews, our own study sought consciously to develop an approach to investigation that was congruent with the topic that we were investigating, and that itself created opportunities for reflection and dialogue. In a context where policy makers have called for a more instrumental relationship between researchers and practitioners (with the former telling the latter 'what works'), we would emphasise strongly the need for a more dialogic and questioning approach to evidence-based practice and policy.

- The main line of further research which our study implies is in the relationship between lifelong learning and social capital. We suggest that this could be operationalised in terms of the sharing of information, the mutual acknowledgement of objectives, and the levels of trust which exist between stakeholders. This is far from being unproblematic. As we have already suggested, policies designed to foster capacity building and investment in social capital may, unintentionally, contribute to the embedding of narrowly-delineated networks and unambitious norms, and researchers as well as policy makers need to acknowledge the down side as well as the up side of social capital. Yet our study has also suggested that social capital may be a helpful concept for exploring patterns of participation and achievement in lifelong learning; it may also provide a focus for careful policy intervention. Exploration of these issues would go some way towards helping Scotland, Northern Ireland and the UK as a whole to develop the reflexivity that is arguably the defining characteristic of a learning society.

Notes

[1] The study on which this paper is based was funded by the Economic and Social Research Council, grant L123251043. We wish to acknowledge the contribution of Caroline Bamford and Lynda Spence in carrying out much of the research on which this chapter is based, and the financial support of the Equal Opportunities Commission Scotland.

[2] We wish to acknowledge the support of the National Institute of Adult Continuing Education, and particularly Alan Tuckett, in making available to us the full draft findings of the survey on which Sargant et al (1997) was based.

[3] It is worth noting that in Scotland, Education and Training was established as a sector-led group itself, with government recognising its distinctive contribution to service-led exports. No parallel initiative existed in Northern Ireland at the time of our study.

[4] In Northern Ireland, this is not only an important field of employment – as it is elsewhere in the UK – but also has for some years played an important role in respect of governance, particularly through its involvement in private/public sector partnerships. It has also acquired a considerable influence as a provider of non-formal education and training for adults.

[5] We considered undertaking a quantitative analysis using a software package such as NUD*IST, but rejected the idea on closer investigation as it was unlikely to add much value to a conventional analysis.

[6] Figures on school education are taken from various Scottish Office, Department of Education Northern Ireland and Central Statistical Office (CSO) publications, including Scottish Abstracts of Statistics and CSO Annual Abstract of Statistics.

[7] Other than NVQ3, Level 3 is taken to be 3 Highers A–C in Scotland, and 2 GCE A levels elsewhere in the UK. Level 4 is a vocational, professional, management or academic qualification at S/NVQ Level 4 or above.

[8] Calculated from data supplied by the Institute of Public Finance Ltd and Scottish Library Association. Institute of Public Finance figures are calculated from their annual compendium of figures (forthcoming).

---

⁹ Calculated from Department of Trade and Industry figures supplied by Professor David Storey of Warwick University.

References

Alheit, P. (1999) 'On a contradictory way to the "Learning Society": a critical approach', *Studies in the Education of Adults*, vol 31, no 1, pp 66-82.

Armstrong, D. (1997) *'Status 0':A socio-economic study of young people on the margin*, Belfast: Training and Employment Agency.

ASCETT (Advisory Scottish Council for Education and Training Targets) (1998) *Annual report*, Edinburgh: ASCETT.

Bamford, C. and Schuller, T. (1999) 'Comparing educational "performance"', *Scottish Educational Review*, vol 31, no 2, pp 122-36.

Beinart, S. and Smith, D. (1998) *National adult learning survey 1997*, Sheffield: DfEE.

Bourdieu, P. (1985) 'The forms of capital', in J. G. Richardson (ed) *Handbook of theory and research for the sociology of education*, New York, NY: Greenwood Press, pp 241-58.

Canning, R. (1999) 'Reinventing Scottish vocational qualifications', *Scottish Journal of Adult and Continuing Education*, vol 5, no 1, pp 25-34.

Coffield, F. (2000) 'Introduction: The structure below the surface: reassessing the significance of informal learning', in F. Coffield (ed) *The necessity of informal learning*, Bristol: The Policy Press, pp 1-11.

Coleman, J.S. (1994) *Foundations of social theory*, Cambridge, MA: Belknap.

Courtney, S. (1992) *Why adults learn: Towards a theory of participation in adult education*, London: Routledge.

Cross, K.P. (1981) *Adults as learners*, San Francisco, CA: Jossey-Bass.

DENI (Department of Education Northern Ireland) (1998) *First destinations of students gaining qualifications from higher education institutions: Northern Ireland 1996/97*, Statistical press release, Bangor: DENI.

Dowswell, T., Millar, B. and Hewison, J. (1999) 'The costs of learning: the policy implications of changes in continuing education of NHS staff', in F. Coffield (ed) *Speaking truth to power: Research and policy on lifelong learning*, Bristol: The Policy Press, pp 46-54.

Eraut, M. (2000) 'Non-formal learning, implicit learning and tacit knowledge in professional work', in F. Coffield (ed) *The necessity of informal learning*, Bristol: The Policy Press, pp 12-31.

Felstead, A. (1996) 'Policy update: identifying gender inequalities in the distribution of vocational qualifications in the UK', *Gender, Work and Organisation*, vol 3, no 1, pp 38-50.

Field, J. (1997) 'Equity and access: adult participation in higher education in Northern Ireland', *Journal of Access Studies*, vol 12, no 2, pp 139-52.

Field, J. (2000) 'Investigating lifelong learning through focus groups', *Journal of Further and Higher Education*, forthcoming.

Field, J. and Schuller, T. (1995) 'Is there less adult learning in Scotland and Northern Ireland? A preliminary analysis', *Scottish Journal of Adult and Continuing Education*, vol 2, no 2, pp 71-80.

Field, J. and Schuller, T. (1999) 'Investigating the learning society', *Studies in the Education of Adults*, vol 31, no 1, pp 1-11.

Gorard, S., Rees, S. and Fevre, R. (1999) 'Two dimensions of time: the changing social context of lifelong learning', *Studies in the Education of Adults*, vol 31, no 1, pp 35-48.

Granovetter, M. (1974) *Getting a job: A study of contacts and careers*, Cambridge, MA: Harvard University Press.

HESA (Higher Education Statistics Authority) (1997) 'Research datapack 7: Regional issues', Cheltenham: HESA.

Knack, S. and Keefer, P. (1997) 'Does social capital have an economic payoff? A cross-country investigation', *Quarterly Journal of Economics*, November, pp 1251-8.

MacEachan, D., Baxter, I. and Robertson, S. (1995) *Graduate employment in Scotland 1983-94*, Edinburgh: University of Edinburgh Careers Service.

McGivney, V. (1991) *Education's for other people*, Leicester: National Institute for Adult Education.

McKeown, M. (1996) 'Anatomy of a myth: the impact of the 1947 Education Act upon Roman Catholic access to academic secondary education in Northern Ireland, 1947–1967', *Irish Education Studies*, vol 16, pp 213-22.

Maskell, P., Eskelinen, H., Hannibalsson, I., Malmberg, A. and Vatne, E. (1998) *Competitiveness, localised learning and regional development*, London: Routledge.

Morgan, D.L. (1997) *Focus groups as qualitative research*, Newbury Park: Sage Publications.

O'Connell, P. (1997) *Adults in training: An international comparison of continuing education and training*, Paris: OECD.

Osborne, R. (1999) 'Wider access in Scotland', *Scottish Affairs*, vol 26, pp 36-46.

Pahl, R. and Spencer, L. (1997) 'The politics of friendship', *Renewal*, vol 5, no 3/4, pp 100-7.

Parry, G. (1997) 'Patterns of participation in higher education in England: a statistical summary and commentary', *Higher Education Quarterly*, vol 51, no 1, pp 6-28.

Putnam, R.D. (1993) *Making democracy work: Civic traditions in modern Italy*, Princeton, NJ: Princeton University Press.

Raffe, D., Biggart, A., Fairgrieve, J. and Howieson, C. (1998) *OECD thematic review: The transition from initial education to working life*, UK background report, Edinburgh: Centre for Educational Sociology.

Riddell, S., Baron, S. and Wilson, A. (1999) 'Social capital and people with learning difficulties', *Studies in the Education of Adults*, vol 31, no 1, pp 49-66.

Sargant, N., Field, J., Francis, H., Schuller, T. and Tuckett, A. (1997) *The learning divide: A study of participation in adult learning in the United Kingdom*, Leicester: National Institute for Adult Continuing Education.

Schuller, T. and Field, J. (1998) 'Social capital, human capital and the learning society', *International Journal of Lifelong Education*, vol 17, no 4, pp 226-35.

Schuller, T., Raffe, D., Morgan-Klein, M. and Clark, I. (1999) *Part-time higher education: Policy, practice and experience*, London: Jessica Kingsley.

Scottish Office (1997) *Statistical bulletin education series, community education statistics 1996-7*, Edinburgh: SOEID.

Sims, D. and Godden, S. (1998) *A study of employers' use of NVQs and SVQs across industrial sectors*, Research Report no 51, Sheffield: DfEE.

Sweeney, K. and Morgan, B. (1998) *Adult literacy in Northern Ireland*, Belfast: Statistics and Research Agency.

TEA (Training and Employment Agency) (1998) *Annual report 1997/ 1998*, Belfast: TEA.

THREE

Learning culture, learning age, learning society: turning aspirations into reality?

Pat Davies and John Bynner

The concepts of 'learning society' and 'lifelong learning' appear in a number of guises in the literature and in policy pronouncements (Coffield, 1999). Our project was concerned with policy and practice: the strategies to bring about a learning society in the wider national sense and to develop a learning culture at the level of organisations, groups and individuals. We focused on a particular feature – *credit-based learning* – and its role in the development of learning cultures at local level.

National policy statements about the Learning Society offer numerous visions of lifelong learning as part of a 'learning culture'. The government's own vision of lifelong learning is set out in the White Paper, *Learning to Succeed*:

> Lifelong learning can enable people to play a full part in developing their talent, the potential of their family, and the capacity of the community in which they live and work. It can and must nurture a love for learning. This will ensure the means by which our economy can make a successful transition from the industries and services of the past, to the knowledge and information economy of the future. It also contributes to sustaining a civilised and cohesive society, in which people develop as active citizens and in which generational disadvantage can be overcome. (DfEE, 1999, p 1)

The underpinning of such lifelong learning by the development of a 'learning culture' is elaborated in the reports of the advisory group under the chairmanship of Bob Fryer (1997, 1999). Such a *lifelong learning culture* (Fryer, 1997) would be characterised by:

- the absence of a 'learning divide' where a minority with qualifications continue to learn throughout their lives and the majority have few or no formal qualifications and do not participate in systematic learning after leaving school;
- a shared responsibility for learning between individuals, employers and the state;
- widened participation and higher levels of achievement – "many more people successfully get to the starting line" (p 5);
- accessible learning: flexible but coherent and coordinated, learner oriented rather than provider oriented;
- an emphasis on home, community and workplace as key places of learning;
- a credit framework where interim achievement is awarded and units of credits can be accumulated into full qualifications according to need;
- a changed language and vocabulary to describe learning (p 13);
- inclusion and social cohesion (p 14);
- a valuing of both formal and informal learning, of learning and achievement as well as qualifications (p 16).

In short, a lifelong learning culture is one where learning is "a normal, accessible, productive and enjoyable (if demanding) feature of everyday life for all people throughout their lives" (p 24). Its foundation lies in participation via local learning opportunities, and within organisations, new forms of learning processes around shared learning goals. Such a culture, implying shared norms and values (Jacobson, 1996), will not be imposed or imported but will comprise the negotiated and shared symbols and meanings (Adlam, 1999) arising through social interaction (Meek, 1994). According to Schein (1991), if no consensus develops there is no culture:

> Basically the founder of the new group starts with some beliefs, values and assumptions about how to proceed and teaches those to new members through a variety of mechanisms. What is for him or her basic reality becomes for the group a set of interim values and beliefs about which they have limited choice. The group then behaves in a certain way based on the founder's beliefs and values, and either succeeds or fails. If it fails, the group eventually dissolves and no culture is formed. If it succeeds, and this process repeats itself, what were originally the beliefs, values, and assumptions of the founders come to be validated in the shared experiences of the group. (p 249)

Hence, culture differentiates communities and groups. In organisations it prescribes 'the way we do things here' (Pheysey, 1993) and the goals to which such action is directed. However, organisations are not monolithic in terms of their culture. In educational organisations in particular, within a given organisation there may be differences between disciplinary and institutional cultures (Välimaa, 1998) and between professional and occupational cultures (Saunders, 1998). Additionally, "changing cultures is a slow and difficult process ... a series of shifts over time" (Fryer, 1997, p 26); it will "require action on many fronts over an extended period, winning people to new ways of working, new priorities and a new sense of what is seen as normal and largely unremarkable" (Fryer, 1999, p 8).

Credit-based learning

The idea of a learning society underpinned by a new learning culture resonates with the claims made for credit-based systems of learning that were developed 'on the ground' in many further (FE) and higher education (HE) institutions as part of the move towards improved learning opportunities and wider access and participation. We focus here on the National Open College Network (NOCN) system, as applied in London, which has a number of different features. It is a system for accrediting and assuring the quality of units of learning based on learning outcomes with flexible delivery mechanisms and a wide variety of forms of assessment. Credits are awarded to learners for small steps of achievement (one credit represents a notional 30 hours of learning time), at four levels: Entry, 1, 2 and 3, which correspond to NVQ levels. The 'credit' acts as a unit of common currency that can be accumulated with others into achievement profiles that serve as qualifications in their own right. Alternatively they can be accumulated into specific kinds of qualifications (such as Access certificates). The main features of the OCN model and for similar models in higher education (Robertson, 1994) are:

- equity and equal opportunities through the targeting of disadvantaged and under-represented groups;
- the promotion of participation and progression by providing a flexible framework for the accumulation and transfer of credit acquired in different learning contexts;

- the promotion of a culture of achievement rather than of failure through the provision of staged developmental awards based on clear criteria, standards and outcomes;
- the valuing of learning outside formal institutions of education and across different qualifications and contexts through the recognition and accreditation of prior experiential learning;
- support for individual responsibility for and planning of learning;
- the promotion of student centred learning and reflective practice; a community of learners.

Our research set out to test some of the claims implicit in the OCN model. First, has credit-based learning contributed to the development of a learning society in the sense of opening up opportunities for *participation* and *progression* to previously disenfranchised or underrepresented groups? Second, is there evidence of the development of a new 'learning culture' in the sense of new norms and values and shared meanings in the organisations in which they have been used? Third, what impact has it had on the way groups and individuals engage with formal learning and the meaning they attach to it?

The evidence we draw on comes from a number of sources. We use the London Open College Network (LOCN) database to establish patterns of participation and progression for learners registered for credit and compare these to the traditional patterns as evidenced in the National Child Development Study (NCDS). NCDS is a national birth cohort study, which followed up the 17,000 individuals born in a single week in March 1958 through to adult life, with surveys at ages 7, 11, 16, 23 and 33 (Ferri, 1993). Through a series of case studies in FE colleges and other organisations we go on to explore the idea of a learning culture at the organisational level, investigating the impact of the introduction of credit-based learning on tutors and learners in different organisational settings. Finally we appraise the role of the OCN credit model in the development of the Learning Society.

Patterns of participation and progression in the London Open College Network

The LOCN database to which we had access comprised 73,940 learners covering the period 1992-93 to 1997-98. It contained information on gender, age group, ethnic group, employment status and the institutions/

providers where the learning experience was undertaken, and also recorded each credit awarded and its level. Because of problems with the database in the first two years due to technical problems in setting up the computerised programmes, and the incomplete records for 1997-98 at the time of our study, our main emphasis is on the period 1994-95 to 1996-97. The period was one of growth: the number of new registrations rose from 12,654 in 1994-95 to 24,302 in 1996-97. In 1997-98 they had reached over 30,000.

Learner characteristics

In all of the years examined, the learners were predominantly female, by a ratio of 2:1. Around half were in the 20-29 age range at the beginning of the period, with some indications of a wider spread across other age groups in the later years. With the exception of the 1996-97 cohort, the 16-19 (traditional FE) age group was always less than one tenth of the cohort. At the other end of the scale, well over this proportion, increasing to one fifth by 1996-97, were over the age of 40.

For those who registered their employment status, the highest proportion – over half – were unemployed, followed by unwaged – about one quarter. At the beginning of the period, less than 1% were in full-time employment and one fifth in part-time employment. By 1996-97, 4% were employed full-time and a quarter part-time. The majority were from ethnic minorities. For example in 1996-97, one fifth were 'White', followed by 'Black', 'Black African', 'Black Caribbean' (30%), of which the largest category (13%) were 'Black Caribbean'. Minorities representing less than one in ten were Indian (3%), Pakistani (2%), Bangladeshi (4%) and Chinese (2%).

The great majority of students (approaching three quarters) were working for their credits in FE and tertiary colleges, with ethnic minority students particularly favouring these. The next most popular venue was adult and community education centres, which appeared to be particularly popular with the youngest (16-19) and the oldest (50+) students. Other kinds of provision that attracted significant proportions of students were voluntary organisations, which accounted for between 5% and 10% of students of all ages in all years. By 1996-97, new providers were also appearing. Most notably 7% of the students were taking their credits through trades unions, an increasingly common base for older students: just over one tenth of 40 to 49 year old students had obtained their credits through the trades union route and nearly one fifth of those over 50. There were no signs of increasing take-up of this kind among one of the other key groups of providers – employers. By 1996-97 among all age groups of students, employers were still accounting for less than 1% of registrations with LOCN.

Participation patterns

One of the key claims of the OCN system is that the flexible delivery and the provision for accumulation mean that learners will be awarded credits over a number of years. The evidence, at least as recorded in the LOCN database, does not support this. Even among those students who had registered in the earliest years of the scheme, the proportion that registered for more than one year never exceeded 15% – including 12% who had registered for no more than two years. It is possible that the same students were coming back into the system in later years with different identifiers in the database, or that their re-registration was outside the time-scale of our study. But what seems most likely – as some tutors suggested – is that many students were using the credit system as a one-off stepping-stone to other post-16 routes to traditional qualifications. The credit route was a means rather than an end in relation to the qualifications they were seeking.

Around one third of those who had registered in 1994 were awarded no credits. Since the system is designed to provide credit for people who have not necessarily successfully completed the whole course but who have achieved the outcomes for small units of learning, this proportion was higher than expected. Further investigation of these data with LOCN officers and course tutors revealed a number of possible explanations. Questions were raised as to whether this represents failure to achieve the learning outcomes or whether there were external reasons why the credits had not been awarded. Learners had to pay for the credits awarded, and tutors suggested that some of them did not consider the expenditure worthwhile, unless they needed the credits for specific and immediate educational or vocational purposes. Thus among access students over the period of study between 80% and 90% were awarded credits, compared with 60-70% among other students. This suggests an area of 'invisible achievement' in the OCN system, which presents difficulties in evaluating its effects. Apparent failure may be no more than an artefact of the recording system, or a reflection of the low value some students place on actually receiving the credits. Some are motivated more by the desire to participate in credit-based learning as a route to other courses and qualifications or for the content of the programme. In their terms success is in completing the course rather than getting the credits for it. (The qualitative research with learners which we report later in this chapter further illustrates this point.)

Of those who were recorded as having received a credit, one tenth had achieved entry level only, and similar proportions level 2 or level 3 only. The most common category was a combination of level 2 and level 3 credits, which reduced from one quarter in 1994-95 to just under one fifth in 1996-97. This trend gives indications of a shift away from traditional access/higher education entry routes through credit in the early years, to a wider spread of learning goals at all levels later.

Another promoted feature of credit-based learning is the opportunity to take credits at different levels in any order. To what extent were learners taking the traditional linear progression routes from lower to higher credits, as compared with moving sideways or up and down through the levels instead? Of those who were registered for more than one year, around two fifths had achieved credits at the same level in two consecutive years. But over the registration periods 1993 to 1995 the proportion achieving a *higher-level* credit in the second year of registration dropped from 37% to 30%. In contrast the proportions achieving a *lower-level* credit in their second year rose from 20% to 30%. Thus while many of the learners registered with LOCN were using the system to follow traditional patterns of progression, there were signs of new and more variable patterns of participation – moving down through the credit levels as well as up.

Participation and progression in the National Child Development Study

The NCDS is a completely representative sample of the British population. In 1991, when the cohort members were aged 33, the sample of 11,400 still participating included 605 who were resident in London. Detailed information was obtained about the cohort members' participation in education and training and the qualifications they gained across the period between 17 and 23 and between 23 and 33 (Bynner and Fogelman, 1993).

We used the national NCDS sample at age 33 as a 1991 baseline against which to compare LOCN students over the period 1994-97. Age 33 was close to the average age of the LOCN sample. If credit-based learning were effective, we would expect to find that disproportionately high proportions of LOCN learners were drawn from traditionally disadvantaged groups. We can use the NCDS data to identify the groups that were educationally disadvantaged under the traditional system and to investigate the factors that were critical to participation and progression.

Compared with the 33% of learners registered with LOCN in 1996–97 who were either employed full-time or part-time, three quarters of the NCDS cohort were in full-time or part-time employment at age 33. Compared with the two thirds of LOCN students who were registered unemployed or unwaged, only 14% of the NCDS cohort were in this category, and most of these were unwaged women at home.

At the time of the 33-year interview, 605 of the NCDS cohort were resident in London, so the question arises – were the differences with LOCN the product of a London effect? Somewhat surprisingly, employment statuses in London were very similar to those in the rest of Britain, with full-time employment being slightly higher in London and unemployment lower. When the analysis was restricted to people who left school at 16, these cross-regional differences largely disappeared. In other words, with respect to employment status, the LOCN sample did represent a distinctly different, more disadvantaged population compared with the population of London as a whole.

One notable difference with the LOCN sample was the lower rates of female participation among NCDS cohort members: 30% of NCDS women cohort members participated in a course leading to qualifications compared with 37% of men. With respect to work-based training the gender gap was larger: 28% of women cohort members had been on one course lasting three days or more compared with 40% of men. Only for traditional adult education courses were more women participating than men (40% of women compared with 26% of men).

Progression routes

Four fifths of the NCDS cohort had participated between the ages of 17 and 23 and two thirds between the ages of 23 and 33. Of those participating, two thirds had gained a qualification between the ages of 17 and 23 and an almost identical proportion of those participating, between the ages of 23 and 33.

As noted earlier, LOCN credits are located at four levels, which coincide with the NVQ/GNVQ standards: Entry Level, Level 1, Level 2, Level 3, with Level 3 equivalent to G/NVQ3 or A level. However, LOCN does not record qualifications at entry, so progression can be observed only within the period of registration with LOCN itself. If we make the strong assumption that people who enter the Entry Level courses have no qualifications to begin with, then we can measure progression.

Taking the periods of assessment as 0-16, 17-20, 21-3 and 24-33, to achieve comparability with LOCN a typology was devised for NCDS based on four categories of achievement at each of these age points: no qualifications (LOCN Entry Level), no qualifications above GCSE Grades 2-5 (NVQ1 standard, LOCN Level 1), no qualifications above GCE O Level (NVQ2, LOCN Level 2), qualifications at GCE A level standard or NVQ3 and above (LOCN Level 3). As we might expect, up to age 20 the most common NCDS combination was Level 1 and Level 2 (NVQ1 and NVQ2). By 33 an equally common combination was Level 2 and Level 3 (NVQ2 and NVQ3+). Notably, few cohort members combined a Level 1 with a Level 3 qualification or had achieved a Level 3 qualification without anything preceding it. It seems likely that many LOCN students through access courses are now able to make this leap. Table 1 compares the distributions of the NCDS cohort and LOCN students across the different qualification levels. Notably, by the time the NCDS sample had reached 33 they were quite similar. In other words despite their educational disadvantage, LOCN students were showing the same qualification levels as the population as a whole.

Table 1: Qualifications awarded: NCDS and LOCN compared (%)

Highest qualification/ credit achieved	NCDS 1991 by 17	NCDS 1991 by 20	NCDS 1991 by 23	NCDS 1991 by 33	LOCN 1996-97
No qualifications	25	23	15	13	10
Level 1	29	30	14	12	21
Level 2	37	38	36	34	25
Level 3	9	10	36	41	43
n (100%)	11,400	11,400	11,400	11,400	24,302

In theory, under a completely open system, any cohort member could have been awarded any combination of credits at different levels over four time-points; this produces 4,096 possible progression routes, different combinations of credits and qualifications achievable across time. For the purposes of illustration, the progression routes constructed for the NCDS cohort are highly circumscribed. We restrict them to one qualification at each age-point; a Level 3 qualification supersedes a Level 2 qualification and so on. We also limit the period of progression to two periods: ages 17–23 and 24–33. Most of the movement occurred in the period between ages 17 and 23. Table 2 shows that two fifths of the cohort members had changed qualification levels over this period – all upwards – compared with only one tenth between ages 24 and 33. The most common changes between the ages of 17 and 23 were from Level 2 to Level 3, followed by from none to Level 2.

Table 2: Improvement in qualifications 17 to 23 and 23 to 33 (%)

Improvement in qualification level	17-23	23-33
0 levels	60	89
+1 level	28	6
+2 levels	8	3
+3 levels	3	2
n (100%)	9,275	10,625

To try to bring the NCDS cohort members closer to LOCN's target student population, we restricted the analysis to those cohort members who left school at 16. Improvement is defined as the percentage of a given group who improved their qualifications over time by one, two or three levels, that is, any change of level counts as improvement.

There were no male-female differences in the percentages that improved. Nor was there any difference in improvement between cohort members resident in London and in the rest of the country. This makes the case for using the whole NCDS sample in the analysis of progression and participation. Some differences in progression were, however, apparent between the participation groups. Notably, between the ages of 17 and 23, apprenticeship on its own or in combination with courses appeared to be closely related to improvement in qualifications (Bynner, 1997). Training on its own was much more weakly related to progression. Between 24 and 33 the same kinds of relationships persisted but were much weaker. Only participation in courses was consistently related to progression. Again, participation in training on its own or in traditional adult education courses was not associated with progression.

Logistic regression analysis

We can extend these findings to incorporate a range of NCDS cohort member characteristics by means of multivariate analysis. We want to find out how strongly each characteristic relates to participation and progression taking account of all other characteristics.

Participation counted as any form of education and training engaged in over each of the two periods 17-23 and 23-33. Progression characterised those people who reported that they had participated and had gained (additional) qualifications through their learning activity over the same periods. To identify the characteristics of those who were first participating and then progressing over these two periods, logistic regression analysis was applied to the data (Bynner and Davies, 2000). This is a form of multiple regression analysis that predicts a 'binary outcome' (ie participated/did not participate) from membership of the categories of a number of predictor variables. The variables used in the analysis were in blocks reflecting well established influences on education at different stages of life starting at birth (eg Parsons and Bynner, 1998; Bynner, 1998; Bynner et al, 2000):

- *birth:* gender; father's social class at birth; age father left full-time education; age mother left full-time education;
- *age 11:* cohort member's reading score at age 11; cohort members' maths score at age 11; number of people per room in family home at age 11; whether owned or rented accommodation at age 11; whether received free school meals at age 11; whether parent took initiative to discuss child with teacher when the child was 11;
- *16+:* age cohort member left full-time education; highest qualification achieved;
- *17-23:* years spent in full-time employment; years spent in full-time education; years spent unemployed; years spent 'at home'.

Between the ages of 17 and 23 the main factors in participation were concerned with educational attainment. Maths score at 11, highest qualification and staying on at school were all strong predictors. Parents' interest in the cohort member's education at age 11 also featured. Men were also much more likely to be participating than women. Of the occupational status variables, years spent 'at home' predicted participation (negatively). In other words, the longer the time cohort members spent at home – which generally applied to women looking after their families – the less likely was their participation in education and training.

The progression indicators extended the picture incorporating the same variables but this time adding in, as we might expect, time spent in full-time education. Again, staying at home appeared to work against progression.

The picture changed slightly for participation and progression between the ages of 23 and 33; this time full-time employment predicted participation and staying at home no longer seemed to be inhibiting it. (This may be because most of those staying at home between 17 and 23 were young mothers.) Participation between 17 and 23 was also a factor in participation from 23 to 33. Reading scores at 11 and highest qualification, coupled with time spent in full-time education, were the only strong predictors of progression. Again, men were far more likely to be participating in education and achieving new qualifications than women.

These findings identify the main features of participation and progression in the traditional system, namely that the more education and opportunities through employment that people had, the more likely they were to be participating and progressing further. Those missing out were those who had tended to do badly earlier and had left school at the minimum age. Women in this category had frequently exited from the labour market early, to have children. These 'inactive' young women and those men and women who were unemployed were the least likely to participate.

Changing the learning culture in organisations

Our qualitative studies addressed the question of whether the introduction of an OCN credit-based learning system had contributed to a cultural shift in the educational institutions and other types of organisation that took it up. We conducted an in-depth case study over a two-and-a-half year period in one FE college where credit was being introduced for the first time, which enabled us to focus on the impact of the changes and to monitor the shifting responses to the initiative as it was occurring. A smaller-scale study was undertaken in another college where the LOCN system had been established for some time, and which therefore enabled us to examine the impact over a longer time frame. These two case studies constituted the major part of the fieldwork and therefore the main focus here.

However, we also investigated the use of LOCN credits in one private sector company, four voluntary sector organisations and three prisons, although these represented a small part of the work of LOCN. In addition, our planned work in relation to trades union provision was supplemented by a project commissioned by the TUC to evaluate the impact of accreditation (Capizzi, 1999). Individual and group interviews with staff and students and observation of a wide range of activities were undertaken in all these settings over the course of the study. A full detailed account of the fieldwork undertaken in each of these contexts is set out in the final report to the ESRC (Davies et al, 1999).

Tutor perspectives

In the FE college that was new to credit, the management had decided to pilot the OCN system and then to roll it out across the college through different types of provision and involving a wider group of teaching staff. The motivations of managers were mixed; we described them as "looking both ways" (Capizzi et al, 1998) – towards, on the one hand, the imperative of a new funding regime and, on the other, towards the social democratic imperative of seeking to achieve greater equity in access to education. Rather than finding a common learning culture surrounding credit to which all teaching staff subscribed, we identified three modes of engagement:

- a compliant mode, in which staff simply applied the technical requirements of the OCN system and which contributed very little to their professional development or innovation in the curriculum;
- an adaptive mode, in which staff adapted credit to their own purposes, using their experience to enrich or expand the curriculum;
- reflective engagement, which was a more innovative mode as staff used credit to enhance their performance in other areas of the curriculum.

Initially, we saw these modes as sequential phases in tutors' involvement with credit-based learning, but while this was the case for some, for others it was not. Some remained in the same mode during our study and others engaged in an adaptive or reflective mode from the outset. It was clear, however, that the introduction of OCN credit had challenged many of the existing beliefs and values of tutors and had opened up the possibility of change. Their responses were shaped largely by their academic discipline, or more frequently by the kinds of learners they worked with. It was clear that the more positive responses – the adaptive and reflective modes – typified those staff who found that features of the credit system matched their own underlying educational values. What existed, therefore, were in Schein's terms (1991) "interim values and beliefs". Rather than a single group sharing the same values and meanings, we found several groups validating their experience in different ways.

In the second FE college, where fieldwork was conducted on a smaller scale, OCN credit was well established, having been in operation in the college for several years. The tutors involved were generally more committed to credit-based learning, mostly in an adaptive or reflective mode. The longer period of using credit had provided more opportunities for their experience to be validated and confirmed; others not sharing their perceptions had moved on. The group that shared a commitment to credit-based provision was larger and did so more securely, but it did not include all the staff of the college.

An all-embracing learning culture would operate not just in educational institutions like FE colleges, but in a wide range of other organisational settings. The LOCN was supported by all the London Training and Enterprise Councils (TECs), and a wider range of other partners, and in principle involved all the FE and community education institutions, voluntary organisations, local authorities and private employers. In practice, as we have seen from the LOCN registration data, hardly any private sector company operated their training provision through the credit system. The one we studied, while exemplary, was a relatively isolated case (Davies, 1999a). In the private sector in particular, the norms and values of management represent the key mediating factor in the development, or not, of a culture which values and rewards learning, and this had yet to embrace credit-based learning. Similarly, we found that in prisons only a small number of prisoners had registered for credit despite considerable efforts on the part of LOCN (Carter, 1999). In these instances the professional, occupational and managerial cultures worked against the introduction of credit, not least because it was seen as offering a qualification of limited labour market utility.

Learner perspectives

The impact of credit-based learning on individual learners was more varied and ambiguous than it was on their tutors. In part this was because, unlike the staff in FE colleges, learners had no experience of the course or programme other than than one that was credit-based. Also, their previous experience of formal learning had often taken place a long time ago or in another country. Their understanding of credit was firmly referenced to the future – what they were intending to do next. None of the learners we interviewed were participating in the programme of learning because it was credit-based, so credit *per se* was not the deciding factor that had engaged them. They had decided to participate for a wide range of reasons that were mostly instrumental: to get any kind of job or a particular kind of job or to get a place in higher education. There were three types of response from learners to the idea of credit and credit accumulation: 'untouched', 'sceptical' and 'persuaded'. The significance of these three types of response lies not in the numbers of learners in each category (this was not a statistical survey), but rather in the relation between their response, their motivation for learning and the way in which accreditation had been used in their programme of learning.

The *untouched* were largely unaware that they were taking a credit-based course and were unable to use the language of credit at the end of a year on the programme: "I don't know really, is it like a merit or a distinction?", or "I didn't listen actually, which didn't help.... It's obvious I don't have any". The first of these quotes comes from a young student who was taking a credit-based course in English as a supplement to a BTEC course and the second from a student who had completed a one-year credit-based drawing and painting course. For these two learners and others like them, the credit they had achieved was irrelevant. What was important was the 'bigger' qualification (BTEC) to which the course was leading or the intrinsic value of the subject (painting). Accreditation of these supplementary programmes had enabled the colleges to provide more learning support and to get funding for it, but of course the students were unaware of this.

The *sceptics* were aware that they were taking a credit-based course and welcomed features of the programme that had been promoted by the credit-based arrangements: continuous assessment, diverse assessment techniques and approaches, accreditation of small steps of achievement, regular feedback, informal relationships between staff and learners, and shared group learning. These features seem to have played a part in encouraging them to continue, largely because they made participation less stressful and a more enjoyable experience than they had expected it to be. They were, however, either unsure or doubtful about the value of the credits in the market place, particularly in the job market: "it's different out there". Nevertheless, they were usually prepared to give credit the benefit of the doubt since they had nothing to lose: "I don't know where it's all going but it might be useful in the long run". (Both these learners were in the FE college introducing credit for the first time.) Similar responses were found among the learners registered for credit in the private sector company: "It's good here, this company knows what it's about 'cos they've set it up and it's been really good. But I don't know if any other employers know about it, whether they'll think it's worthwhile".

The *persuaded* were mostly found on access programmes and on the trades union courses. In both the idea of credit was central to the programme and discussed at length between tutors and learners. Learners on access programmes were required to put together packages of credits at different levels from different parts of programmes based on different forms of assessment. Consequently, they needed to monitor their own achievement in terms of credit carefully over the period of their course – one or two years. Application to higher education also confronted them with the various ways that OCN credits were viewed by the universities.

For the trades union programmes, considerable debate had taken place before the programmes were accredited. There was concern that the award of credit for individual achievement might undermine the collective goals of the programme and that the credits might come to be a required qualification for trades union representatives. Thus it was always stressed that submitting their work for formal assessment was voluntary; no one on the programme was obliged to 'go for the credit' (Capizzi, 1999). They were also mostly politically aware, and acknowledged that 'out there' LOCN credits might not have the recognition and status that other types of qualification had. Nevertheless, they believed that the various features of the credit-based provision had enhanced the value of their learning, that they had been 'really learning' in new and interesting ways, and that the assessment methods had increased the 'shelf-life' of their learning. Despite its voluntary nature, around 97% of learners registered for trades union programmes through LOCN were awarded credit (Bynner and Parsons, 1998).

Conclusions

In general the case studies did not support the view that the move from non-participant to participant in learning was a direct result of the availability of credits. As we have demonstrated, some learners were unaware that they would be or had been awarded credits. However, various features of the credit-based programmes – in particular the forms of assessment – seemed to encourage continued participation and to improve the quality of some participants' learning. Learners' understanding of credit was shaped largely by their own goals and motivations and their experience of the programme of study. As we have shown, tutors adopted a variety of different stances towards credit, which mediated the experience of the learners. Learners were therefore 'improvising' (see Fowler, 1997 for a discussion of regularised improvisation) within a culture shaped by their own horizons for action (Hodkinson and Sparkes, 1995) and by their tutors' professional and political cultures.

Lessons for the development of the Learning Society

Has the OCN system of credit-based learning made a contribution to the development of a learning society? In so far as such a society depends on the establishment of a learning culture, the evidence is mixed. Our data covered almost a three-year period, but this remains a relatively short time span in terms of transforming cultures and building a learning society, and we examined only a relatively small corner of it. Nevertheless, there are a number of pointers that we can draw from our data. At the beginning of this chapter we posed three key questions about the claims made for credit-based learning that we explored in order to examine its impact, and we return to those now.

First, has credit-based learning opened up opportunities for participation and progression to previously disenfranchised or under-represented groups? There is convincing evidence from the analysis of LOCN data and the participation and progression patterns of the NCDS cohort that the OCN system was highly effective in targeting traditionally non-participating groups, and those who had not acquired the building blocks of post-16 participation from earlier educational achievement. It could, of course, be argued that the numbers are small in terms of the total adult population of London; nevertheless they have increased each year and continue to do so. In addition, they were predominantly unemployed or unwaged, women and/or from ethnic minority groups, and they were increasingly studying at lower levels, which suggests that they had few or no formal qualifications. In short, they were precisely those people who in the past have been classified as non-participants or even non-learners. There was evidence too of a widening range of take-up at different levels:

an increase in registrations for credit at Entry and Level 1 and in the proportion following more complex patterns of credit at diverse levels. The flexibility of the LOCN system was therefore increasingly addressing a wider range of individual needs and offering certification for types and patterns of learning that previously had not been counted as formal learning.

The gender imbalance among learners registered for LOCN credits is particularly significant because of the relatively low level of accredited education and training that women received in the past compared to men (see, for example, Bynner and Fogelman, 1993). Men are the prime beneficiaries of the traditional system where, as we have shown, the 'more education you have had the more you will continue to receive'. Nevertheless, the apparent special attraction of LOCN to women (which also applied to traditional adult education) does raise questions of how it might be made more appealing to groups, such as unemployed men, who currently do not take advantage of it to the same extent. Evidence from this study indicates that the effectiveness of the OCN credit system lies largely in its utility as a tool to target particular groups with appropriate types of provision. As such there is no reason why it should not be used to meet the needs of particular groups of men. The expansion of accredited courses for trades union representatives and health and safety officers is one way in which more men are already being involved.

Second, is there evidence of the development of a new learning culture in organisations where credit-based learning has been introduced? At an organisational level, the picture was varied, with new thinking in parts of some colleges, trades unions and voluntary organisations and no impact in others such as private employers and prisons. Even in the FE college where OCN credit-based learning had been established for some years, there remained some staff who were unconvinced or unsure about what they were doing and why, and in the other college most were still responding to what was basically a management inspired initiative. However, there were also examples of very positive results. In one private sector company the LOCN system had been used strategically by management to provide training and work incentives for 'those at the bottom of the heap' in terms of their place in the hierarchy and in terms of their skills and qualifications, and the success of the scheme was recognised in a national training award. Among the trades unions, the adoption of the Open College system of accreditation had prompted a wide-ranging debate about the purpose of the training in relation to individual and collective needs. In FE, the introduction of the LOCN system in one college, and its review and modification in the other, had prompted individual and group review of the curriculum and reflection on the practice of teaching and learning. Thus, even if the organisation as a whole had not moved to embrace credit-based learning, its introduction had unfrozen existing practice, and its development had shifted parts of an organisation to new values, moving it some way towards a learning culture.

Third, what impact has credit-based learning had on the way groups and individuals engage with formal learning and the sense they make of it? The case study data drawn from interviews with learners echoed different kinds of engagement and different kinds of motives and uses of credit. The 'untouched' knew nothing much about credit and were not interested in receiving the award – their motives lay elsewhere, in an interest in the subject itself or in the support it provided for other kinds of learning and qualifications. However, their access to these learning opportunities had been made possible by the colleges' use of the credit arrangements even though these remained largely invisible to the learners. The 'sceptics' doubted the value of the credits in the longer term or outside the environment of the college, but nevertheless saw intrinsic value in the credit-based arrangements in the programmes they were currently undertaking, and were encouraged to continue participating as a result. The 'persuaded' were convinced that various features of the credit-based system had enhanced and deepened their learning in significant ways and had increased its 'shelf-life'. They were also persuaded that the value of the credits they had earned would be recognised beyond the immediate context of their current learning and would enable them to progress to other forms of education and training if they chose to do so. Learners took these different positions largely on the basis of the role played by the credit-based programme within the totality of their learning project. The untouched had no immediate use for the credits (although they did for the programme of study); the sceptics saw the potential but were unconvinced that others outside the educational context shared their view; and the persuaded had a clear view of the value of the credit to their learning and to progression opportunities.

A model for change?

Coffield has suggested that in order to bring about a learning society we need *inter alia* to introduce a new model of change and that this must involve a strategy to include teachers in the planning, "as well as encouraging teachers' ideas for reshaping the system to bubble up from below" (Coffield, 1999, p 495). With its roots in the adult education tradition (Davies, 1999b), credit-based learning is such a bottom-up reform that for several years it struggled for recognition and has been taken up by policy makers relatively recently. Our evidence suggests that credit-based learning has contributed to the development of a learning culture by widening participation, facilitating diverse patterns of progression and challenging the professional and organisational cultures in providing institutions. However, it is not a 'quick fix' or a strategy that is equally effective in all learning contexts for all learners. Neither can it gain parity with other qualifications unless it connects with other changes and challenges to the *status quo*. A national credit framework (eg Kennedy, 1997; Fryer, 1997, 1999; DfEE, 1999) is needed to bring the idea to fruition and fully exploit the possibilities offered, and in particular to underpin the status of qualifications acquired in this way (Davies, 1999c).

The idea of a credit framework that could accommodate all qualifications in a single map and describe them in similar ways so that they could be compared, transferred, accumulated and widely understood, has been on the agenda for some time – for example, the then Further Education Unit was coordinating a debate on the topic in 1992 (FEU, 1992). More recently, the Qualifications and Curriculum Authority (QCA) has been attempting to convert debate and consultation into action, but progress is slow (Davies, 1999c). The difficulty of establishing such a framework arises from the need to resolve the differences between the various kinds of qualification. Coffield (2000) has set out the various models of a learning society identified by projects in this programme of research and elsewhere and it is clear that different qualifications are underpinned by different models. NVQs emanate from a 'skills growth model' (Rees and Bartlett, 1999), based on the belief that the improvement of the skills of the labour force is a critical determinant of the international competitiveness of the economy. Learning at and for work therefore constitutes the primary focus of development (Ball, 1995). The NOCN credit-based system has its roots in a 'democratic' rather than an 'economic model' (Coffield, 1997; Davies, 1999b). The structure of the Open Colleges at national and local level is based on collaboration between a wide range of different kinds of institutions – colleges, universities, and private, public and voluntary sector organisations – representing providers, consumers and stakeholders. This is echoed in the 'social learning' model (Coffield, 2000) that underpins the programmes of study accredited by Open

Colleges and stresses the strength of collective learning for both individuals and groups. In its totality therefore, the Open College at local level seeks to generate a learning culture of the kind identified by Coffield as a "local learning society". As we have seen, such a project is not without its difficulties and cannot be achieved quickly, but there is evidence that a shift in this direction is well under way.

However, the NOCN credit-based system and the NVQ system have developed independently of one another, with little or no cross-fertilisation. While these accreditation mechanisms remained separate the differences of ideology and ownership and the differences between the models of a learning society that underpin them could be fudged. This approach to the management of change is not uncommon. Indeed, the 'manipulation of ambiguity' is a recognised strategy for furthering educational reform (Davies, 1997). However, since the reforms and changes in funding for further and adult education that followed the 1992 Further and Higher Education Act, this strategy has become increasingly difficult to sustain (QCA, 1999a, 1999b). As the attempts to convert the idea of a credit framework into a reality have progressed, the deeper differences between the models have become more explicit. Thus the task of finding a framework to accommodate them both (and others, such as A levels) has been very slow. Without an effective framework of qualifications, the outlook for the further development of the NOCN system of credit and a wider acceptance of the value of such credits is limited. The effectiveness of credit-based learning in contributing to the development of a learning society is therefore critically dependent on deciding what type of learning society we are trying to create.

References

Adlam, R. (1999) 'We need a night shift: notes on the failure of an educational design for police managers', *Educational Action Research*, vol 7, no 1, pp 51-62.

Ball, C. (1995) 'Learning does pay', in D. Bradshaw (ed) *Bringing learning to life*, London: Routledge, pp 18-32.

Bynner, J. (1997) 'Use of NCDS data on post-16 educational progression and participation in the study of credit-based learning', Paper presented to 'The Impact of Credit-based Learning on Learning Cultures Advisory Forum', City University, February.

Bynner, J. (1998) 'Education and family components of identity in the transition from school to work', *International Journal of Behavioural Development*, vol 22, pp 29-53.

Bynner, J. and Davies, P. (2000) *Post 16 credit-based learning in the learning society*, mimeo, London: Centre for Longitudinal Studies, Institute of Education,.

Bynner, J. and Fogelman, K. (1993) 'Making the grade: education and training experiences', in E. Ferri (ed) *Life at 33: The fifth follow-up of the National Child Development Study*, London: National Children's Bureau, pp 36-59.

Bynner, J. and Parsons, S. (1998) 'Participation and progression in LOCN', Paper presented to the 'The Impact of Credit-based Learning on Learning Cultures Advisory Forum', May.

Bynner, J., Joshi, H. and Tsatsas, M. (2000) *Obstacles and opportunities on the route to adulthood: Evidence from rural and urban Britain*, London: Smith Institute.

Capizzi, E. (1999) *Learning that works: Accrediting the TUC programme*, Leicester: NIACE.

Capizzi, E., Carter, J. and Davies, P. (1998) 'Making sense of credit: FE staff managing change', *Journal of Access and Credit Studies*, vol 1, no 1, pp 40-52.

Carter, J. (1999) 'Turning prison education inside out', *Prison Report*, no 49, p 28.

Coffield, F. (1997) *Can the UK become a learning society?*, Fourth Annual Education Lecture, London: School of Education, Kings College.

Coffield, F. (1999) 'Breaking the consensus: lifelong learning as social control', *British Educational Research Journal*, vol 25, no 4, pp 479-99.

Coffield, F. (2000) 'Introduction: A critical analysis of the concept of a learning society', in F. Coffield (ed) *Differing visions of a Learning Society: Research findings, Volume 1*, Bristol: The Policy Press, pp 1-38.

Davies, P. (1997) 'Number crunching: the discourse of statistics', in J. Williams (ed) *Negotiating access to higher education: The discourse of selectivity and equity*, Buckingham: Open University Press and SRHE, pp 47-64.

Davies, P. (1999a) 'A new learning culture? Possibilities and contradictions in accreditation', *Studies in the Education of Adults*, vol 30, no 3, pp 10-20.

Davies, P. (1999b) 'Inclusion and exclusion: credits and unités capitalisables compared', in F. Coffield (ed) *Why's the beer always stronger up North? Studies of lifelong learning in Europe*, Bristol: The Policy Press, pp 43-52.

Davies, P. (1999c) 'Mickey Mouse or michaelmas: a false dichotomy for an inclusive framework of qualifications', *Widening Participation and Lifelong Learning*, vol 1, no 2, pp 33-40.

Davies, P., Bynner, J., Capizzi, E. and Carter, J. (1999) *The impact of credit-based systems of learning on learning cultures*, Research Report, London: City University.

DfEE (Department for Education and Employment) (1999) *Learning to Succeed: A new framework for post-16 learning*, Cm 4392, London: DfEE.

Ferri, E. (ed) (1993) *Life at 33: The fifth follow-up of the National Child Development Study*, London: National Children's Bureau.

FEU (Further Education Unit) (1992) *A basis for credit?*, London: FEU.

Fowler, B. (1997) *Pierre Bourdieu and cultural theory: Critical investigations*, London: Sage Publications.

Fryer, R. (1997) *Learning for the twenty-first century*, First report of the National Advisory Group for Continuing Education and Lifelong Learning, London: NAGCELL

Fryer, R. (1999) *Creating learning cultures: Next steps in achieving the learning age*, Second report of the National Advisory Group for Continuing Education and Lifelong Learning, London: NAGCELL.

Hodkinson, P. and Sparkes, A.C. (1995) 'Markets and vouchers: the inadequacy of individualist policies for vocational education and training in England and Wales', *Journal of Education Policy*, vol 10, no 2, pp 189-207.

Jacobson, W. (1996) 'Learning, culture and learning culture', *Adult Education Quarterly*, vol 47, no 1, pp 15-28.

Kennedy, H. (1997) *Learning works: Widening participation in further education*, Coventry: Further Education Funding Council.

Meek, V.L. (1994) 'Organisational culture: origins and weaknesses', in D. McKevitt and A. Lawton (eds) *Public sector management: Theory, critique and practice*, Open University Reader, London: Sage Publications, pp 265-80.

Parsons, S. and Bynner, J. (1998) *Influences on adults' basic skills*, London: Basic Skills Agency.

Pheysey, D.C. (1993) *Organizational cultures: Types and transformations*, London: Routledge.

QCA (Qualifications and Curriculum Authority) (1999a) *Consultation on flexibility within the national qualifications framework*, London: QCA.

QCA (1999b) *Flexibility for adult learners: Report on the outcomes of consultation*, London: QCA.

Rees, T. and Bartlett, W. (1999) 'Models of guidance services in the learning society: the case of the Netherlands', in F. Coffield (ed) *Why's the beer always stronger up North? Studies of lifelong learning in Europe*, Bristol: The Policy Press, pp 21-30.

Robertson, D. (1994) *Choosing to change: Extending access, choice and mobility in higher education*, London: Higher Education Quality Council.

Saunders, M. (1998) 'Organisational culture: electronic support for occupational learning', *Journal of Computer Assisted Learning*, vol 14, pp 170-82.

Schein, E.H. (1991) 'What is culture?', in P.J. Frost (ed) *Reframing organizational culture*, London: Sage Publications, pp 243-53.

Välimaa, J. (1998) 'Culture and identity in higher education research', *Higher Education*, vol 36, pp 119-38.

FOUR

Teaching and learning in higher education: issues of innovation

Andrew Hannan, Harold Silver and Susan English

Aims and origins

The ethics protocol for phase one of the *Innovations in Teaching and Learning in Higher Education* project[1], launched in September 1997, began with the following statement:

> The past decade has seen increased attention to methods of teaching and learning, and the 1997 Dearing Report, *Higher Education in the Learning Society*, has further emphasised the need for innovative responses to the challenges facing higher education. The agenda for these changes has included increased student numbers and diversity, the promotion of lifelong learning and a learning society, and satisfying the requirements of employment and citizenship. The project aims to examine and interpret the innovative responses of higher education in the recent period to these pressures and opportunities. It will seek to analyse the sources, nature and implementation of recent and current innovations, the obstacles and life histories. It will explore the meanings attached to innovation as process and product. It will therefore attempt to identify:
>
> - the motives, sources of ideas, successes and failures of innovators in a range of subjects in a variety of institutions, and implications for staff satisfaction and rewards;
> - the characteristics of innovations generated by individuals, institutions, internally and externally available funding, external scrutiny, national policies and programmes, international models and research;

- the factors (inter-personal, institutional and structural) which do or do not stimulate and support innovation;
- the contribution of new developments in communication and information technologies to innovations in teaching and learning;
- innovation as creation, adaptation, transfer, development, dissemination;
- the contexts of innovation, including those of finance and institutional scale and structure.

Although curriculum change, modularisation, assessment methods, access and emphases on skills and learning outcomes, for example, relate to teaching and learning, these will be contingent rather than central features of the project. The focus will be on those innovations that seek to shape the learning interface of students with teachers, one another, the technologies and materials. These include such processes as problem based learning, open learning, independent learning, distance learning and computer based or supported learning.

This first phase of the project was thus focused mainly on 'the experiences of innovators' with respect to a wide range of innovations, and was carried out largely by means of an interview survey. As such, it had grown from a much narrower proposal that had initially set out to investigate the impact of the Partnership Trust Awards and the experiences of those who had been rewarded by the scheme[2]. The project as finally launched still differed significantly from the other 13 in *The Learning Society Programme* because of the degree to which its aims were predetermined (as specified in the original brief provided by the sponsors), the manner in which it was divided into two 12 month phases and the fact that other agencies in addition to the Economic and Social Research Council (ESRC) provided the funding. In practice, the two-stage structure allowed for considerable flexibility, with the aims for the second phase being developed during the first. Funding from other agencies in addition to the ESRC (the Higher Education Quality Council in phase one and the Higher Education Funding Council for England and the Department for Education and Employment in phase two) also allowed for inputs from 'users and beneficiaries' that were of considerable value to the project. Nevertheless, the uncertainties introduced into the funding and the negotiations required with such a range of funding bodies introduced delays and other problems of a kind not experienced by other projects in *The Learning Society Programme*.

In the second phase, which began in October 1998, the case study investigations focused on selected aspects of institutions which work on the first phase had suggested could be of especial interest to questions of climate, framework and culture. The concept of 'organisational culture' and its associated range of literature were of particular interest, including that which addressed the various sub-cultures found in organisations and institutions. The research involved an examination of the theory and practice of sub-units such as departments, schools and faculties and the work of the middle managers who had responsibility for them. An attempt was made to gauge the impact of such factors in terms of the promotion or inhibition of innovation in teaching and learning.

The stated objectives for phase two included: to explore institutional climates/frameworks in higher education that support or inhibit innovation in teaching and learning, and to continue the exploration of 'new patterns of teaching and learning' begun in the first phase and needing further understanding. It was important to examine how institutions embed, or fail to embed, innovations in teaching and learning, and the operation of institutional sub-structures that are intended to affect, or that impinge on, institutional or individual efforts to innovate in teaching and learning. The latter meant considering educational development units or their equivalent, staff development units, teaching and learning committees, and the work of senior management responsible for teaching and learning, as well as the impact of national policies on institutional approaches to the support of innovations in teaching and learning.

Methodology

Phase one

The main purpose of the first year was defined in the remit for the project as "to identify the characteristics of successful innovations in teaching, learning and assessment practices in higher education...". The project was to indicate "which factors ... stimulate and those which inhibit innovation". The first-year work was to explore the experiences of innovators, and the second year would examine 'institutional climates'. The focus was to be on undergraduate programmes. Although it proved impossible entirely to separate the first and second-year emphases, the project did focus in its first year overwhelmingly on innovators and innovations.

It was important at the outset to explore previous discussions and interpretations of 'innovation' that would be relevant to a project focusing on teaching and learning. There were boundaries to be established with curricular and management or administrative innovation, which might be influential for teaching and learning. A substantial annotated bibliography was therefore produced, together with the working paper entitled *The languages of innovation: Listening to the higher education literature* (Silver, 1997). The relevant literature on higher education itself was sparse. In recent decades much of the discussion of innovation has focused on the use of 'audio-visual aids', 'educational technology' and 'communication and information technology', and underlying most of the discussion in general are unquestioned assumptions about what constitutes innovation. The literature seemed to leave open, for example, questions about the relevance of past experience of innovation to one of the key developments of recent years – the widespread adoption by innovators and institutions of new technologies. It was equally clear from the literature that it was important to understand at what levels and under what pressures and incentives innovation took place and survived, or failed to survive.

A second working paper, *'Innovation': Questions of boundary* (Silver et al, 1997) paid particular attention to the question of 'levels' and innovation as a response to institutional and societal changes. These changes – structural, cultural, economic and technological – seemed to influence not only the nature and life histories of innovations, but also how they might be perceived by all the actors and witnesses concerned. Although the focus of the first year of the project was 'the experiences of innovators', and the study of institutional frameworks was to be a focus of the second year, a consideration of how innovation occurred and was 'managed' at different levels within institutions could not be avoided. What was, in fact, an 'innovation' had to be approached within the changing academic, social and political environments of an institution, as well as within the policy frameworks of national government, quasi-governmental agencies and influential organisations of employers, educational pressure groups and others.

Since the focus of the first year of the project was to be on innovators and innovations in teaching and learning at the undergraduate level, the initial task was to decide at which higher education institutions there were clusters of likely people. Institutions to visit were chosen on the basis of the frequency of their appearance in various indices of innovations such as Enterprise in Higher Education projects, lists of Partnership Trust Award winners and the Teaching and Learning Technology Programme (TLTP) directories, books and conferences. Efforts were made to include a wide geographic spread and a rough balance of representation from old and new universities. As a result of this process interviews were conducted at the following institutions, 15 in all:

University of East London
University of Glasgow
Heriot-Watt University
University of Leeds
University of Lincolnshire and Humberside
Middlesex University
University of Nottingham
Oxford Brookes University
University of Plymouth
University of Portsmouth
Queen's University of Belfast
University of Salford
University of Wales, Cardiff
University of Wales College of Medicine
University of York

(Full details of the sampling process are given in Appendix A of Silver et al, 1997.)

Universities were asked to arrange interviews for the researchers with those people identified from various publications as 'innovators' and to suggest the names of others who were involved in significant innovation (those introducing new methods of teaching and learning in undergraduate programmes) and those in the institution who had particular or general responsibility for such matters. In terms of subject identity the interviewees can be categorised as follows (see Table 1).

Obviously crucial to all this is what is meant by 'innovation'. It was decided not to be too demanding about this. It was not just a matter of looking for mould-breakers who had made global breakthroughs. The project team were interested in those who had introduced methods of teaching and learning new to their own situation, their own course, department or institution. These were planned rather than accidental changes, designed, but not guaranteed, to improve teaching and learning. The project was interested in the small as well as the large scale, in one-

Table 1: Phase one interviewees: subject identities

Category	Frequency
Clinical and pre-clinical	4
Science	39
Professions allied to medicine	8
Engineering and technology	19
Built environment	8
Mathematical sciences, IT and computing	19
Business and management	13
Social sciences	15
Humanities	17
Art, design and performing arts	3
Education	9
Central management	20
Support services	47
Total	**221**

module innovations as well as those introduced across an institution or even on a national level, in the unfunded individual initiative as well as nationally funded projects. There was a particular focus on the learning/ teaching interface, in the *methods* of teaching and learning, in 'pedagogy'. Obviously wider structural changes such as semesterisation and modularisation were part of this, but the focus was on the mode of delivery and the methods of discovery, the learning support structures, the ways of teaching and of learning. Although curriculum changes and the impact they had on pedagogy were also relevant, an attempt was made not to be diverted from the primary focus on efforts to introduce new methods of teaching and learning, even though the distinction was not always an easy one to make.

A total of 221 interviews were conducted and taped and notes were made. The tapes were intended as a back up, and the notes were typed and subsequently analysed (using HyperQual) alongside supporting documentation relating to the work of individual innovators and to institutional policies concerning teaching and learning. An initial analysis of the information collected was discussed on a return visit to the institution where the pilot study had been conducted and at a mini-conference with representatives from each of the universities we had visited. The general content of the findings was confirmed by these meetings, which also provided guidance for the second phase of the project.

Phase two

A number of the second phase research questions posed in the early specification and then revisited had necessarily arisen to varying extents in the first phase, including "the criteria by which success or failure are to be assessed", identifying "new patterns of teaching, learning and assessment", models of good practice and dissemination processes. The priority focus for the second phase was clearly to be on how/whether innovations become embedded in institutions, the institutional structures and cultures that supported or inhibited innovation in teaching and learning, and lessons from the impact of national and institutional policies.

It was proposed that a highly focused, intensive study be conducted of a relatively small number of institutions. Messages from the first phase research on 15 institutions of all types across the UK would be important, but it was now proposed that five institutions be selected, four from the first phase list and one other. The exception was the Open University (OU), which, because of its dispersed character, it had not been practicable to include in the first phase, but which could be very important for the second phase. The OU was significant because of new developments in its use of distance learning and partly because of its particular organisation and methods of operation. Of the remaining four institutions, it was proposed that three be in England and one in Scotland. The English universities would include one of the 'older' universities (Nottingham was chosen), one '1960s' university (Salford) and one 'new' university (Middlesex). The Scottish university would be Glasgow. The selection of four first-phase institutions would enable impressions and insights from the first phase visits to be tested more systematically on the second. The vice-chancellors (the 'principal' in the case of Glasgow) of all five universities readily agreed to their university being named in the outcomes of the research. As in the first phase, an ethics protocol protected the universities in such matters as confidentiality and an undertaking was given not to name individuals or enable them to be identified (unless with their prior consent).

The design of the study was to incorporate 'top-down' and 'bottom-up' approaches. The former would involve an examination of relevant policy making; responsiveness to external policies and programmes; the directions in which teaching, learning and assessment were driven, the reasons for doing so and the mechanisms chosen; the control of funding and support processes; the machinery of implementation. The focus of these 'framework' investigations would therefore be the operation of the relevant committees in these universities, the roles of specific, responsible individuals, the roles of faculty committees and deans, and departments. The essential questions would relate to how policy and practice were shaped at these various levels, and the interview pattern (and possibly attendance at committee or other meetings) would therefore be determined in each case by the particular structure and distribution of authority.

The 'bottom-up' approach would focus on ways in which proposals for innovation were fed into the system by members or groups of staff. It would cover their perception of the processes involved, time-scales, obstacles and outcomes, and reasons for innovations becoming, or failing to become, embedded at the appropriate (course, departmental or other) level. Questions addressed included the impact of the Research Assessment Exercise (RAE) and other pressures on the willingness and ability of staff to innovate in teaching and learning. This type of interview would build on the experience of interviewing such individuals in the first phase (and some re-interviewing could be helpful). The intention for 'bottom-up' interviews, however, was to base them on random sampling of teaching staff, not on identified innovators as in the first phase. The concept of focus groups was adopted for this purpose.

As a result of this approach a total of 117 individual interviews took place (34 at Glasgow, 17 at Nottingham, 21 at Middlesex, 22 at Salford and 23 at the Open University), with a rough balance of top-down and bottom-up interviews at each institution. A decision had been made to choose one discipline found in all five institutions, thus controlling to some extent for differences determined by subject-specific factors. 'English' or a cognate area was chosen in each institution, and a second subject area was intended to be in some way unique or prominent in the university visited. At Glasgow this was Medicine, at Nottingham Biological Sciences, at Middlesex Business Studies, at Salford Electrical and Electronic Engineering, and at the Open University Technology. The focus groups at each university were based on this selection, and staff were invited on a random basis within the departments selected to such a group discussion. Depending on the availability of staff and other factors, two such groups took place at Nottingham and at Middlesex, and one each at Glasgow, Salford and the OU, with a total of 30 randomly selected teachers of undergraduates involved. In a small number of cases members of the research team were present at meetings of relevant committees or other groups.

As in the first phase, full handwritten notes were made during each interview and discussion, and most of the individual interviews were also tape recorded. The discussion groups, however, were not taped after the first such meeting, when we were asked to turn off the machine in order not to inhibit the participants. Also as in the first phase the notes were typed up and entered for analysis on HyperQual stacks. Analysis was based on data collected in this way, but also from documents and reflection after each visit. An extensive case study report was written on each institution and the parts relevant to individual departments were submitted to departmental 'gatekeepers'. Once these were cleared the full report for each institution was submitted to an institutional 'gatekeeper' (the vice-chancellor or nominee) before being corrected and sent to every member of staff who had been interviewed or who had taken part in a discussion group, with an invitation to comment in answer to the following questions:

• Is our description of your university accurate?
• Have we included all the important issues and, if not, what have we left out?
• Of the issues we have identified, which do you consider to be the most important?

An intention to return for a round-table discussion of the final case study report at each institution proved to be possible only for the first institution visited (Middlesex) because of long delays in the gatekeeping process. Our account of each institution has been very largely accepted as accurate by staff at different levels of seniority.

An additional thread to the methodology for the second phase was a continued analysis of the literature. The theoretical underpinning identified in the first phase continued to be an active element in the work of phase two, but additionally an extensive, annotated bibliography was produced on *Organisational culture and innovation in higher education*, addressing the literature on both organisational culture and related concepts of importance in investigating the place of innovation in higher education institutions (Silver, 1998). Although much of this literature was American, and originated in studies of industrial and other companies, it pointed to relevant and helpful work on, for example, cultures and sub-cultures (Allaire and Firsirotu, 1984; van Maanen and Barley, 1985; Louis, 1985, 1990; Schein, 1985, 1996; Meek, 1988), and aspects of leadership and management (Kimberly, 1981; Handy, 1985). A small but vitally important literature addressed some of these areas in relation to the management, leadership and culture of higher education institutions (Cohen and March, 1974;

Clark, 1984, 1987; Becher, 1984, 1989; Chaffee and Tierney, 1988; Schuller, 1992; Middlehurst, 1993; McNay, 1995; Sporn, 1996).

Findings

Innovations and innovators

Innovation, while something new to a person, course, department, institution or higher education generally, could also be something already established elsewhere. The implication for the project, however, was that an innovation was a departure from what had been done before in that situation. It is not always obvious whether an innovation is an act of creation, adaptation or imitation. What is adopted and modified may be an idea or a practice, and implementation may be a single episode (for example, the reorganisation of a seminar procedure) or a continual process of renewal. A new way forward in one place may have been abandoned in another for a more promising alternative. "Innovation in teaching and learning" is itself a difficult vocabulary. An innovation in the former may not result in any change in the latter. There is no necessary relationship between the two. An innovation in students' learning procedures may be independent of any 'teaching' in its traditional sense, and may be mediated by the use of technology.

A wide variety of types of innovation was identified by those we interviewed, across most subjects in very many different sorts of programme. Table 2 indicates the innovations with which those we interviewed were involved (the numbers indicating frequency).

However, there were other projects that do not neatly fit under any of these headings. It is also apparent that these categories overlap, that some innovations might be included in more than one and that several staff were involved in a range of innovative projects of different types.

The analysis of the first phase, with regard to the innovators and their innovations, led to the following conclusions:

* Innovators rarely saw themselves as 'innovative people' but were driven to innovate by their background (eg further education or industry), picking up ideas (including on courses and training), student numbers and diversity, curriculum change (including modularisation), student boredom, funding opportunities, Teaching Quality Assessment (TQA) and other external stimuli.

Table 2: Phase one: types of innovation

Types of innovation

1	Making use of computers (web, Internet, Intranet, computer-aided learning, computer-based learning, computer-mediated communication)	77
2	Skills (personal, transferable, key, core, employability, communication and problem solving)	45
3	Team projects, group learning (cooperation and collaboration)	40
4	Student presentations (individual or group)	16
5	Interactive seminars or lectures	16
6	Work-based learning	16
7	Problem-based learning	16
8	Resource-based learning (packages, booklets, etc)	14
9	Distance learning or open learning	12
10	Peer-tutoring, mentoring or assessment	9
11	Others (eg student-directed learning, learning journals/ portfolios, profiling, reflective practice)	18

- Young staff (especially in old universities) waited to feel secure before innovating; some staff wanted to use prior experience to improve 'inherited' situations in higher education. In general they felt under external pressures, facing difficult teaching challenges.
- The main categories of innovation, as Table 2 suggests, were: group/ team work; live projects; simulations; student (often group) presentations of many kinds; skills development affecting the teaching/learning relationship; experiments with interactive lectures and seminars; self, peer and group assessment on various bases; other types of innovation involving departmental, faculty or institutional policy or endorsement (eg work-based learning, problem-based learning, resource-based learning). Independent learning and greater student responsibility for their learning were subsumed in most of these.
- Innovators were often a minority, not necessarily successful, and although their innovations were not always original, they were seen as new or radical *in their circumstances*. They invariably began with the aim of

improving student learning and/or overcoming some of their own teaching difficulties in new situations and/or taking advantage of new opportunities (including financial opportunities).

- There were widely varied colleagues' and students' perceptions of the nature and value of an innovation, often difficulty in winning over colleagues, who sometimes came round when they saw that it 'works', but would stay aloof because of research pressures.
- There was widespread emphasis on the importance of support/sympathy from senior colleagues – not always forthcoming.
- Some colleagues saw innovators as eccentric or even dangerous, depending on a variety of factors, but including the kind of innovation (eg computer-aided learning or work-based learning) and how threatening it was to conventional teaching.
- There was often greater interest (notably when an innovation was subject-specific) and take-up in other institutions, some invitations to speak within the institution, but more likely elsewhere.
- Differences between research cultures (mainly, but not only, old/new universities) and departmental/faculty/institutional politics, as well as in their support structures for teaching and learning, were important.
- There was much staff criticism of centralised policy and decision making. Some innovations were, however, generated by institutional policy (notably on information technology). Institutions were commonly producing policy documents on teaching and learning, but staff were suspicious of their seriousness.
- There were mixed, but mainly supportive, views of the involvement of educational development services or learning support units in teaching and learning innovation.
- Strong emphasis was placed on the importance of seed corn funding, and widespread approval of the impact of Enterprise in Higher Education as a catalyst.
- There were mixed views about the value of TQA, but there were many expressions of approval of its 'shaking up' effect.
- Use of information technology in innovations was extensive, aimed at replacing or supporting conventional teaching. It often needed sustained institutional support, or involvement with a national strategy such as the Teaching and Learning Technology Programme. There was therefore a strong link between individual and institutional (and wider) initiatives.
- The use of distance learning was accelerating, most strongly at postgraduate level, and for both postgraduate and undergraduate courses for on-campus and off-campus students.

- Tensions were clear between research and teaching and learning activity. Efforts to conduct research on teaching and learning resulted in some cases in inclusion in an RAE education unit of assessment, and elsewhere incorporation into other subject units of assessment (and in some cases active discouragement).
- Recent moves to raise the profile of teaching (either innovation or excellence) for promotion and other forms of recognition (including prizes) were widely discussed, but there was much staff cynicism or 'wait and see' attitudes.
- Partnership Trust Awards (1989-95) had in some cases helped to legitimate teaching and learning innovation, in other cases nothing had happened as a result of an award. Awards by professional and other bodies were sometimes seen as important.
- There was an obvious welcome on the part of large numbers of people interviewed for the opportunity to discuss their work with the project team, reflecting in many cases the lack of interest within their institutions.

Given the widespread and growing interest in distance learning in higher education, the position as seen in phase one of the project is worth summarising. Nine of the 15 universities visited offered some distance education (DE) courses, including pre- and post-degree courses, but only four included some undergraduate courses at a distance (or modules within courses). Some had invested in new DE designs, offering a different learning experience from the traditional Open University text-based model. Although the number of undergraduate courses being offered was small, the idea of developing DE was currently under investigation or being encouraged by some universities, often with the appointment of a director, coordinator or adviser with a brief including DE. Five such people were interviewed in different institutions, and it was apparent that open and distance learning methodologies were beginning to be employed with campus-based students. Generally the methods being used in the 21 DE examples encountered (projects, courses or modules) were at an experimental stage.

The institutions

The limits of the sample in the second phase of the project (although we were able to draw also on the first phase of the study) have to be borne in mind. The same applies to an important implication of investigating at the level of departments or other basic units, including the random sampling of teachers of undergraduates. This meant that the focus of discussion was not only directly on innovation as in the first phase, but also on the practices and perceptions of teaching and learning in general, and of aspects of the functioning of institutional structures in relation to teaching and learning. The following were the main direct findings from the case studies:

- In the past half century there seem to have been, mainly but not only in teaching and learning, three interlocking themes, which have to some extent been overlapping phases in the history of innovation within institutions of higher education. These have been marked by 'individual innovation' (drawing on the ideas of enthusiasts), 'guided innovation' (often supported by institutional funds derived from national programmes and somewhat loosely connected to guiding notions about improving teaching and learning) and 'directed innovation' (driven by institutional imperatives often aimed at maximising returns on investment in new technologies or promoting more student-centred learning partly for reasons of efficiency).
- Innovations in teaching and learning were taking place within a context of often quite radical changes in institutional structures, changes that served as important frameworks for the perceptions of interviewees at all levels.
- Middle managers (heads of departments/schools and deans of faculties/ schools) were crucial if the implementation of institutional policies on teaching and learning was to be achieved. Considerable differences among departments, schools or faculties were apparent, and successful practice in teaching and learning and relevant policy implementation often depended on reliable institutional monitoring procedures. The characteristics of these basic and intermediate units were significant elements in the responses of interviewees within them.
- The extent and nature of institutional commitment to teaching and learning cannot be categorised solely on the basis of 'post-1992' and 'pre-1992' universities. In the other *Learning Society Programme* project with an HE focus, Dunne et al (2000) similarly found that contrasts between 'new' and 'old' universities had been exaggerated, finding little difference between them in practice despite the tendency for 'new' universities to make more commitments to innovation in teaching and learning in policy statements and strategic plans.

- At institutional, faculty or departmental levels, major obstacles to the general development of teaching and learning strategies could arise. They included: a strong emphasis on research and the RAE; staff attitudes based on tradition and unquestioned assumptions; and student resistance to change, as a result of pre-entry expectations and pressures, for example, from part-time employment which placed limits on the time available.
- Institutional cultures are immensely difficult to analyse, given that they are the result of often widely different attitudes and approaches by different levels of staff and by students, competing interpretations of policy, and competing commitments (to the institution and to the discipline, to research, to teaching and administration, to short-term needs and to those of promotion and career). The result is often a complex picture of tensions and consensus. There are important differences affecting teaching and learning between those institutions which had defined themselves and settled into their definition and those which are in the process of achieving this. Adequate consultation about institutional policies may not lead to innovative changes in teaching and learning, but these are less likely without it.
- It was possible to detect a 'culture of teaching and learning' or a 'culture of research', or a mixture of the two. It was not possible to detect a 'culture of innovation', since the intentions and outcomes of institutional policy and individual initiatives depend on substantially different factors and these may (but do not necessarily) point in different directions. In relation to the difficulties of determining such a culture of teaching, competing and conflicting pressures and attitudes were particularly apparent.
- Innovation in teaching and learning is more likely if the institutional policies on such matters are understood and trusted, and if there is adequate central support for their implementation through both structures and means of delivery. Promised recognition of and rewards for innovation and/or excellence in teaching and learning have to be credible.

Before we turn to some other general considerations that emerge from this investigation, we can highlight some policy implications that emerge from the above analysis.

Implications for the funding councils, the Department for Education and Employment and the Institute for Learning and Teaching (ILT)

- We found institutions that were independently developing their own policies for recognising developments in teaching and learning, and were aware of directions in which national policies and pressures were moving. It was clear that these could benefit from targeted national funding that could usefully experiment with different ways of supporting the enhancement of teaching and learning and directly rewarding (for example, through sabbaticals or the equivalent of readerships and chairs) those who successfully introduce innovations.
- The pursuit of excellence in teaching and learning could benefit from greater attention to the role of innovation, a study of which could usefully be incorporated within the training of all academic staff. All partners in higher education need to have a broad understanding of the origins and purposes of innovation of different kinds and at different levels – individual, team, institutional, national, disciplinary and technological.
- The future of innovation in teaching and learning has to be seen in national, institutional and, crucially, individual terms, particularly taking account of the needs of those at the point of contact with students.
- Successful innovation in teaching and learning is possible where a balance with research is maintained. It was possible in the project to find evidence of a strong commitment to research alongside an equally strong commitment to improving teaching and ensuring effective student learning, sometimes in practice as well as in principle. However, a commitment to research was not necessarily associated with a commitment to its use for the enhancement of teaching. Research which enhances teaching and learning in higher education needs to be recognised, promoted and rewarded. Any future RAE should incorporate mechanisms to encourage this.

Implications for higher education institutions

In attempting to promote innovation in teaching and learning, account should be taken of the following aspects of institutional culture.

Innovation in teaching and learning is most likely to take place when:

- the innovator has encouragement or support from the head of department, dean or other person in authority;
- the institution has a policy establishing parity between research and teaching and learning, including for purposes of promotion, and the policy is reflected in practice;
- colleagues and people in authority show an interest in disseminating the outcomes of innovation;
- resources are available either through the department or an innovations or similar fund or an education development unit.

Innovation is most likely to be obstructed by:

- low esteem of teaching and learning, compared with research;
- lack of recognition and interest by colleagues and people in authority;
- institutional or other policies and action plans laying down firm directions that preclude individual, alternative initiatives;
- excessively bureaucratic procedures for approval, support and resources;
- quality assessment procedures that inhibit risk taking.

Institutions of higher education, in reviewing their structures and support systems, need also to have in mind the possible longer-term implications of teaching and learning styles for employment, participation in lifelong learning and contribution to a learning society of the policies and practices they promote.

Themes and challenges[3]

UK higher education institutions (HEIs) are expanding their number and range of students, aiming to meet new requirements in terms of the eventual employability of their graduates and to provide 'lifelong learning' for a 'learning society'. Alongside these newer demands, more traditional aims for higher education – the development of 'critical thinking' – persist. All of this needs to be accompanied by the maintenance if not the raising of 'quality' in both teaching and research, with little hope of extra public funding and with a requirement for continuing 'efficiency gains'. Chief among the various means by which these demands are to be met is the hope that methods of learning and teaching can be developed and adopted that will meet the needs of more, and more diverse, students, within resource constraints. Innovations in pedagogy are looked for that will both enhance the quality of the student learning experience and reduce its demands on staff time, with information and communications technology (ICT) being widely seen as the means of achieving this. HEIs have had to develop learning and teaching strategies and have adopted, or are adopting, relevant management and development structures. An understanding of the nature of pedagogy in HE is of particular importance and has far-reaching implications. Any study of this topic needs to give special prominence to the processes of change, the challenges being made to conventional approaches to teacher–learner interaction and the claims being made for new pedagogies (student-centred, ICT-based or ICT-mediated, etc).

Central to such understanding has to be an emphasis on the dynamics of higher education. The focus of this project has therefore been on changes in institutions, for the managers and academics who work in them and the students who study in them, and on changes in the conditions for learning. The former raises a wide variety of issues about the features of institutions that enable them to be or become 'learning communities', or hinder or prevent them from doing so. The latter raises issues about how these contexts influence teacher–learner interaction, including how they impact on teachers' perceptions of their professional roles and the possibility and desirability of changing them. In both cases there are profound issues of intention and potential, definition and redefinition, and the bases on which continuing processes of change can be conceived and tested. The project has touched on these interrelated institutional and pedagogical issues, which operate at a number of levels:

Macro level – the external world of national policies that impact on higher education teaching and learning, for example quality assurance, the Institute for Learning and Teaching (ILT) and funding arrangements that drive the development of strategies to improve teaching.

Meso level – HEI policies and the organisational and operational strategies to implement such policies.

Micro level – classroom (including, for example, laboratory and ICT) practitioners and their location in particular disciplinary cultures.

Central to this typology are binding forces (or tensions) such as those of academic professionalism and strategies for understanding and shaping 'high quality' teaching, influenced by national initiatives as well as the structures and cultures of basic units and the skills and motivations of individual teachers.

Of vital importance to the project was the analysis based on three trends that have emerged in the recent history of British higher education – 'individual', 'guided' and 'directed' innovation – which were concepts employed to make sense of some of the shifts in the nature of innovation that reflected developments in the interplay between such forces (Silver, 1999).

Thus, in the changing picture of higher education from the 1950s, the 'stand-up lecture' became a focus of debate. The new 'green fields' universities, the Open University and the Council for National Academic Awards and the polytechnics then came into existence. Innovation within universities and colleges was largely the product of individuals, focusing on small group teaching or educational technology. From the late 1970s in particular, overlapping this 'individual innovation' was 'guided innovation', under the impact of structural changes which were themselves a response to change in the wider system of higher education and government policy. Innovation was becoming institutionalised, and new maps were being drawn in response to the use of computers and new technologies (and 'guided innovation' often meant 'guided new technology development'). Governments were increasingly investing in such change and in Britain the Enterprise in Higher Education (EHE) initiative was at the frontier of development, a cascading model of change that did, however, meet with strong counter-reactions, producing a range of innovations that originated with individuals or the teaching-oriented units of institutions, often promoting student-centred initiatives. The importance of EHE in this period of 'guided innovation' was considerable, and its messages have still not been properly heard.

Later national programmes to promote the use of information and communications technology were more prescriptive as to projects and outcomes. EHE paradoxically offered opportunities, but also profoundly influenced the trend towards policy-driven frameworks for innovation, which were to close off or discourage individually determined directions. 'Guided innovation' was being rapidly merged into forms of 'directed innovation', with incentives to innovate increasingly located, in the 1990s, within national government policy and funding frameworks, and hemmed in by research priorities. The need to innovate at any level, in new circumstances, emerged from a configuration of factors: the old forms of lecture and seminar were seen by many staff not to be working; student numbers and diversity challenged the efficacy of old forms of assessment; modular and semesterised courses were influencing learning styles as well as curricular structures; higher education outcomes were coming under various kinds of critique. There were good reasons, of course interpreted differently at different levels, to recognise the importance not only of good teaching, but also of changes in teaching to match student needs. Subsequent measures adopted by many institutions and by the national decisions of the funding councils and the ILT may point to the emergence of a fourth, 'post-directed' phase of development, or at least one with more open opportunities.

If we focus on the possibility of individuals continuing to take initiatives to promote improvements in teaching and learning, we are faced with a number of challenges:

- There are obvious problems regarding choice of the sort of innovation and perceptions of its purposes, and what someone sees as an innovation to improve student learning may be seen by someone else as ideological or budget-cutting or a waste of time. The challenge here is what *can* be done, possibly because the old way is simply not working, or there has been a radical change in student background and diversity.
- How do we know if an innovation will be beneficial for students, particularly given changing student circumstances, constituencies and expectations? The difficulty is that judgement and rapid decision cannot be made on the basis of market research and only rarely on the basis of any other research. Is it possible to translate into action a hunch or a hope or a conviction that students will benefit, even though there may be resistance from some students to non-traditional methods?
- Institutional cultures, statuses and priorities are profoundly different, depending on their histories, the ways in which they have responded to the pressures and requirements of recent years, and to their place in 'the market'. In some institutions traditional methods do remain dominant and relatively unchallenged. The difficulty is in judging the position of teaching and learning and of innovation within the institution as it has been or is becoming in rapidly changing circumstances.
- There is a serious issue to be faced, therefore, in terms of the priorities and plans of the institution, the faculty or the department. Does the innovation fit within the relevant rolling plans and the directions defined

for supporting finance? Can it therefore be done? Even if innovation involves or may result in research on teaching and learning, this is still problematic since such 'non-discipline' research is still rarely seen as respectable or rewarding.

- What kind of support, if any, may be needed, what obstacles may need to be overcome? Is support available and likely to be forthcoming?
- There is a challenge to know whether to be tempted by the available funding, which may determine the direction in which to go. Since the early days of EHE this has become an increasing dilemma, as institutions have themselves become more directive or prescriptive, and the problem lies in weighing one sort of innovation that is not funded against another that may attract resources. What one wishes to do, which may raise all kinds of difficulties, may come into conflict with what can more easily be done.
- There are personal issues to do with recognition, including promotion. Not only innovation in teaching and learning, but an interest in teaching and learning as such, may reduce promotion prospects. The increasing emphasis nationally and within institutions on equal recognition of teaching and research raises a major concern – that of judging how real such policies are in practice.
- Finally, the question 'Why bother?' has to be answered. Potential or experienced innovators are likely to argue as follows:

    "The RAE lies ahead and I still have 3¾ articles to write."
    "Everyone in authority wants me to do something else."
    "I have too much administration and no time."
    "Innovation generally means an up-front investment of time, and though there may be sabbaticals for research, I won't get one for teaching and learning."
    "People think I am eccentric."

These are salient issues for innovators or would-be innovators, and we have found them in one form or combination or another in all the institutions we have visited. Of course, some of these issues may not be challenges at all. For example, what an institution or faculty wants may be what an individual also wants, and may have been consulted about. It may be possible to persuade colleagues or a department to adopt the teaching and learning initiatives proposed by individuals. On the whole, however, we have found innovators and innovation projects relating to teaching and learning to be often isolated, low status and treated with suspicion, echoing the findings of Dunne et al (2000) who also discovered that innovators were often not supported by their colleagues and that there was little evidence of planning for future change at the departmental level.

This is particularly true of research-driven universities, although we have found important exceptions, and universities that in many respects look similar may have very different approaches to the extent of support they wish to give (and are willing to be seen to give) to the enhancement of teaching and learning.

That there have been profound changes affecting innovation over the past decade is beyond doubt, given the changes in funding and accountability and quality machineries, the greater centralisation of decision making, a new managerialism, the loss of community and collegiality – all of which and related vocabularies have been regularly used by those we have interviewed. It is important to note that critical comments of this kind are sometimes accompanied by recognition that the real problem lies with policies and pressures coming from outside the institution. But the question is whether we have now reached a plateau, or whether there are real prospects of further change. Teaching and learning *are* being talked about and made the subject of national and institutional policies, and the Dearing Report (NCIHE, 1997), and responses to it, have played a part. Structures to support teaching and learning are in place in most of the institutions we visited. These include the appointment of pro-vice chancellors responsible for teaching and learning, committees for teaching and learning at institutional or faculty or other level, and so on, and although structures do not necessarily tell us a great deal, they do indicate changes of emphases in the recent past. People who do the teaching, however, often see these as without relevance or impact.

The Higher Education Funding Council for England (HEFCE) has seen the need to put more, albeit still relatively modest, funds into subject support for teaching and learning (modest by comparison with the funding of research). The Institute for Learning and Teaching is in existence, and in 1999 the ESRC launched the first phase of its £11½ million Teaching and Learning Research Programme. The latter was not targeted specifically on higher education, and there is much that is positive in that fact – given the opportunities the programme offered for linking teaching and learning in higher education and in the remainder of the formal education system, as well as in all the other locations of the 'learning society'. It is not clear whether all of this means a real shift in the environment for innovation in teaching and learning, or whether it is just a temporary recoil from the excesses of the RAE and the growth of research cultures. The different kinds of innovation and levels of decision making for innovation will continue to raise the question of *whose* innovation is concerned. All of these recent and current moves could end up with more *institutional* or *system-wide* innovation, not necessarily with any greater opportunity for individual initiatives. There is, of course, an argument for harnessing the energies of individual innovators for wider, possibly institutional initiatives, given the difficulty of individuals disseminating their work. The main challenge, however, is to know whether the individual innovator and the individual initiative at the level of student–teacher encounter will nevertheless be able to survive.

The reasons for addressing these issues go beyond the immediate processes of teaching and learning. Fundamental is the frequent realisation that, for one reason or many, in very many contexts the old ways are not working, and that what are needed are new ways to sustain motivated learners who are more autonomous and more able to take responsibility for their own continued learning. Old models of what it means to be a student, and therefore what it means to be a teacher, are changing. The vocabularies of innovation are extensive and relate not only to improved learning, but also to *improved access* to learning, to changing the format and rhythm of learning in order to cater for mature and part-time students, to make it possible for students to interrupt and resume their studies and to make choices that mesh with their experience and aspirations.

A focus on the learning experience of students points to immediate outcomes in terms of knowledge, skills and understanding and success in the forms of assessment that lead to degrees. But it also points beyond the degree, to the students' own lifelong learning, and to their ability to support others for lifelong learning in the workplace and in society. Innovations that point students in that direction are also situating higher education institutions more securely in a learning society. All levels of innovation have a part to play in the preparation of students for creative roles in a learning society. These are issues that go unrecognised in most policy making for the development of Higher Education. The HEFCE, even while launching its imaginative learning and teaching strategy under its Teaching Quality Enhancement Fund, and emphasising the need "to continue to support the development of innovative learning and teaching methods", justified the latter as necessary "to maintain a leading edge in higher education worldwide" (HEFCE, 1999, p 5). It did not take account of the role of innovation at the higher education level in helping to prolong creative learning into life beyond the degree, and into the influential roles graduates play in the world of work. The government's 1998 policy document for *The Learning Age* pointed to the larger part higher education could play in terms of skills, more places, a wide range of courses, high standards, improved participation, and collaboration with others to contribute further to the economy (DfEE, 1998, pp 49-50). It showed no interest, however, in *how* people learn, and the implications of their passive or active learning for their future roles in society. The assumption here, as in much policy literature, has been that education and its benefits are to be 'delivered'. Fortunately those with a more creative approach to teaching and learning still have a voice, and the hope is that it will increasingly be heard.

Notes

[1]When the project was launched, 'teaching and learning' was still the most familiar vocabulary, changing to 'learning and teaching' mainly following the Dearing Committee on *Higher Education in the learning society* (NCIHE, 1997).

[2]The Partnership Trust had for seven years (1989-95) conducted annual programmes of awards to successful innovators in higher education. Each award was sponsored by a major employer of graduates or some other body concerned with the quality of undergraduate education, in a subject area in which it had a particular interest. The winners of these cash awards were in a wide variety of disciplines and institutions, and ranged in seniority from department head to young lecturer. In 1996 the Trust agreed with the Economic and Social Research Council (ESRC) and its *Learning Society Programme*, and also the then Higher Education Quality Council, a research specification for a project on teaching and learning in higher education, and bids to run the project were invited to be made to the ESRC.

The specification set out the main purposes of the proposed project, which was conceived in two parts – a first phase (or year) to be concerned with the experiences of some successful innovators, and the second phase with 'institutional climates which further or inhibit innovation'. The focus was on undergraduates. At that stage of project planning the aim was to address the experience of innovators who had won Partnership Trust awards. The Trust, which had discontinued its awards programme, was to be involved in funding the first phase, but withdrew its funding before the project was launched. The Department for Education and Employment and the Higher Education Funding Council for England later joined the ESRC in funding the second phase. A research team based at the University of Plymouth submitted the winning bid for the first phase, and was later confirmed as the team to carry out the second phase.

The aims of the project have therefore to be considered in two parts, each one of which was based on research directions and questions formulated by the ESRC's *Learning Society Programme*, into which the new project was integrated. At the outset and in practice these were addressed and interpreted by the research team, also within the context of an advisory group, chaired by the Director of *The Learning Society Programme*.

[3] The analysis presented here draws partly on a recent research proposal co-written with Melanie Walker, George Lueddeke and John Brennan.

References

Allaire, Y. and Firsirotu, M.E. (1984) 'Theories of organizational culture', *Organization Studies*, vol 5, no 3, pp 193-226.

Becher, T. (1984) 'The cultural view', in B.R. Clark (ed) *Perspectives on higher education: Eight disciplinary and comparative views*, Berkeley, CA: University of California Press.

Becher, T. (1989) *Academic tribes and territories: Intellectual enquiry and the cultures of disciplines*, Buckingham: Open University Press.

Chaffee, E.E. and Tierney, W.G. (1988) *Collegiate culture and leadership strategies*, New York, NY: Macmillan.

Clark, B.R. (1984) 'The organizational conception', in B.R. Clark (ed) *Perspectives on higher education: Eight disciplinary and comparative views*, Berkeley, CA: University of California Press.

Clark, B.R. (1987) *The academic life: Small words, different worlds*, Princeton, NJ: Carnegie Foundation for the Advancement of Teaching.

Cohen, M.D. and March, J.G. (1974) *Leadership and ambiguity: The American college president*, Boston, MA: Harvard Business School Press.

DfEE (Department for Education and Employment) (1998) *The Learning Age: A renaissance for a new Britain*, Cm 3790, London: The Stationery Office.

Dunne, E., Bennett, N. and Carré, C. (2000) 'Skill development in higher education and employment', in F. Coffield (ed) *Differing visions of a Learning Society: Research findings, Volume 1*, Bristol: The Policy Press, pp 105-38.

Handy, C.B. (1985) *Understanding organizations*, New York, NY: Facts on File.

HEFCE (Higher Education Funding Council for England) (1999) *Teaching quality enhancement fund: Funding arrangements*, Bristol: HEFCE.

Kimberly, J.R. (1981) 'Managerial innovation', in P.C. Nystrom and W.H. Starbuck (eds) *Handbook of organizational design, vol 1: Adapting organizations to their environment*, Oxford: Oxford University Press.

Louis, M.R. (1985) 'An investigator's guide to workplace culture', in P.J. Frost et al (eds) *Organizational culture*, Beverly Hills, CA: Sage Publications.

Louis, M.R. (1990) 'Acculturation in the workplace: newcomers as lay ethnographers', in B. Schneider (ed) *Organizational climate and culture*, San Francisco, CA: Jossey-Bass.

McNay, I. (1995) 'From the collegial academy to corporate enterprise: the changing cultures of universities', in T. Schuller (ed) *The changing university?*, Buckingham: Open University Press.

Meek, V.L. (1988) 'Organizational culture: origins and weaknesses', *Organization Studies*, vol 9, no 4, pp 453-73.

Middlehurst, R. (1993) *Leading academics*, Buckingham: Open University Press.

NCIHE (National Committee of Inquiry into Higher Education) (1997) *Higher education in the learning society: Report of the national committee* (Dearing Report), London: NCIHE.

Schein, E.H. (1985) *Organizational culture and leadership*, San Francisco, CA: Jossey-Bass.

Schein, E.H. (1996) 'Culture: the missing concept in organization studies', *Administrative Science Quarterly*, vol 41, no 2, pp 229-40.

Schuller, T. (1992) 'The exploding community? The university idea and the smashing of the academic atom', in I. McNay (ed) *Visions of post-compulsory education*, Buckingham: Open University Press.

Silver, H. (1997) *The languages of innovation: Listening to the higher education literature*, http://www.fae.plym.ac.uk/itlhe.html.

Silver, H. (1999) 'Managing to innovate in higher education', *British Journal of Educational Studies*, vol 47, no 2, pp 145-56.

Silver, H., Hannan, A. and English, S. (1997) *'Innovation': Questions of boundary*, http://www.fae.plym.ac.uk/itlhe.html.

Sporn, B. (1996) 'Managing university culture: an analysis of the relationship between institutional culture and management approaches', *Higher Education*, vol 32, pp 41-61.

Van Maanen, J. and Barley, S.R. (1985) 'Cultural organization: fragments of a theory', in P.J. Frost et al, *Organizational culture*, Beverly Hills, CA: Sage Publications.

Publications of the project

Hannan, A. and Silver, H. (2000: forthcoming) *Innovating in higher education: Teaching, learning and institutional cultures*, Buckingham: Open University Press.

Hannan, A. and Silver, H. (1999) 'Innovation motivation', *Times Higher Education Supplement*, 25 June, p 29.

Hannan, A., English, S. and Silver, H. (1999) 'Why innovate? Some preliminary findings from a research project on "Innovations in teaching and learning in higher education"', *Studies in Higher Education*, vol 24, no 3, pp 279-89.

Silver, H. (1998) 'Why can't you just lecture to us?', *Teaching and learning*, Nottingham: University of Nottingham, autumn, p 1.

Silver, H. (1999) 'Managing to innovate in higher education', *British Journal of Educational Studies*, vol 47, no 2, pp 145-56.

Silver, H. and Hannan, A. (2000) 'Bright sparks across the divide', *Times Higher Education Supplement*, 18 February, p 38.

Silver, H., Hannan, A. and English, S. (1999) 'Innovations in teaching and learning in higher education: A focus on Middlesex', *North Circular* (Middlesex University), vol 82, no 6, pp 5-6.

The project website (at http://www.fae.plym.ac.uk/itlhe.html) contains the following:

- *The experiences of innovators: A report of the first year* for a 'mini-conference' held on 24 June 1998. Also published on the Internet in *EducatiON-LINE* (see http://www.leeds.ac.uk/educol)
- *The languages of innovation: Listening to the higher education literature*, Working Paper 1, also published in *EducatiON-LINE*
- *'Innovation': Questions of boundary*, Working Paper 2, also published in *EducatiON-LINE*
- *Innovations in teaching and learning in higher education; An annotated bibliography*, also published in *EducatiON-LINE*
- *Organisational culture and innovation in higher education: An annotated bibliography of organisational culture and related concepts of importance to investigating the place of innovation in higher education institutions*, also published in *EducatiON-LINE*
- *Aspects of distance learning and the use and impact of information technology*, a paper given at The Romanian Internet Learning Workshop, 2nd Annual Conference, 17-22 July 1998
- *Re-inventing innovation*, a keynote address given at the conference on 'Managing Learning Innovation: The Challenges of the Changing Curriculum', held at Lincoln University Campus, University of Lincolnshire and Humberside, 1-2 September 1998
- *Mechanisms for change: Thoughts from 'Innovations in teaching and learning in higher education'*, extracts from a short talk given to the Higher Education Quality and Employability Division (DfEE) conference on 'Educational Change within Higher Education', London, 2 December 1998
- *The challenges of innovation*, a talk given to 'The history 2000 conference (FDTL)', Bath Spa University College, 15 April 1999.

FIVE

Participating in the Learning Society: history, place and biography

Gareth Rees, Stephen Gorard, Ralph Fevre and John Furlong

Economic change and the Learning Society

There has been a remarkable renewal of governmental concern with education and its organisation over the past couple of decades in Britain (and, indeed, elsewhere). Through much of the 1980s, it was schools and schooling which provided the focal point of policy makers' attention (for example, Ball, 1990). More latterly, the focus has widened to encompass a broader conceptualisation of 'lifelong learning', which certainly continues to embrace the compulsory phases of education, but also includes activities in further and higher education, as well as continuing education and training throughout adult life (for example, Coffield, 1999). This is not to suggest, of course, that this shift in policy emphasis has produced a coherent strategy with respect to education and training through the life course (a point to which we return later). Nevertheless, the change is unmistakable. For example, the creation of a Minister for Lifelong Learning within the Department for Education and Employment (DfEE), along with equivalent positions in the devolved Scottish and Welsh administrations, signals a formal acknowledgement of its significance. Similarly, a plethora of official reports and other policy statements on lifelong learning have flowed from government departments in recent years. Especially since the election of the New Labour administration in 1997, official pronouncements about lifelong learning have proliferated spectacularly. There have been three substantial reports (Kennedy, 1997; Fryer, 1997; NCIHE, 1997), a major Green Paper (DfEE, 1998) and most recently a White Paper on the reorganisation of post-16 education and training (DfEE, 1999). Certainly, lifelong learning has come to occupy a position which – symbolically at least – is at the centre of government strategy (Ainley, 1998; Tight, 1998).

What is involved here is more than a narrowly technical adjustment to the organisation of educational provision. It is instructive, for example, that the key Green Paper was given the portentous title, *The Learning Age: A renaissance for a new Britain* (DfEE, 1998). What is suggested, then, is a transformation in learning opportunities, which is crucial to effecting a profound restructuring of wider social and economic relations. The intellectual basis for this is provided, in turn, by what has become a widespread consensus about the emergent requirements of the economy. Simply put, it is now widely argued that the production and distribution of knowledge are increasingly significant processes in the determination of economic competitiveness and development, which are reflected, in turn, in economic growth, employment change and levels of welfare. The capacity of both organisations and individuals to engage successfully in learning processes of a variety of kinds has come to be regarded as a crucial determinant of economic performance (for example, Lundvall and Johnson, 1994). For some commentators, this implies nothing less than a fundamental transition from an industrial to a knowledge-based or *learning society* (OECD, 1996; Leadbeater, 1999). Clearly, alternative accounts of the nature of the Learning Society are possible and many have been propounded at length in the literature (Gorard et al, 1998a). However, the ideological impact of this particular version derives precisely from the fact that it is rooted in a coherent – albeit contested – analysis of contemporary patterns of economic and social change.

The proponents of this sort of analysis recognise, of course, that the development of the Learning Society (even defined in these terms) involves a complexity of economic and social processes. On the one hand, it holds the promise of increased productivity and an improved standard of living. On the other, it simultaneously implies that individuals and organisations face major challenges in adjusting to new circumstances. The emergent forms of economic activity affect the characteristic nature of work and the types and levels of skills required in the economy. As a result, the security and general quality of jobs are being radically altered, with profound implications for the welfare of individuals. Accordingly, it is recognised that the nature of access to learning opportunities has implications not only for general economic competitiveness, but also for the employability of individuals and the consequent impacts on their standards of living. In this way, then, this dominant view takes the effective organisation of learning opportunities to be crucial to both economic growth and social cohesion (Brown and Lauder, 1996)[1].

The policy implications of this analytical consensus are, of course, profound. If an economy like Britain's – where factor costs are fairly high – is to be competitive, employers need to pursue innovative and technology-intensive strategies for the production of goods and services that have high value-added. Employees require not only good levels of general education, but also the capacity to adapt flexibly to changing skills requirements throughout their careers. Moreover, educational institutions should be organised in ways which ensure that these standards of general education are attained and also that the renewal of skills through continuing education and training is facilitated (for example, Ashton and Green, 1996). As Coffield (1997, 1999) has argued, however, one of the striking features of British policies is that they have concentrated very much on the implications of this analysis for educational institutions and for individuals. For example, the long-term preoccupation with raising 'standards' in schools and colleges is a clear reflection of the former. Equally, the emphasis in initiatives such as the University for Industry, Individual Learning Accounts and the National Grid for Learning is on the need for individual workers to acquire the necessary skills and competences (Gorard and Selwyn, 1999). And it is this latter preoccupation that is of particular concern in what follows.

History, place and biography: participation in lifelong learning

As we have argued at greater length elsewhere, this emphasis on individuals reflects a model of participation in lifelong learning, which is based on a highly simplistic version of human capital theory (Rees et al, 1997a; Fevre et al, 1999a). Hence, according to this model, individuals participate in lifelong learning according to their calculation of the net economic benefits to be derived from education and training (Becker, 1975). Given the dominant consensus about the general direction of economic change towards more knowledge-based forms of production, it follows that a worker will seek to participate in lifelong learning in order to capitalise on the benefits which will flow from skills renewal and development. Hence, the principal issue which government policy needs to address is to ensure the removal of the 'barriers' which prevent people from participating in education and training. These include 'situational' factors, such as finance and lack of time because of other commitments, as well as the features of educational institutions which make them unresponsive to potential learners (McGivney, 1990). Achieving a learning society thus comes to be defined in these rather simple terms.

We wish to argue that this sort of thinking involves an unwarranted abstraction of economic processes from the wider social system. In reality, individual behaviour in economic markets of any kind is embedded in social relations which are shaped by social norms, interpersonal relationships, family and community structures and so forth. Hence, rather than adopting a *universalist* form of explanation (such as human capital theory), we seek to explore the ways in which the determinants of participation in lifelong learning vary systematically over time and from locality to locality (Rees et al, 1997a). Viewed from this perspective, of course, creating a learning society – even one defined in terms of essentially economic considerations – becomes a much more complex process. Nevertheless, we concur with Coffield (1997) that the development of an adequate social theory of lifelong learning – however complex – is a necessary condition of creating a learning society, however conceived.

The temporal and spatial variations in empirical patterns of participation have been widely acknowledged. However, their analytical implications have been less fully explored. Understanding why these patterns take the form they do requires an analysis of the shifts which have taken place in the structure of learning opportunities available in given areas (through, for example, changes in educational provision or labour market conditions), as well as how access to these opportunities is constrained by the social and cultural resources which different social groups command. Moreover, the relationships between these kinds of structural conditions and actual participation are further mediated, not only by the knowledge about learning opportunities which is socially available, but also by the beliefs and attitudes which are held in respect of them (Fevre et al, 1999a). Previous research suggests that the latter 'learner identities' also vary systematically over time, and spatially, reflecting complex patterns of individual, family, community and wider determinations (Rees et al, 1997a).

Accordingly, understanding the determinants of participation in lifelong learning involves tracing out the interactions between the social relations which are specific to particular places, patterns of historical change, and the experiences which constitute individual biographies. In what follows, we explore some of these issues by reference to the results of an empirical study of patterns of participation in lifelong learning in industrial South

Wales over the past 100 years or so. In particular, we draw on the results of a large-scale questionnaire survey, in-depth semi-structured interviews with a sub-sample, and extensive archival analysis (see Appendix to this chapter for a detailed account of the methodology). Focusing on a single region has allowed a detailed reconstruction of the changes which have taken place in patterns of lifelong learning and how these are related to shifts in the economic structure, as well as transformations in social relations more widely. Clearly, industrial South Wales provides a context in which changes of these kinds have been especially marked and rapid (Gorard, 1997).

Patterns of lifelong learning trajectories

We explore empirical patterns of participation in lifelong learning through the concept of 'trajectories'. At one level, what is involved here is the attempt to describe characteristic sequences of learning episodes through the life course by aggregating individual experiences into a set of typologies (Banks et al, 1992). However, there is a clear analytical element too. Hence, the 'trajectory' which people join is largely determined by the resources which they derive from their social background. Moreover, an individual's capacity to take up whatever learning opportunities are available is constrained by his or her previous history in this respect. However, 'trajectories' do not simply reflect the constraining effects of structured access to learning opportunities. The individual educational experiences of which they are comprised are simultaneously the products of personal choices, which themselves reflect 'learner identities'. What is central to an adequate analysis, therefore, is to produce an account of the *interaction* of 'learner identities' and the individual choices to which they give rise, with wider structural parameters (Rees et al, 1997a).

Our questionnaire survey permitted the construction of 1,104 individual education and training histories. These were subsequently aggregated into a typology of 11 'lifelong learning trajectories' which encompassed almost all of the individual variations. This was further aggregated into a five-fold typology, and it is the latter which is used here. Table 1 summarises the frequencies of the five 'trajectories'.

The 'immature trajectory' describes the small number of respondents who have yet to leave full-time education (and they are not used in the discussion which follows). The 'non-participants' are those who reported no extension of their education immediately after ending compulsory

Table I: Frequencies of the lifelong learning trajectories

'Trajectory'	Frequency	%
Non-participant	339	31
Transitional	222	20
Delayed	144	13
Lifelong	353	32
Immature	42	4

schooling, no continuing education in adult life, no participation in government training schemes and no substantive work-based training. The 'transitional learners' reported only the continuation of full-time education or a period of initial work-based training immediately after completing compulsory schooling. Those on the 'delayed trajectory' have a gap in participation between leaving school and at least 21 years of age, but followed by a minimum of one substantive episode of education or training. The 'lifelong learners' reported both transitional participation and later episodes of education and training – albeit of varying kinds – as well.

It is significant that this lifelong trajectory accounts for almost a third of respondents, neatly balancing the 'non-participants'. On the other hand, for a substantial minority of respondents, their experience of lifelong learning ended with initial schooling. Although this conclusion needs to be qualified in light of the evidence from the semi-structured interviews (see below), it nevertheless confirms other accounts of the size of the task confronting policy makers seeking to promote lifelong learning (for example, Beinart and Smith, 1998).

Changes over time in learning trajectories

There is also considerable evidence that the pattern of typical trajectories has changed very substantially over time. The archival research, for example, shows that, during the early decades of the century in South Wales, the dominant forms of formal, post-school learning were employment-based and largely restricted to men. Within coalmining, the pervasive method of acquiring knowledge and skills was through working under the tutelage of an experienced worker, usually an older family member. This came to be supplemented by organised evening classes, which enabled individuals to acquire the technical qualifications which became necessary for career advancement in the industry (and which were consolidated during the period after nationalisation in 1947). However, with the intensification of conflict between miners and owners during the interwar years, the nature of participation was transformed through the rise of 'workers' education', aimed at raising political awareness and feeding the labour movement with activists, a pattern which was not replicated even in other coalfield areas (Burge et al, 1998).

Although the nature of the evidence is different, the pattern of trajectories has also changed significantly during the period since the Second World War. Disaggregating the total sample (which covered the age range 15 to 64) from the questionnaire survey into age cohorts allows a mapping of these changes. Hence, there has been a clear trend away from non-participation over the period since the oldest respondents left school. The proportion of each cohort reporting no formal learning has therefore decreased (despite the greater number of years in which participation was possible for the older groups). However, the increase in post-school participation which this implies is reflected mainly in the substantial rise in the proportion of 'transitional learners', primarily reflecting increased investment in initial schooling. Indeed, later participation in learning has actually decreased in overall frequency, duration and the proportion funded by employers (Gorard et al, 1999a).

Moreover, when these changes are analysed separately for men and women, distinctive patterns emerge. For men, the increase in post-school participation took place chiefly for those completing initial education during the 1950s and 1960s, while for women, it occurred a decade later, for those finishing school during the 1970s and 1980s. The increase in participation for men is attributable to the growth of 'lifelong learners', although only up until the 1980s. For women, in contrast, the increase is the result of more 'transitional learners'. Hence, gender remains a significant determinant of participation in lifelong learning, even where it has been eliminated as a determinant of extended initial education.

Again, there are interesting implications here. These patterns of change raise questions about conceptualisations of the 'learning society' exclusively as a desirable future state, yet to be achieved (as is most commonly the case in contemporary discussions). They discount the possibility that elements of past practice in education and training were superior to the present, or that the development over time of participation in learning may be distinctly non-linear, especially for particular population groups. Certainly, for those men who left school in South Wales during the 1950s and 1960s – a period of full employment, relative affluence and settled welfare state provision – their situation with respect to lifelong learning was significantly better not only than that of their female contemporaries, but also than that of those who have left school during the marketised 1980s and 1990s (Rees, 1997).

The determinants of learning trajectories

To begin to explain this changing pattern of participation in lifelong learning, logistic regression analysis can be used to identify those characteristics of respondents which enable good predictions of which trajectory they later follow. These characteristics are thus tentatively identified as social determinants of patterns of participation (Gorard et al, 1998b). For example, a respondent who is a 50 year old woman, born and still living in Neath-Port Talbot, whose father was unqualified and in an intermediate-class occupation and whose mother was unwaged, whose family religion was Anglican, who attended secondary modern school and left with no qualifications, who herself has an intermediate-class occupation, and who does not have a hobby requiring study or practice, is estimated by our analysis – and using only these data – to have a 16% predicted probability of being a 'lifelong learner'. This is confirmed by her survey responses, which report no education or training since leaving school.

The full model includes over 40 independent variables which have a (statistically) significant impact, but the sense of these can be summarised in terms of five broad factors.

Time

When respondents were born determines their relationship to changing opportunities for learning and their social expectations. For example, a number of older respondents reported having experienced quite radical changes of job, with no training provided to equip them to cope with their new position, something which was believed to be much less likely today. As one of them put it:

> "Nobody worried about things like that then. It's quite a new thing, isn't it?"

Similarly, the salience of educational qualifications was widely perceived to have increased as a consequence of shifts in the nature of employment. One father, for example, contrasted his own experiences with those of his son.

> "... so they kept me back from my 11-plus ... I didn't go to school that day.... As soon as I was old enough to work, they wanted me to work.... [But] he's not coming out of school until he's 18, you know. It's as simple as that, because we know how important it is, especially today."

It is significant that respondents with similar social backgrounds from different birth cohorts exhibit different tendencies to participate in education and training.

Place

Where respondents are born and brought up shapes their access to specifically local opportunities to participate and specifically local social expectations. Those who have lived in the most economically disadvantaged areas (such as Blaenau Gwent) are least likely to participate in lifelong learning. This reflects both sharp inequalities in the availability of learning opportunities between different localities, as well as differences in values and attitudes. However, those who have moved between regions are even more likely to participate than those living in the more advantaged localities.

It is not too much of a simplification to say that those who are geographically mobile tend to be participants in lifelong learning (of some kind), while those who remain in one area tend to be non-participants. One of our respondents, for example, had left school at 15 to enter employment in the local colliery, along with all his friends.

> "... but that was closed then, in 1969. I had an accident just before it shut and it was while I was out that Llanilleth shut."

He was clear that none of the local jobs now required any special skills or qualifications, and that there was little point in his seeking out alternative employment elsewhere, even though the opportunities may have been better. As he put it:

"I'm not brainy enough, I suppose. Well, I never looked to be honest."

Gender

Men consistently report more formal learning than women. Although the situation is changing (see below), these changes are different for each gender. Women are still less likely to participate in lifelong learning, but are now more likely to be 'transitional learners'. Staying on in education after 16 and undertaking some form of initial training (including apprenticeships) is now relatively evenly distributed between young men and women. However, among our respondents, participation in learning later in life is *increasingly* the preserve of males, especially in respect of work-place training and despite the shift away from male-dominated employment in the region (Gorard et al, 1998c, 1999a).

Women's participation in lifelong learning is clearly constrained by the expectations placed on them by their parents and by their husbands and children. And this seems to have changed rather little over the hundred years or so covered by our study. A particularly vivid example of the contemporary salience of these factors is provided by a respondent who had succeeded in gaining the first formal qualification in her family ever.

"Well, I found work then [as a management trainee]. We moved away to Birmingham, up there. But Steve [her husband] didn't like it up there. And he was promised a job here, so we came back. But it fell through and then the kids came along."

Her husband has been unemployed ever since. Our respondent now works as a packer, helps with a local play-group, is learning Welsh and taking further qualifications in childcare. She still looks after the children.

Family

Parents' social class, educational experience and family religion are perhaps the most important determinants of participation in lifelong learning. Family background is influential in a number of ways, most obviously in material terms, but also in terms of what are understood to be the 'natural' forms of participation (as is indicated by the importance of family religion) (Gorard et al, 1999b). As one respondent explained:

"My mother and father would have been devastated if I hadn't passed [the 11-plus], totally devastated. My father was a collier, but the attitude in our house was if you don't learn, you won't get on, and you'll go down the colliery."

In contrast, for a number of respondents, the influence of family on participation was negative. For example, a man of 56 recalled how his father had pre-empted all the major decisions about his transition from school at 15 years of age.

"He organised the job for me and took me out of school, before I could try ... I wanted to stay in school ... to try my O levels.... But you couldn't get an apprenticeship over 17, so he said ... 'I've got a job for you in W.H. Watts.'"

Initial schooling

Experience of initial schooling is crucial in shaping long-term orientations towards learning, and in providing qualifications necessary to access many forms of further and higher education, as well as continuing education and training later in life (although see below). There are important 'age effects' here, however, relating especially to the reorganisation of secondary schooling in the maintained sector. For the older age groups, the 11-plus was a clear watershed. Those who did not sit the examination, as well as those who failed it, were especially affected. Even within the later comprehensive school system, there remained a keen awareness among respondents of the impact of different forms of school experience. As one explained:

"Well, I didn't take no exams at all because I wasn't very good in school. When I left school, then I did, the job I wanted was to be a care assistant. But I can't, 'cause I didn't get the papers."

What emerges from these sorts of account, moreover, is the extent to which experiences of compulsory schooling exert continuing impacts on how individuals define themselves in relation to learning opportunities later in life (a point to which we return below).

Learning through the life course

It is important to note that all of these factors reflect characteristics of respondents which are determined relatively early during the life course. This can be expressed more formally, as the variables were entered into the logistic regression function in the order in which they occur in real life. Hence, those characteristics which are set very early in an individual's life, such as age, gender and family background, predict later lifelong learning trajectories with 75% accuracy. Adding the variables representing initial schooling increases the accuracy of prediction to 86%. And this rises to 89% and 90% respectively, as the variables associated with adult life and with respondents' present circumstances are included.

The analytical implications of this are profound. It provides strong empirical support for the utility of the concept of 'trajectory' in analysing participation in lifelong learning. Not only is there a clear pattern of typical trajectories which effectively encapsulates the complexity of individual education and training biographies, but also, which trajectory an individual takes can be accurately predicted on the basis of characteristics which are known by the time an individual reaches school-leaving age. This does not imply, of course, that people do not have choices, or that life crises have little impact, but rather that, to a large extent, these choices and crises occur within a framework of opportunities, influences and social expectations that are determined independently. At this level of analysis, it is this framework which appears most influential.

These conclusions, however, should be qualified in the light of more detailed modelling of the determinants of lifelong learning trajectories. Hence, where the logistic regression function is constructed to distinguish between those forms of participation which occur immediately after compulsory schooling and those which occur later in life, different factors are highlighted (Gorard et al, 1998d). It is possible to predict the former much more accurately than the latter on the basis of those characteristics of respondents which are set by the end of initial schooling (age, place of birth and gender are most significant, along with regular attendance at school and sitting – although not necessarily passing – school-leaving qualifications). For later participation, while some of the determinants are the same, their *relevance* is not. For example, those with no qualifications are more likely to return to learning later in life than those who do not achieve the 'benchmark' equivalence of five GCSEs, the opposite of the situation with respect to participation immediately after school. Moreover, many of the determinants of later participation are different and reflect the changing circumstances of adult life in terms of family relationships, access to learning opportunities through employment and so on. These results offer important correctives to the conventional view of participation in lifelong learning, summarised by Tuckett (1997) as "if at first you don't succeed, you don't succeed" (see also Gorard et al, 1999a).

Learner identities

When the focus of analysis shifts to individuals' own accounts of their experiences of education and training after school (derived from the semi-structured interviews), it is not surprising that it is their very diversity which is initially most striking. Necessarily, respondents tend to emphasise the specificities of their learning histories, the particular family circumstances or labour market shifts to which they had to react and so on. Certainly, there are no *simple* patterns in these individual accounts, even among those who follow the same trajectory.

This complexity is at least consistent with the theoretical framework which was sketched earlier, where the *choices* made by individuals over participation in learning constitute a key element. Equally, however, for the respondents themselves, any choices which were made are perceived to have been heavily constrained by external circumstances. Perhaps most obviously, many older women describe the ways in which the learning opportunities available to them were limited by local employment, social expectations as to what was appropriate or by a 'forced altruism' with respect to family commitments (themes which are reproduced for earlier periods in the archival analysis). Even the younger women respondents frequently provide similar accounts, confirming the points made earlier about the very partial nature of changes in women's trajectories over time (Gorard et al, 1998c). Moreover, for a number of those – women and men – who *had* participated actively in post-school learning (albeit mainly in the form of conventional further and higher education), this is seen as a product of what was normatively prescribed within the family or, less frequently, the wider community, rather than their own active choice (Gorard et al, 1999a). Certainly, it is clear that, to make sense of individuals' learning histories, it is necessary to understand the ways in which learning opportunities were understood when decisions over participation were being made. Moreover, there is strong evidence that these 'social constructions' of opportunities, in turn, are shaped by a range of contextual influences.

One of the clearest exemplifications of the latter relates to the impacts of the experience of compulsory schooling. 'Success' or 'failure' at school lays the foundation for what appears to be an enduring 'learner identity'. It is striking, for example, how numerous respondents who had experienced the 11-plus examination testified to its major and often long-term effects. For example, a respondent explained that he had left school at the earliest opportunity to be a coalminer; only passing the 11-plus would have offered an alternative:

> "It's just the normal thing, I think, around here, unless I went to a grammar school or whatever."

For respondents too young to have gone through the tripartite system, although 'success' and 'failure' are less starkly defined, it remains the case that they identify positive experiences of schooling as crucial determinants of enduring attitudes towards subsequent learning. For many individuals, then, the significance attached to 'doing well' at school, within families and even the wider community has long-term consequences. In particular, while 'passing' the 11-plus is certainly not a sufficient condition for becoming a 'lifelong learner', a number of respondents do attribute their post-school education and training to the influences of their adolescent experiences of the traditional grammar school, especially in the wider context of the South Wales coalfield, where the conventional non-conformist emphasis on the intrinsic value of education continued to be influential (Gorard et al, 1999a). As one respondent recalled, for example:

> "When I was in school, we won the Urdd Eisteddfod play 10 years on the trot.... Mind you, look at the people we had there.... We had debating societies every Monday and we had to prepare a speech.... You were influenced by your peers as well, not just your parents.... And I think it held you in good stead later on ... you were never afraid to stand in front of an audience."

In contrast, those who 'failed' at school often come to see post-school learning of all kinds as irrelevant to their needs and capacities. Hence, not only is participation in further, higher and continuing education not perceived to be a realistic possibility, but also work-based learning is viewed as unnecessary. There is thus a marked tendency to devalue formal training and to attribute effective performance in a job to 'common-sense' and experience (Fevre et al, 1999b). While this is certainly not confined to those whose school careers were less 'successful' in conventional terms, it is a view almost universally held among this group of respondents. For example, one of our respondents had left school at 14 and gone straight into a successful career in British Steel Tinplate, despite having no formal qualifications or even training:

> "You learn as you get along.... You got to train yourself and you use your hands and ears. No one came along and said 'you mustn't do this' or 'you mustn't do that'.... I mean common-sense will tell you not to do certain things.... I can pick up most things purely by watching someone else doing it...."

In reality, of course, it is difficult to interpret the implications of these findings. Reluctance to acknowledge a significant role for formal training may not impair an individual's ability to do a job, especially where the requirements are minimal. Conversely, there is considerable evidence from the semi-structured interviews that many people are able to acquire substantial knowledge and skills – both inside and outside of employment – *without* formal training (Fevre et al, 1999b; Gorard et al, 1999c). This observation is further elaborated in the work of another of the projects within *The Learning Society Programme* (Eraut et al, 1998). Here again, the evidence from one of our respondents will have to suffice:

> "I haven't got a GCE or a BSc or whatever they're called these days ... but as I say you don't have to be academic to be able to do things.... It's the same with the French polishing, you see. I used to do it as a favour. I got a book from the library. I had a blind chappie who was a pianist, like, and he used to tune pianos and doing them up. He asked me if I knew anything about polishing and I said 'not the foggiest'. So I went to the library, got a book on it. We got the French polish and promptly went into business. It was just a sideline when I was working for the printers."

Concluding comments

What emerges very clearly from our study is that the model which currently underpins official versions of the learning society in Britain is not compatible with the realities of actual patterns of participation in lifelong learning and their determinants. Certainly, people make choices about their participation in education and training after school. However, these are not framed exclusively in terms of the economic benefits which will accrue from such participation. Rather, they reflect deep-seated attitudes towards learning in formal settings, such as educational institutions and work places. These 'learner identities', in turn, are predominantly formed early in life through the influences of family and the experiences of compulsory schooling. Hence, non-participation is largely a product of the fact that individuals do not see education and training as appropriate for them and these views, in turn, are structured by factors which occur relatively early in life. Hence, policies which simply make it easier for people to participate in the kinds of education and training which are already available (for example, removing 'barriers' to participation, such as costs, time and lack of childcare) will have only limited impacts.

This also suggests, of course, that 'lifelong learning' should mean precisely that. The relationships between initial education and training and developing lifelong learning are highly complex. We have seen, for example, that the considerable growth in participation immediately after the completion of compulsory schooling has not been paralleled by the expansion of continuing participation through life. Whether this changes in the future is dependent on the development of 'learning careers' which extend 'from cradle to grave'. Accordingly, it follows that priority should be given to the facilitation of lifelong progression routes, rather than focusing on *either* initial *or* continuing education and training. Certainly, the current 'front-loading' of public investment into initial schooling is called into question, if the objective is to produce a learning society based on lifelong learning. Moreover, major issues are also raised about the appropriateness of a curriculum and teaching methods that are driven by criteria of raising 'standards' measured in terms of formal qualifications, if the objective is to produce self-motivated and self-directing learners equipped to participate in learning through adult life.

The significance of a truly lifelong perspective is further emphasised in the results of our modelling of the determinants of learning trajectories. As we have seen, if we know an individual's age, place of birth, gender and family background, we can predict his or her pattern of participation in education and training after school with 75% accuracy. If we also know the details of compulsory schooling, the accuracy of our prediction rises to 86%. Moreover, these results also indicate that policies which seek to improve access to opportunities for education and training are likely to have limited impacts unless they are integrated within wider strategies to combat social exclusion. Combating social exclusion through improvements in individuals' employability brought about by participation in lifelong learning can only be partially effective, because this participation is structured profoundly by patterns of social disadvantage. 'Joined-up government' is a necessary condition of progress here.

Finally, there are clear divergences between the way in which lifelong learning is seen by our respondents here and the view embodied in policy. Even in the case of learning in the workplace, formal education and training is often down-played in favour of 'common-sense' and, by implication, the extensive learning which takes place in *informal* ways. And this appears to have been almost unaffected by the introduction of competence-based National Vocational Qualifications, as well as the other initiatives by government and firms to raise the profile of training (Fevre et al, 1999b). Moreover, contrary to our initial expectations, our study uncovered a vast amount of learning taking place wholly outside of the formal arena of education and training. It is true there are some indications of a growing acknowledgement among policy makers of the significance of informal learning in the workplace, the family and community settings (for example, Fryer, 1997). However, for these insights to be fully integrated into policy development would require the adoption of a vision of the Learning Society which continues to encompass the needs of individuals to engage effectively with the world of work, but which extends beyond the current preoccupation with the purported role of human capital in ensuring economic competitiveness.

Appendix 1: The study methodology

The study is based, then, on an extended examination of *one* of Britain's most important industrial regions, South Wales. There were three principal methods of data collection. These were: (i) a questionnaire survey, (ii) semi-structured interviews, and (iii) archival analysis.

Questionnaire survey

The sample for the questionnaire survey was drawn from three localities (Blaenau Gwent, Bridgend and Neath-Port Talbot) chosen to reflect the diversity of social and economic conditions in industrial South Wales. Within each site, sampling was focused on three electoral divisions, again selected to represent local conditions. Household lists were identified from electoral registers and an initial sample of some 880 respondents (one from each household) was derived by means of repeated systematic sampling. This sample was stratified so that respondents were divided equally between men and women; and span the age range 35 to 64 years old evenly. A booster sample of around 220 respondents was drawn from the children of members of the initial sample, to allow detailed exploration of family relationships. This sample was also divided equally between men and women and covered the age range 15 to 34 years old evenly. The primary response rate was 74% and this was supplemented by substitution; 1,104 usable questionnaires were completed.

The questionnaire was designed to collect data of four principal kinds: the social/demographic characteristics of individual respondents, detailed histories of respondents' post-compulsory educational and training careers, simplified histories of respondents' employment careers, and simplified histories of the educational and training careers of respondents' children. Information on individual histories was collected on a modified "sequential start to finish date of event basis" (Gallie, 1994, p 340).

Following extensive preliminary analysis, there were two major elements in analysing the data derived from the questionnaire survey. Firstly, the complexity of the 1,104 individual education and training histories was reduced by converting each one into a sequence of episodes (an educational programme, new job, etc) in which participation in education and training did or did not occur. These sequences, in turn, were classified into 11 'lifelong learning trajectories', which describe almost all of the variations in individual histories. For most analyses, these can be further grouped into only five types of 'lifelong learning trajectories'.

Secondly, logistic regression analysis permits the identification of those characteristics of individuals (independent variables) which provide good predictions of which 'lifelong learning trajectories' they follow (dependent variable). This method of analysis is especially fruitful, as independent variables may be added into the regression function in the order in which they occur in real life: that is, the statistical procedure models exactly the social phenomenon it is analysing ('trajectories') (Gorard et al, 1998b).

Semi-structured interviews

A 10% sub-sample, representing the characteristics of the main sample, provided the basis for 105 extended, semi-structured interviews. The interviews were tape recorded and transcribed.

These interviews again focused on the respondent's recollections of how his or her education and training career unfolded. However, here it was the ways in which this is understood by respondents which provide the focus. Although respondents were encouraged to speak freely on these issues, interviewers followed an *aide memoire* to direct the discussion to a predetermined analytical agenda.

Archival analysis

The full historical range of the study was made possible by the analysis of materials held in the South Wales Coalfield Archive. The tape transcripts of oral history interviews held in the Archive, although carried out originally with different objectives in mind, provided a primary source of data on the nature and determinants of participation in education and training during the first half of the twentieth century. (See Appendix I of Burge et al, 1998.)

Acknowledgements

The study on which this chapter is based was funded by the Economic and Social Research Council (grant L123251041) as part of its *Learning Society Programme*. It also received financial support from the West Wales Training and Enterprise Council and the then Gwent and Mid Glamorgan Training and Enterprise Councils (now part of TEC South East Wales). None of these organisations has any responsibility for the views expressed, which remain the responsibility of the authors alone.

We should also like to acknowledge the contributions made to the study by our colleagues in the Department of Adult and Continuing Education at the University of Wales, Swansea, Alan Burge, Hywel Francis and Colin Trotman; and in the Cardiff University School of Social Sciences, Jane Salisbury, Trevor Welland and, in particular, Paul Chambers and Emma Renold.

Finally, we should like to commend publicly the part played by Frank Coffield as Director of *The Learning Society Programme*. He was a model of constructive criticism and friendly encouragement. His work contributed considerably to whatever success our project has achieved.

Notes

[1] Social cohesion has been more significant in official discourses about lifelong learning since the return of the New Labour administration than under the previous Conservative ones. It has also been more important at the level of the European Union (Rees et al, 1997b).

References

Ainley, P. (1998) 'Towards a learning or a certified society? Contradictions in the New Labour modernization of lifelong learning', *Journal of Education Policy*, vol 13, pp 559-74.

Ashton, D. and Green, F. (1996) *Education, training and the global economy*, Cheltenham: Edward Elgar.

Ball, S. (1990) *Politics and policy making in education: Explorations in policy sociology*, London: Routledge.

Banks, M., Bates, I., Breakwell, G., Bynner, J., Emler, N., Jamieson, L. and Roberts, K. (1992) *Carers and identities*, Milton Keynes: Open University Press.

Becker, G. (1975) *Human capital: A theoretical and empirical analysis*, Chicago, IL: University of Chicago Press.

Beinart, S. and Smith, P. (1998) *National adult learning survey 1997*, London: DfEE.

Burge, A., Francis, H. and Trotman, C. (1998) 'In a class of their own: adult learning and the South Wales mining community 1900-1939', Working Paper 16, Cardiff: School of Education, Cardiff University.

Brown, P. and Lauder, H. (1996) 'Education, globalization and economic development', *Journal of Education Policy*, vol 11, pp 1-25.

Coffield, F. (1997) 'A tale of three little pigs: building the learning society with straw', *Evaluation and Research in Education*, vol 11, pp 1-15.

Coffield, F. (1999) 'Breaking the consensus: lifelong learning as social control', *British Educational Research Journal*, vol 25, pp 479-500.

DfEE (Department for Education and Employment) (1998) *The Learning Age: A renaissance for a new Britain*, London: The Stationery Office.

DfEE (1999) *Learning to Succeed: A new framework for post-16 learning*, London: The Stationery Office.

Eraut, M., Alderton, J., Cole, G. and Senker, P. (1998) *Development of knowledge and skills in employment*, Research Report no 5, Brighton: University of Sussex Institute of Education.

Fevre, R., Rees, G. and Gorard, S. (1999a) 'Some sociological alternatives to human capital theory and their implications for research on post-compulsory education and training', *Journal of Education and Work*, vol 12, pp 117-40.

Fevre, R., Gorard, S. and Rees, G. (1999b) 'Necessary and unnecessary learning: the acquisition of knowledge and "skills" in and outside employment in South Wales in the 20th century', in F. Coffield (ed) *The necessity of informal learning*, Bristol: The Policy Press, pp 64-80.

Fryer, R. (1997) *Learning for the twenty-first century*, First report of the National Advisory Group for Continuing Education, London: NAGCELL.

Gallie, D. (1994) 'Methodological appendix: the social change and economic life initiative', in D. Gallie, C. Marsh and C. Vogler (eds) *Social change and the experience of unemployment*, Oxford: Oxford University Press, pp 335-46.

Gorard, S. (1997) *The region of study: Patterns of participation in adult education and training*, Working Paper 1, Cardiff: School of Education.

Gorard, S. and Selwyn, N. (1999) 'Switching on the learning society? Questioning the role of technology in widening participation in lifelong learning', *Journal of Education Policy*, vol 14, pp 523-34.

Gorard, S., Fevre, R. and Rees, G. (1999c) 'The apparent decline of informal learning', *Oxford Review of Education*, vol 25, pp 437-54.

Gorard, S., Rees, G. and Fevre, R. (1999a) 'Two dimensions of time: the changing social context of lifelong learning', *Studies in the Education of Adults*, vol 31, pp 35-48.

Gorard, S., Rees, G. and Fevre, R. (1999b) 'Patterns of participation in lifelong learning: do families make a difference?', *British Educational Research Journal*, vol 25, pp 517-32.

Gorard, S., Rees, G., Fevre, R. and Furlong, J. (1998a) 'Society is not built by education alone: alternative routes to a learning society', *Research in Post-Compulsory Education*, vol 3, pp 25-37.

Gorard, S., Rees, G., Fevre, R. and Furlong, J. (1998b) 'Learning trajectories: travelling towards a learning society?', *International Journal of Lifelong Education*, vol 17, pp 400-10.

Gorard, S., Rees, G., Fevre, R., Renold, E. and Furlong, J. (1998c) 'A gendered appraisal of the transition to a learning society', in R. Benn (ed.) *Research, teaching and learning: Making connections in the education of adults*, Leeds: SCUTREA, pp 62-7.

Gorard, S., Rees, G., Fevre, R. and Furlong, J. (1998d) 'The two components of a new learning society', *Journal of Vocational Education and Training*, vol 50, pp 5-19.

Kennedy, H. (1997) *Learning works: Widening participation in further education*, Coventry: FEFC.

Leadbeater, C. (1999) *Living on thin air: The new economy*, London: Viking.

Lundvall, B.A. and Johnson, B. (1994) 'The learning economy', *Journal of Industry Studies*, vol 1, pp 23-42.

McGivney, V. (1990) *Education's for other people: Access to education for non-participant adults*, Leicester: NIACE.

NCIHE (National Committee of Inquiry into Higher Education) (1997) *Higher education in the learning society: Main report* (The Dearing Report), London: NCIHE.

OECD (1996) *Transitions to learning economies and societies*, Paris: OECD.

Rees, G. (1997) 'Making a learning society: education and work in industrial South Wales', *Welsh Journal of Education*, vol 6, pp 4-16.

Rees, G., Fevre, R., Furlong, J. and Gorard, S. (1997a) 'History, place and the learning society: Towards a sociology of lifelong learning', *Journal of Education Policy*, vol 12, pp 485-97.

Rees, G., Gorard, S., Fevre, R. and Furlong, J. (1997b) 'Lifelong learning, labour markets and social cohesion', Paper presented to the ECER Annual Conference, Frankfurt, September.

Tight, M. (1998) 'Education, education, education! The vision of lifelong learning in the Kennedy, Dearing and Fryer reports', *Oxford Review of Education*, vol 24, pp 473-86.

Tuckett, A. (1997) 'An election shopping list for lifelong learning', *Times Educational Supplement*, 14 March.

SIX

Skills in the British workplace

David Ashton, Alan Felstead and Francis Green

Context

Although the study of education has long been recognised to have an economic aspect, in that education is in part an investment for future monetary gain, it was not until around the middle of the 1980s that the pivotal role of education and training policies as economic policies began to be widely canvassed. Much cited studies by Finegold and Soskice (1988), Reich (1988), Marshall and Tucker (1992) and others highlighted the salience of achieving a highly skilled workforce in an increasingly global economic environment. The British education system was diagnosed by many as failing the economy, except perhaps at the highest level of university participation. Deficiencies in intermediate skills were identified (eg Steedman and Wagner, 1987; Daly et al, 1985), and in recent years the alarmingly large proportion of British workers lacking basic skills has been castigated (Murray and Steedman, 1998).

Following recognition of this problem, many policy changes have been enacted. To highlight just a few, we may cite the introduction of the National Curriculum in 1988, the switch from O levels to GCSEs, the setting up of employer-dominated Training and Enterprise Councils (TECs) for the delivery of work-based training[1], the attempt to simplify the system of vocational qualifications via the NVQ system and, at the enterprise level, the introduction of Investors in People.

Coincident with these changes, although only partly as a result of policy, there has been a radical shift in individuals' attitudes to education, as reflected in sharply rising participation rates beyond the compulsory school leaving age. Whereas in 1985 only 67% of 16 and 17 year olds in England participated in some form of education or training, by 1995 that figure had risen to 83%, with all of this growth being due to an increase in the proportion who remained in full-time education. Since 1979 student numbers have doubled and the proportion entering higher education has risen from one in eight in 1979 to almost one in three in 1995 (DfEE, 1997). Work-related training participation has changed also, in that the proportion of employees taking part in training has risen from around 11% in 1985 to 15% in 1998. The total volume of training – as measured by time spent in training – has probably not changed much, because courses have become shorter (Felstead et al, 1999b). Nevertheless, the volume of employer-provided continuing training in Britain is above average in European terms (Green, 1999). These various developments ought to lead us to expect an increasing supply of skills in the workforce, as less qualified workers retire and are replaced by newly qualified and trained young workers.

At the same time, there are cogent reasons to expect an increase in the demand for skilled workers by employers. On the one hand, national markets are increasingly being opened up as companies go global and as trade barriers are progressively lowered in successive rounds of trade negotiations. Simultaneously, the emergence of growing but still very poor nations as industrial competitors reduces the relative demand for lower skilled workers in the rich nations (Wood, 1998). On the other hand, and in line with the balance of evidence so far, modern technologies and forms of work organisation are argued to be complementary with high skills (Machin and Van Reenen, 1998). Information technology, biotechnology and other innovations require relatively more highly qualified workers often displacing less skilled workers. There is also case study evidence of increasing need for problem-solving skills, for the ability to deal with non-routine and abstract issues, to handle decisions and responsibilities, to operate effectively in groups and to acquire system-wide understanding of production processes (Hirschorn, 1984; Bertrand and Noyelle, 1988). An important channel through which these new skills are acquired may be the workplace itself rather than the external education and training system. It is only recently that work-based learning is coming to be recognised as a potential key source of rising skills (see evidence below; also Eraut et al, 2000).

It is against this backdrop that we carried out an investigation into the skills of the workforce, as part of the ESRC's *Learning Society* research programme. In this chapter, we examine the extent to which Britain might be considered a 'learning society'. In such a society we would expect:

- aggregate skills to be increasing;
- these skills rises to represent society's conscious or unconscious response to the changing technological and global environment;
- the market for skills to be effective in providing signals and incentives for workers (or potential workers) to acquire the necessary skills;
- *all* workers to have access to the channels of skill acquisition, with especially lower-skilled workers enabled to catch up and, most crucially, avoiding a further polarisation of society driven by a widening skills gap between rich and poor.

A prior objective of our work was to develop the methodology available to economists and social scientists for measuring skills in survey work, building on existing approaches. With this achieved, the aim was to design a new survey which could then provide a backbone of statistical evidence for the *Learning Society* research programme. Although the programme ranges well beyond the issue of skills, it is in this area that the evidence is thinnest. New evidence about the detailed pattern of skills in Britain could also constitute a benchmark for future analyses, so as to track the changing pattern of skills in much more detail than hitherto possible. In this chapter we use the survey to address some of the key indicators of a 'learning society' identified above.

However, it is important to note at the outset that we did not examine the skills of unemployed or economically inactive people. This restriction meant that our conclusions in respect of the distribution of skills are only partial; arguably, the major proximate source of social exclusion is the lack of opportunity to do paid work. The reasons for the limitation were partly financial: we wished to devote finite funding to a large sample of employed people. Nevertheless, concentration only on employed people facilitated a methodology of skills measurement that revolved largely around jobs – something that would have been difficult to apply consistently to those without current jobs.

The chapter continues as follows. In the following section we describe our methodology in some detail. Since we intend this methodology to serve as a possible base for further studies, we have also provided a full description elsewhere (Ashton et al, 1999). The subsequent four sections assess the overall trajectory of skill change, the drivers of change, the market value of different skills and the changes in the distribution of skills. Armed with this evidence the chapter concludes that there are signs that Britain is on the road to a 'learning society'. However, there are also areas of concern and disadvantage that need to be tackled before Britain can truly claim to have achieved the status of a 'learning society'.

Developing an integrated empirical concept of skill

One of the unique contributions of this research was the development of a new methodology for the analysis of skills. This methodology drew on different academic traditions and integrated them to provide a new set of tools for intellectual enquiry in this area. Hitherto our knowledge of skills has been derived from three main sources: the discipline of economics with its concern with measuring the incentives to acquire skills, sociology with its concern for locating the functions of skill in a social context, and psychology with its concern to understand the process of acquisition of skills. Our aim was to draw on these three disciplines in order to create a genuine interdisciplinary approach to many of the issues surrounding the acquisition and use of skills. This meant drawing on three very different theoretical traditions, each with its own set of assumptions and methodologies.

In the economics literature the dominant approach to understanding the impact of education and training (ET) has been framed by the human capital approach, which regards ET as an investment that can be treated (apart from the issue of property rights) in the same way as physical capital. One can identify returns to investments in education and training at the individual, organisational and societal levels. As such this has formed the basis of a cost benefit methodology and is the most all-pervasive framework to inform national policy debates and the work of international bodies such as the World Bank and the International Labour Organisation. Theoretically, economists regard skills as acquired faculties that generate higher productivity and hence higher wages or better employment prospects.

One of the drawbacks with the conventional approach in economics is that it treats the concept of skill as relatively unproblematic. In general, it is used to refer to those technical attributes of individuals which are rewarded in the labour market. Owing to this relatively narrow conceptualisation and to a preference for 'hard' (ie quantitative) data, economists have typically used proxies for skill for which such data were easily available. These proxies include qualifications, and years of education, of training, of job tenure and of general work experience. Our project retained the quantitative approach, but aimed to broaden and improve the conceptualisation of skill.

Sociologists have usually ignored the work of economists in their approach to the issue of skills. Their theoretical origins look to the work of Marx, Weber and Durkheim, where the focus is on the social construction of skills and their function in the economy and wider society. One focus of attention in sociology concerns the ways in which skills are used by groups as weapons in their struggle to further sectional interests, be it those of trade unions (Parkin, 1974), professions (Johnson, 1972) or males (Cockburn, 1983). This has led to a concern with the ways in which different groups construct skills and use them in inter-group struggles within the wider society. This work has shown how the label 'skilled' can be used as a means of furthering the status, wealth and power of groups independently of the actual content of the job in question.

A second focus of interest has been on the ways in which the system of production is changing and how employers utilise the skills of employees. This has given rise to a tradition of research, stemming in part from the work of Braverman (1974), on the process of de-skilling and the links between skills, technology and changes in the workplace (Wood, 1989). Some of the main issues of debate here concern the decline of craft skills under capitalism, the introduction of new technology, and the emergence of new forms of post-Fordist production methods and their impact on the composition and distribution of skills within the wider society. This debate has recently expanded to incorporate the impact of globalisation on organisational forms and the 'new' skills they demand from the labour force. This has led to a widespread acceptance of the assumption that employers are introducing 'flat hierarchies', smaller units of employment, team work, quality circles and other high performance management techniques (Keep, 1998). Within this tradition, two dimensions of skill – substantive complexity and autonomy/control – both capture the theoretical arguments and describe a number of the empirical studies (Spenner, 1990). From the economist's angle, a problem with such concepts is the difficulty encountered when trying to find quantitative measures to test the sociological theories.

Within psychology, the concept of skill has been examined in more detail than in both the other disciplines. Different schools of thought within psychology have adopted a wide range of diverse approaches and foci in the conceptualisation and investigation of skill. Much of the early research on skill was in the sphere of learning theory or general behaviour theory with a focus on motor skills. Under the influence of the behaviourist tradition, interest in motor skill remained a persistent theme within experimental psychology for the next half century, culminating in Fleishmann's (1966) landmark research, which provided a widely adopted taxonomy of psychomotor abilities. Meanwhile, the emergence of cognitive and developmental psychology as established fields of study led to greater interest in the acquisition and development of cognitive skills, following the tradition established by Piaget (eg 1952).

In the latter half of the century, occupational psychologists (known as 'industrial/organisational' psychologists in North America), have utilised the term 'skill' to cover both motor and cognitive capabilities of the individual, particularly as applied in the workplace. These researchers have regarded skill as one sub-category of the human attributes or KSAO's (Knowledge, Skills, Abilities and Other characteristics) required for effective performance of jobs. Gatewood and Field (1990) proposed the following definitions of knowledge, skills and abilities in order to make inferences concerning employee specifications for a job:

- Knowledge: a body of information, usually of a factual or procedural nature that makes for successful performance of a task.
- Skill: an individual's level of proficiency or competency in performing a specific task. Level of competency is typically expressed in numerical terms.
- Ability: a more general, enduring trait or capability an individual possesses at the time when he or she first begins to perform a task.

A different categorisation system derives from research in the area of job training. The Industrial Training Research Unit (1981) proposed five types of learning summarised by the acronym CRAMP:

- Comprehension: knowing why, how and when things happen.
- Reflex skills: skilled physical movement and perceptual capacities.
- Attitude.
- Memorisation.
- Procedural: following a procedure (eg, operating a petrol pump).

A different but parallel approach to the understanding of skill within occupational psychology has been through the use of job analysis techniques. Job analysis refers to the systematic collection of information about jobs, including the objectives of the job, and the tasks that need to be performed to achieve those objectives. Worker-orientated job analysis procedures have focused on describing the psychological or behavioural requirements of the job, although writers such as Harvey (1991) have argued forcefully that the development of person specifications (the documenting of human characteristics necessary for effective task performance) should be regarded as an entirely separate activity from the job analysis itself.

Notwithstanding Harvey's exhortations to the contrary, a number of worker trait inventories, such as the Job Element Method (JEM) (Primoff and Eyde, 1988), the Ability Requirement Scales (ARS), now called the Fleishmann Job Analysis System (FJAS), (Fleishmann and Mumford, 1988) and the Threshold Traits Analysis System (Lopez, 1988), have been developed to assist employers in specifying the human attributes or KSAOs required for effective job performance.

Perhaps the most widely recognised job analysis tool is the Position Analysis Questionnaire (PAQ) developed by McCormick et al (1972). The PAQ consists of nearly 200 items organised into six major divisions:

* information input;
* mediation processes (ie the mental processes of reasoning, decision making etc);
* work output (the physical activities engaged in and the tools used by the worker);
* interpersonal activities;
* work situation and job context;
* miscellaneous aspects.

One problem with the PAQ is that it requires a fairly high level of reading ability on the part of the respondent. A British questionnaire developed in an education and training context that partially addresses this issue is the Job Components Inventory (JCI), which is targeted at a broader range of jobs across the full spectrum of the economy (Banks, 1988). Another job analysis questionnaire developed in a commercial setting is the Work Profiling System (WPS) (Saville and Holdsworth, 1998).

Methodology

As would be expected, having defined the concept of skills in different ways, each of these schools of thought gave rise to different approaches to the measurement of skills. The economists' primary concern and their main achievements have been in developing an appropriate econometric methodology for estimating the determinants of participation in, and the rate of return to, various types of education or training programme. Where skills are measured more directly in economists' research, they are typically associated with formal educational qualifications (as for example in the National Institute's seminal contributions on international comparisons) or derived from conventional classifications of workers. Where qualifications are clearly inappropriate, for example in the government's attempts to identify 'skill shortages', then recourse is made to employers' 'hard-to-fill vacancies'. Similarly, economists will use the existence of such 'skill shortages' as an indication of non-optimal levels of training by employers, owing to the presence of externalities associated with job mobility (allowing another firm, other than that providing the training, to reap part of the benefit). These measures also raise serious questions of interpretation (Green and Ashton, 1992; Green et al, 1998a). Most commonly, by adopting these proxies economists avoid the problem of measuring skills directly.

Sociologists have adopted a range of methodologies for the measurement of skills (Spenner, 1990), the most common being the case study and the social survey. The case study methodology has been used to examine the social construction of skills and the relationship between skills, new technology and new organisational forms. This has been useful in highlighting the ways in which workers are able to utilise the label 'skilled' to sustain their position in the labour market when the content of their job has been routinised and deskilled (Cockburn, 1983). It has also been extensively used to demonstrate the ways in which technology can be used to either enhance employees' skills or to diminish them (Wood, 1989). Finally, it has also been used to identify the new skills which are associated with new technology and new forms of work organisation (Frenkel et al, 1995; Thompson et al, 1995). This methodology always faces the problem of generalising to larger populations, especially as case studies often reveal evidence of contradictory trends.

The social survey has been used successfully to identify the social aspects of skill in an attempt to link skill acquisition with the social organisation of work, for example attempts to identify the extent to which jobs offer 'autonomy' and provide the respondent with 'discretion' in the exercise of work tasks and therefore the opportunity for intellectual development (Kohen, 1969). Similarly, sociologists have used the survey method to address the question of changes in skill use over time and to measure the extent of upskilling and deskilling (Gallie and White, 1993).

As we have already seen, psychologists have developed the most detailed techniques for measuring the skills of individuals and those demanded by different types of work. These were frequently developed for such immediate practical purposes, such as helping improve the selection and matching process and for providing a more 'objective' measure of differences between jobs/job evaluation. The aim was to provide a more 'objective' measure of responsibilities and skill to inform the payment systems used by large employers. The techniques usually involved a questionnaire but one which was devised after detailed analysis of specific cases. One disadvantage was that these techniques are largely focused on identifying skills as personal characteristics of individuals, thereby ignoring the social dimension of skills. Another disadvantage is that the lead was taken by commercial consultants rather than academic psychologists. The methods developed have been suitable for meeting particular clients' needs, thus concentrating on specific occupations and involving substantive participation by the clients. On occasion, however, it has proved possible for researchers to make good secondary use of data originally gathered for commercial purposes (Cappelli, 1993).

It is our contention that the analysis of skill has been one of the more pointed casualties of the drawing and closing of disciplinary boundaries. Although each of the three disciplines just mentioned have come to regard 'skill' as a major variable in their own scientific research programmes, language and exclusivity have often prevented communication and inhibited progress in understanding the central role that skills and skill formation are playing in modern societies. Nevertheless, perhaps because of the imperatives of economic growth and the increasingly widely held belief that skills must somehow be central to securing 'competitiveness', there is now considerable pressure to make progress in this field.

An interdisciplinary approach

Our objective was to draw on the different disciplinary backgrounds to develop measures of skill which could be used in a large nationally representative survey. The first issue to be tackled in developing the questionnaire was the conceptualisation of 'skill'. The categories to be utilised would have to be adequate to apply to all types of work likely to be found in the country. Moreover, in pursuit of this objective we were confronted with the classical dilemma between conceptualising skills as an attribute of the individual or of the broader social relationships within which the person is embedded by virtue of their job (Attewell, 1990).

We decided to attempt to construct an inclusive/comprehensive conceptual framework of the skills, human characteristics and personal attributes, abilities, qualities, attitudes and competencies most commonly regarded as important for effective performance of jobs, and which also incorporated the dimensions most frequently referred to in policy discourse and/or the economics/sociology literatures. The working definition of 'skill' initially adopted for the project was therefore:

- personal characteristics, influencing the quantity and quality of work performance, including abilities, attitudes, knowledge, motivation and competences.

We were aware that this would mean that we would have conceptualisations of skill which extended far beyond that which psychologists have conventionally regarded as skills, but this broad definition makes no presumption about the source of these skills and enables us to explore skills acquired as a function of situational factors such as the organisation of the work process. This, in turn, enabled us to address the issues and policy discourse which underpinned our core research questions.

In order to construct the required conceptual framework we drew on the broader situational factors discussed above and on two main fields within the psychology literature. These were:

- The job analysis/job evaluation literature, which focuses on the tasks that individuals need to perform in order to achieve work objectives. Here we focus on the models which formed the underlying structure of existing job analysis questionnaires such as PAQ, WPS, and JCI, and also the major factors incorporated within job evaluation systems such as the Hay system.
- The literature on generic job competences, rather than the more specific competences discussed within the Management Charter Initiative or National Vocational Qualifications literatures. The latter was concerned with competences which are too closely tied to performance in particular jobs for our purpose of capturing a full range of skills across a very broad ranging sample. Instead, we examined a wide range of different generic competence models for both managerial and non-managerial staff.

We also introduced all the standard variables from the labour economics literature, including pay, educational qualifications, training and occupational designation. With regard to the situational factors, key issues from theory and from case studies suggested exploring the impact of task variety, autonomy and the level of responsibility exercised at work. In addition, there was a danger that, if we relied only on existing psychological work on skills, we would fail to address the important question of 'new skills' which many commentators were claiming to be increasingly important – most prominently, information technology, teamworking, and problem-solving skills. These skills are frequently linked to the emergence of new organisational forms and for this reason we included a number of questions designed to identify those organisations at the forefront of change.

The final framework at which we arrived for the operationalisation of the concept of skill is given in Figure 1. Inevitably, the results we discuss below do not cover all items of interest in the framework.

Approaches to measurement

The next stage was a consideration of alternative approaches to measurement of the different constructs. Approaches other than self-report assessment of skills were initially considered, including objective ability testing through the use of psychometric instruments and the use of others' (eg supervisors') ratings of the skill range and level of the target individuals. However, these were rejected as practically impossible. Nevertheless, the use of a self-report methodology raised some fundamental issues that affected the survey design.

Of particular concern were the issues of social desirability responding and self-referencing of standards, which might systematically bias the data collected in unidentifiable ways. The main strategy we adopted was to assess skills through questions about the skill requirements of respondents' jobs, rather than directly asking respondents to evaluate their own range and level of skill. The rationale is that being asked to describe one's job is much less bound up with an individual's self-esteem than being asked to assess one's own competence. Nevertheless, one of the costs of the survey method, in contrast to the in-depth studies that job analysts can undertake in commercial practice, is that one does not have the opportunity to verify the nature of the job through consultation with line-managers and colleagues[2].

Figure 1: Conceptual framework of skill

A *Intellectual*
    Verbal – reading
    Verbal – writing
    Numerical
    Abstract/spatial
    Problem solving
    Planning
    Checking
B *Interpersonal*
    Communicating
    Teamworking
    Supervising/managing
C *Physical*
D *Knowledge*
    Technical/specialist
    Information technology
E *Motivation/reliability/initiative*
    Motivation/effort
    Reliability
    Initiative
F *Attitudes/working environment*
    Organisational commitment
    Employment commitment
    Autonomy/discretion/decision latitude
    Responsibility for things and persons
    Routinisation/skill variety
    Subjective effort
    Working conditions
    Organisational culture and climate

For all the skills items investigated in this way we drew on job analysis procedures by asking about the importance of different activities, following a well established precedent in the job analysis literature. Since we needed to cover a wide range of groups in society, we restricted the Likert-scale of responses to five points. An important aspect of our Skills Survey (SS) was the inclusion of several questions that had been asked of respondents to previous British surveys – in particular the Social Change and Economic Life Initiative (SCELI) respondents in 1986 and Employment in Britain (EIB) respondents in 1992. Several questions, on both skill and related areas, were replicated word for word as far as possible, including any accompanying prompts, use of show cards and response sets. Repeating questions allows comparisons over time to be made[3].

The survey

Management of the survey was sub-contracted to Social and Community Planning Research (SCPR), who conducted all piloting, fieldwork and raw data preparation in consultation with the research team, according to a tender specification. A representative sample in Great Britain was drawn, comprising 2,467 employed individuals aged 20 to 60, interviewed in person at home for an average of 45 minutes. The response rate was 67.1% (see Ashton et al, 1999 for full details).

Construction of skill indices

Several skill measures were obtained from the responses. In this section we describe the derivation of the relevant indices used below. In addition to conventional indicators of occupation and qualifications, we use both broad measures of job skills and many detailed measures which are grouped using principal components analysis into skill types.

One measure of broad job skill is the qualification level needed. However, an increase in required qualifications may also reflect increased use of qualifications by employers to screen job applicants and may not be reflective of jobs becoming genuinely more demanding. Therefore, further questions were asked to explore this dimension. Indicators such as the training time required for particular types of work and the time required to do it well were used to reflect the different levels of complexity and knowledge inherent in different types of work[4]. While these three measures of broad skill capture outcomes of somewhat different processes of skill acquisition, they are highly correlated with each other across jobs.

Autonomy is seen as a skill, in part because if employees are to act without close supervision they must know what tasks are to be done and how to do them. Autonomy is also a reflection of trust by the line manager in the conformity of the employee to appropriate effort norms. For these reasons, autonomy remained an important focus of our enquiry.

Following the self-reported job analysis approach, we had 36 detailed questions about the types of activities involved in a wide range of jobs with respondents being asked to rank them on a five-point scale, from 'essential' to 'not at all important or does not apply'. Examples of the activities included caring for others, making speeches or presentations, using a computer, analysing complex problems and planning the activities of others. The questionnaire focused on 36 activities designed to cover the tasks carried out in a wide range of jobs.

To proceed with the analysis, we subjected all activities (excluding the one related to computer use which was further embellished by a question relating to the sophistication of usage) to a principal components analysis. That analysis generated eight components, using conventional criteria (Ashton et al, 1999), from which were derived component scores as standardised variables with mean zero and unit standard deviation. The average scores for respondents in each occupational group are shown in Table 1, for the components identified as problem solving, professional communication, client communication and horizontal communication (components not shown in the table are manual skills, planning skills, verbal skills and numerical skills). The first column is an index of computer usage sophistication, where the index could range from zero (not used) to four (advanced usage, as for example with programmers). Note that the scores are positive for higher status occupations: in other words, the skills measures are positively correlated as expected with a crude broader occupational classification of skills. The table also shows that each skill index is greater for those with more education, but the skill difference between men and women can be positive or negative depending on skill type.

Skill changes in Britain

As outlined in the introduction, both demand factors and the changes in the education system lead us to expect an increase in skill levels during the recent era. Our principal method for assessing changes is to compare our broad skills measures with those obtained in identical fashion from the SCELI survey of 1986[5].

Table 2 shows a rise in skills over the period 1986 to 1997. In terms of the proportions of jobs where some qualification was required, this rose from 61.6% to 68.5%. To counter the possible objection that this merely represents credentialism, we also note that the proportions 'using' degrees rose from 7.5% to 10.6%. Moreover, the finding of skills rises is confirmed by the two other independent broad job skill measures. In 1997 people were doing jobs that required longer learning time and for which they had had longer training time than their equivalents in 1986. This basic finding is robust[6]. It confirms the findings of Gallie and White (1993), and is inconsistent with the thesis of widespread ongoing deskilling.

Table 1: Skills indices in 1997, by occupation, by gender and by educational attainment level

| | Computing | Problem solving | Communication | | |
			Professional	Client	Horizontal
Average skill levels among:					
Managers etc	1.7	0.14	0.43	0.52	0.23
Professionals	2.1	0.15	0.88	0.13	0.33
Associate professionals	1.9	0.31	0.42	0.23	0.19
Clerical	1.9	0.16	-0.54	-0.18	0.08
Craft etc	0.9	0.46	0.07	-0.28	-0.33
Personal and protective	0.6	-0.49	-0.19	0.02	0.39
Sales	0.9	-0.37	-0.60	0.91	-0.23
Operatives	0.7	-0.04	-0.36	-0.60	-0.35
Other	0.2	-0.94	-0.36	-0.68	-0.50
Average skill for those:					
Qualified to at least NVQ3 level	1.8	0.15	0.31	0.14	0.14
Qualified below NVQ3 or not qualified	0.9	-0.12	-0.27	-0.10	-0.08
Average skill levels among:					
Men	1.37	0.11	0.13	-0.03	-0.10
Women	1.22	-0.12	-0.18	0.04	0.13

The computing skills index ranges from 0 to 4; all other indices have an average of zero for the whole sample. See text and Ashton et al (1999) for details of definitions.

Table 2: Broad skills measures, 1986 and 1997

% of jobs

	All		Men		Women	
	1986	1997	1986	1997	1986	1997
Qualifications required	61.6	68.5	69.1	71.0	51.5	65.3
Degree used*	7.5	10.6	9.8	11.1	4.4	10.0
Long training	22.4	28.9	30.1	33.6	11.9	23.2
Short training	66.0	57.0	58.4	53.9	76.4	60.9
Long learning time†	24.3	24.3	43.2	30.9	11.7	17.0
High learning time†	27.1	21.4	18.2	15.5	38.4	28.0
Much choice‡	53.9	46.2	57.9	50.1	48.5	40.7
Loose supervision¶	34.9	27.2	38.0	28.0	30.8	26.3

Notes:

* By 'using' a degree is meant that a degree is both required now for getting the job *and* judged to be 'fairly necessary' or 'essential' for doing the job competently.
† Employees only.
‡ 'A great deal of choice' over work methods.
¶ Supervised 'not at all closely'.

Nevertheless, the broad skill rises are not all that great. The period we cover, just over a decade, is not all that long, and one ought not to extrapolate after this period to conclude that upskilling is an inevitable long-term tendency in the British economy. Moreover, there are two factors that call into question the extent to which these changes could be counted a success story.

First, there has not been any increase in the autonomy enjoyed by the average British worker. If anything, workers in 1997 were more constrained over the way they carry out their work, and more closely supervised, than in 1986. Even here the changes are not very large, and the cyclical factor (1997 being a year of much lower unemployment than 1986) might bias downwards the change in autonomy. Nevertheless the much-heralded post-Fordist worker, with supposedly greater flexibility in the workplace, does not appear to be exercising any greater personal control through that flexibility. In so far as autonomy is one of the elements of skill defined within sociology, this type of skill is not responding to the exigencies of the global economy.

Second, even with our main broad measures of skill that have been rising, we cannot easily assess how the rise compares to changes in other

Figure 2: Qualifications mismatch, 1986

Highest qualification held and required, % of jobs

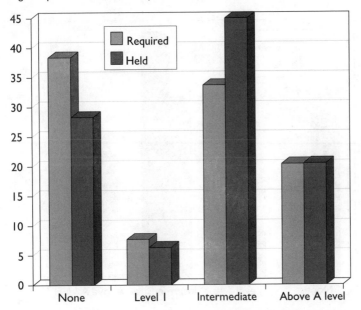

industrialised nations. It seems likely that other economies are also benefiting from a rising skills base, although that judgement pertains largely to changes in qualifications held (Green and Steedman, 1997). We can, however, address one of the main problems picked out in the 1980s – the lack of intermediate skills in Britain.

Figure 2 shows the match, at the aggregate level, between the supply of employed people holding qualifications at different levels and the requirements of the employers for qualifications[7]. The picture is one of excess supply at the intermediate level: that is, whereas 34% of employers would require an intermediate qualification (defined here as Levels 2 or 3), 45% of employed people have achieved one. At higher levels, there is a broad match between supply and demand. Thus the deficiencies, in relation to other European industrialised nations, in respect of intermediate qualification was as much one of low demand as of low supply – consistent with the notion of a low skills equilibrium. Figure 3 shows the position in 1997. While the demand for intermediate qualifications, at 35%, has hardly risen, the supply has risen a little to 48%, with the result that the picture of excess supply at the intermediate level remains the same. The

Figure 3: Qualifications mismatch, 1997

Highest qualification held and required, % of jobs

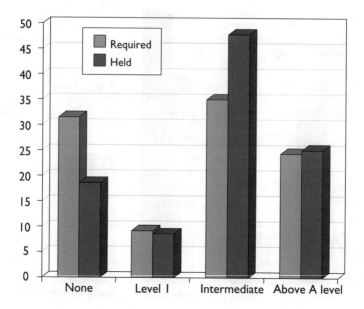

increased requirements for qualifications have mainly come at the top and the bottom end of the spectrum. Recent evidence suggests that Britain's deficiencies (in relation to other economies) in intermediate level skills have not been resolved (Lloyd and Steedman, 1999). Figure 3 suggests that the problem remains one of deficient demand as well as deficient supply.

We conclude that work skills on aggregate increased, but that this increase does not necessarily guarantee the competitiveness of the economy in terms of its skills base. The rise is consistent with the notion of a learning society, but it is now necessary to examine the sources of skill rises, and the extent to which the rises are widely spread among the employed population.

Where do skill rises and 'new skills' come from?

To gain some insight into the processes whereby people come to be doing more skilled jobs, we addressed two related issues. First, we examined

Figure 4: Skills and sector

% of jobs with short learning time, 1986 and 1997

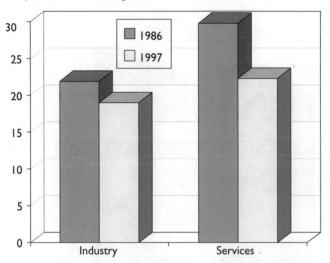

possible factors on the demand side that might have been expected to generate increased skill requirements by employers. Second, we examined factors that were associated with individuals' exercise of 'new' skills and their experience of skills rises. Although these different sets of factors are related, this approach enabled us to pick out the more important separate sources of pressure on either side of the market.

On the demand side, we first examined whether the opening up of trade could be driving the skills rise. Consistent with most, but not all, previous literature, our main finding is that trade played no significant part in the skills rise. Perhaps the single most telling indicator is that skills rose as fast or faster in services as in industry (predominantly manufacturing), as Figure 4 illustrates. The manufacturing sector as a whole has been most exposed to trade and competition with emerging low wage/low skill economies. If the influence of trade were the prime cause, we should expect the demand for low skilled workers to fall fastest in that sector (Wood, 1998). This finding remains robust, even if we include highly tradable service sectors such as finance, and even after controlling for other factors influencing skills (such as establishment size) in a multivariate analysis (Green et al, 1999).

Next, we examined the influence of technology. One way of doing so is to introduce data on research and development (R&D). High R&D

Figure 5: Skills and computer usage

% of jobs requiring qualifications, 1986 and 1997

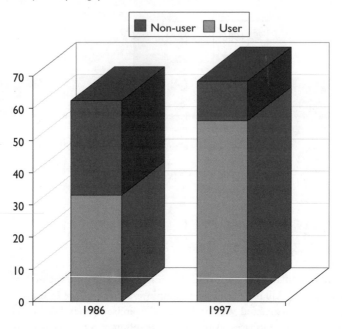

intensity is an indicator of being a high technology industry, with presumably larger than average technological change. Unlike previous analyses (eg Machin and Van Reenen, 1998) we could find no evidence that skills rose fastest in industries with high R&D intensity. However, another representation of technology is indicated by computer usage. Since 1986 there has been a rapid expansion in the use of computerised or automated equipment (especially PCs) in the workplace. Although we cannot track this change perfectly, a simple variable measuring whether or not the job involves computers turns out to be associated with large differences in skill. Using this simple variable, all the rise in skill between 1986 and 1997 is associated with expanded computer usage. Figure 5 illustrates this finding in respect of the requirement for qualifications: for non-users of computers, the proportions of jobs requiring qualifications has even decreased. We confess that we have been a little surprised about the strength of this finding. The ability of rising computer usage to 'explain' most or all the upskilling is robust to variations among our measures of skill and computer usage. We do not conclude that computers were an entirely exogenous factor causing the skills rise. Rather, the increasing supplies of skills were associated with and utilised by this pervasive new technology. Indeed, the significance of the technology, like other great innovative waves in history, lies in its pervasiveness; computers are not confined to particular industries or groups of workers. Moreover, the changing use of computers is likely to be associated with changes in work organisation which themselves have skills implications. So the fact that the computing variable shows up so strongly in this statistical analysis does not preclude that changes in organisational characteristics have also had an impact on skills. A further finding, reported in Green et al (1999), is that part of the skills rise between 1992 and 1997 is associated with an increased use of quality circles in the workplace.

The larger than expected association of computer usage also means that there has been insufficient attention in the research community to this fundamental change in work in Britain and elsewhere. None of the regular representative surveys has tracked the changing extent and sophistication of computer usage at work in Britain over the 1990s. The future role of computers will need to be measured more satisfactorily, if we are to understand adequately any future changes in the skills of the workforce.

If the expansion of new technology is the overwhelming source on the demand side for the rising deployment of skills in Britain, what factors are associated with individuals acquiring more skills? Is it just that, with the expanding education system, we see a happy matching of increased supply with the rising demand? Or are employers themselves contributing to the changes? We have already seen the problem of a continuing mismatch at intermediate level in the aggregates of required and achieved qualifications, suggesting that employers' role in engendering a low level of intermediate skills may be important. By not demanding higher skills, individuals get the message through the labour market and so may lack the incentive for acquiring them. As has been well shown by Soskice (1994), the lack of demand for skilled craft workers and consequent lack of availability of apprenticeships (by comparison with Germany) has historically fed through to a lack of study incentives in schools among non-college bound young people.

To address these issues, we examined the antecedents of 'new skills', comprising computing, problem solving, social and communication skills, and teamworking. We focused on three sources of skills: the education system, previous training (either on or off the job), and the individual's current job. In a single cross-section study, it is not possible to disentangle two separate processes: the acquisition of skills and the gaining of the particular job. Thus, a certain education may land you in a certain type of job, but you may also have acquired certain types of skills which are not used much in that job (see Bynner, 1994). Our working assumption is that if a job involves certain activities then the individual has the minimum skills to carry out those activities (despite the inevitable exceptions). The question is, where were those minimum skills acquired?

Our statistical analysis reveals that, as might be expected, individuals' prior education and training are indeed positively associated with their 'new skills', although different types of education and training are linked with different skills. For example, teamworking skills are strongly associated with on-the-job training but not with off-the-job training or with prior education. Education appears, by contrast, to be most important for computing skills.

However, the most striking finding is that the current employers' policies and characteristics have a remarkably strong association with new skills. We defined three types of organisation according to the presence or absence of the following features: an appraisal system, use of quality circles, a suggestion scheme, meetings to inform employees, meetings to consult with employees about company policies, and registering with Investors in People. A 'modern' organisation we arbitrarily defined as one which deployed at least five of these characteristics. A 'traditional' organisation was one which utilised at most one. The remainder, with a few of these characteristics, we classified as 'middling'. Our main finding is that jobs in 'modern' organisations involved significantly higher levels of 'new skills' than 'middling' or *a fortiori* 'traditional' organisations. This finding comes after allowing for many other associated factors in a multivariate analysis, and is robust to lots of different ways of parcelling the data responses. Consistent with the conclusion that 'modern' organisations are linked with the use of 'new' skills, we also found that the extent of skills increase was greatest for people working in 'modern' organisations (Ashton and Felstead, 1998). Confining our attention to those who remained with the same firm, Figure 6 illustrates the point: the proportion of jobs where the jobholder reports an overall skills rise over five years was 73% in 'modern' organisations compared with just 32% in 'traditional' organisations.

We cannot definitely conclude that the features of the 'modern' organisation themselves create the higher levels of skill. It is likely that 'modern' organisations will have a recruitment policy that will emphasise candidates with aptitudes and abilities suitable for their organisations.

Figure 6: skills and organisational characteristics

% of jobs with skills rising by type of organisation, 1997

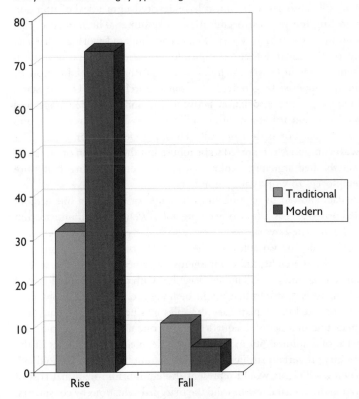

Nevertheless, our finding is consistent with the growing body of evidence that allocates a strong role to work-based learning in the process of upskilling. In that context, it is salutary to note that less than a third of employed people worked in 'modern' organisations according to our definition.

Are skills rewarded in the labour market?

If individuals are to acquire skills, it is hard to see how this can be accomplished satisfactorily without ensuring their cooperation in the process. In a predominantly capitalist economy, an important motivation for the acquisition of skill is the economic return. Skilled jobs need to afford greater pay or other forms of job satisfaction than unskilled jobs if the supply of workers is not to dry up. The same may be said for particular types of skill. Hitherto, economists have devoted a great deal of attention to estimating the returns to education or training. The human capital earnings function, which relates pay to schooling and work experience, is one of the most widely established empirical generalisations in economics. Yet little is known about the skills that the education or training is supposed to generate. Recent research in the United States has found a positive association between pay and computer usage, and between pay and reading/writing skills, but no link between pay and customer contact or arithmetic skills (Holzer, 1998; Krueger, 1993). The link with computers is reported to be robust, but the question of causation is not established; arguably, employers may have been assigning their more able employees to work with computers.

Our data allowed us to look into the value of skills in a much more detailed way than has hitherto been possible. We utilised all information from the detailed work activities reported by our respondents, as summarised in our variables for the level of complexity of computer usage, and by the eight skill components described above in the second section. These multiple skill indices, together with other controls designed to pick up aspects of jobs that might be linked to otherwise unobserved skills, constituted the explanatory variables in a hedonic wage equation. The principle of a hedonic equation is that one attempts to account for the price of a commodity in terms of the detailed characteristics of the commodity. If certain strong free market assumptions were to hold, the estimated coefficients would represent the equilibrium marginal cost of generating those characteristics and the marginal valuations by consumers. In the case of labour, the price is the wage, and the characteristics are those of the job. Since we do not expect free market assumptions of perfect competition to hold in the labour market, one should regard the coefficients as 'reduced form' outcomes of the interaction of both supply and demand factors, and not assume that they estimate the cost of supplying the skills. However, the analysis does allow us to identify a positive value (if there is one) for each skill, hence to estimate the gross return to acquiring jobs that use those skills.

Our main findings are summarised in Table 3. Most strikingly, computer skills are highly valued in the British labour market. Even after allowing for many other skills (including education measures) and job characteristics in an extremely rich data set, the premium for using computers at just 'moderate' levels of complexity (compared to non-users) is 13% for both

Table 3: The value of skills

Marginal pay premium[*], %

	Men	Women
Computing level (comparator: non-user)		
Simple	3.8	6.5
Moderate	12.6	12.7
Complex	16.9	10.7
Advanced	20.6	15.3
Skill components, effect of a 10-point skill rise:		
Problem solving	5.9	4.6
Professional communication	5.5	4.8
Client communication	(0)	(0)
Horizontal communication	(0)	(0)

[*]Estimated coefficients from hedonic wage equations. Controls include: all other skills measures, quadratics in work experience, job tenure and establishment size, over-education, under-education, marital status, permanent/temporary job, part-time/full-time, whether job is gender-segregated (male and female), union recognition and membership, public/private, self-employment/employee, regional dummies. All positive estimates are significantly different from zero at the level of 90% or above.

sexes. By 'moderate' is meant, for example, the skill of using a word processing package (respondents were given examples such as this to aid their responses). Thus, while it is acknowledged that computer specialists – especially those involved in recent years in clearing the millennium bug from old computer systems – can command higher pay, our results indicate that the pay benefits of using computers extend far wider. Given that the financial costs of acquiring computer skills are unlikely to be all that high, there is a clear incentive for individuals to acquire computing skills.

Table 3 also shows substantial positive impacts from the deployment of problem-solving skills, and from professional communication skills. These findings confirm the importance attached by employers to these types of skills. They also show that there may be an incentive for individuals to acquire these skills, providing that the costs do not exceed the expected gains.

However, there is no significant premium attached to either client communication skills or horizontal communication skills. From this we may conclude that there is no pay incentive for individuals to acquire such skills, and that it may therefore behove employers to fund the acquisition of these skills by their employees if they find that the skills are beneficial for the company. There remains a question as to why – if they are beneficial – the employers do not reward such skills with more pay. One possibility is that employees cannot easily demonstrate such skills and, by threatening to quit, lever up their pay (something easily done in the case of computing skills). It may still be significantly helpful for individuals to improve their communication skills, in order to gain employment: on this we have no evidence. Nevertheless, the message of this finding is that improvements in non-professional communication skills need to be brought about by employers, in the course of training and other work-based learning.

Are skills becoming more polarised?

Although we have shown that, with certain caveats, the aggregate skill level has been increasing in Britain, not everybody has experienced skills rises. The question at issue is whether there is a tendency on average for those with higher skills to pull away faster than the rest, thereby widening the gap between the skill-rich and skill-poor. A particular strong version of the polarisation thesis would suggest that low-skill groups have experienced an average decline in their skills. If either this strong version, or even a weak version synonymous just with increasing skills inequality, is valid, we are a long way from becoming a learning society.

As stated in the introduction, one of the strongest mechanisms of social exclusion – unemployment – was not investigated as part of this project. Nevertheless, we are able to examine whether there is any polarisation among the skills of employed people. In previous work, Gallie (1991) had found evidence of increasing skills inequality in the 1980s, whereby many more of those in higher occupation classes were reporting skill rises than of those in lower-status occupations.

However, in this study we found no strong evidence of polarisation in workforce skills, and some indication of the converse (Felstead et al, 1999a). One indication of skills equalisation is seen by considering the different changes in men's and women's jobs. As Table 2 shows, for every broad measure of skill, women's jobs entailed less skills than men's in both 1986 and 1997, but the gap substantially narrowed over the period.

Looking, for example, at the requirement for any qualification (see Figure 7), men's skills rose according to this measure by a paltry two percentage points to 71%, while women's skills rose by 14 points to 65% in 1997.

Figure 7: Skills and gender

% of jobs requiring at least some qualifications, 1986 and 1997

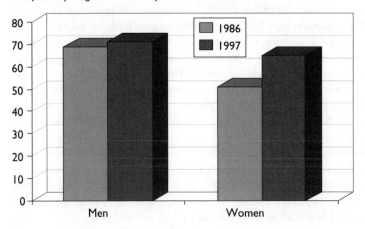

Figure 8: Skill change by occupation

Average rise in computing skills and in 'new skills', for those staying in same occupation, 1992-97

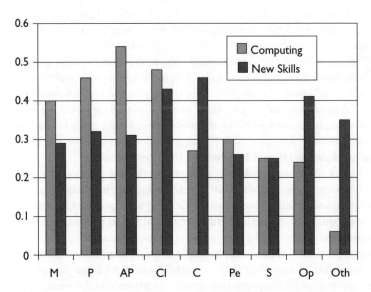

M=manager; P=professional; AP=associate professional; Cl=clerical; C=craft; Pe=personal; S=sales; Op=operatives; Oth=other.

Figure 8 looks at polarisation from a different perspective, here using the more detailed skills measures available only in the Skills Survey. We were able to compare respondents' skills with those in their jobs of five years' earlier (assuming they had one). Confining ourselves to those who did not change occupation over the period, the figure shows the change in the level of deployment of 'new skills' (comprising computing, problem solving, teamworking and communication and social skills). As can be seen, these skills have risen in all occupations, some more than others. But there is no special tendency for those in lower-status occupations to have had below-average rises in new skills. The only group which has a significantly lower rate of increase in 'new skills' is that of female part-timers, which suggests that the gulf between full-time and part-time work may be widening (Felstead et al, 1999a). Nevertheless, overall new skills have become more equally distributed among jobs over the period. Thus, the coefficient of variation of new skill, a conventional measure of inequality, was 0.42 in 1992 but fell to 0.34 in 1997.

Figure 8 hints at a possible polarisation in computing skills, in that higher status occupations have gained more computing skills. However, the overall utilisation of computing skills has become more equal, with the coefficient of variation falling from 1.12 to 0.87.

There *are* sectors that do not seem to have benefited from skill rises as much as the rest. For example, neither the wholesale nor the health sectors experienced substantive rises in broad skills between 1986 and 1997 (Green et al, 2000). Nevertheless no industry or occupation appears to have experienced a fall in skills. The only group that experienced significant falls over 1992 to 1997 were those who had had full-time jobs in 1992 then switched to part-time work. The majority of this group were women, and although we did not collect family history details it seems likely that for many in this group the decision to switch to part-time work is conditioned by family or local circumstances.

The lack of any major evidence of increasing skill inequality may appear as unexpected, even paradoxical, given the known inequalities in the education and training system and the fact that pay continued to become more unequal over this period. However, several factors potentially resolve the paradox.

First, even if education and training is unequal, everyone in work has the possibility of acquiring skills at work. Second, while pay inequality has risen in general, the period has seen a convergence in the average pay of men and women. If we confine attention in particular to full-time workers, a part of this convergence is explained by the narrowing of the skills gap (Green et al, 1998b). Third, it is incorrect to assume that pay differentials have widened solely because of observed (or unobserved) skills divergence. Institutional changes are also significant, especially during the Thatcher era. The decline of unions, the concomitant decentralisation of wage bargaining and adjustment of norms have all been features of the previous two decades. Institutional differences have been used to explain the divergent nature of inequality trends across nations (Blau and Khan, 1996).

Conclusions

Are we, then, moving towards becoming a learning society? Even if our rather simple criteria, suggested in the introduction, are accepted, there can be no simple answer to this question. Although information about skills is crucial to understanding the effects of learning, it throws only indirect light on learning processes, which are also central to understanding the Learning Society. We have also been self-limited by our concentration on employed people. Our excuse has been the central (although not exclusive) role attributed to workforce skills in maintaining competitiveness in a modern economy. Until recently, there has been rather little known of a quantitative nature about skills in Britain (or elsewhere). Given the importance attached to skills, this might seem odd to an observer from outside the world of social science.

Our project has attempted to build on previous work to develop a new methodology for measuring skills to analyse the distributional and growth pattern of both broad and detailed skills, and to provide a benchmark for future comparisons. We have found that work skills in Britain have increased according to three separate ways of measuring them: via qualifications required to get and do jobs, via the training time required, and via the learning time required. Only in respect of autonomy, which is one element of the sociologist's definition of skill, has there been no rise (and probably a fall) in skill. We have also found no strong evidence of a skills polarisation among employed people. Women's jobs, which on average have entailed lower broad skills than men's jobs, have been closing the gap on men's jobs, although female part-time workers have not participated as fully as other groups in the growth of new skills. Computing skills appear to have risen most for higher status occupations, but overall computer usage at middling levels of sophistication has spread more widely across the workforce.

Indeed, computer usage has turned out to be a crucial factor in the upskilling of the British workplace. Not only has computer usage expanded greatly, it is associated with a substantive pay premium even after allowing for many other variables that affect pay. It is hard to avoid the conclusion that this particular skill has been in continually increasing demand over the recent period. Our understanding of what this, most radical, transformation of work is doing to the labour market, and its implications for a learning society, will be greatly enhanced if researchers are able to continue to monitor the effects of information technology over the coming decade.

Our project also raises issues which public policy should address. If Britain is to become a 'learning society' then it can ill afford to have such a substantial section of the labour force as female part-timers without access to the means of enhancing their skill levels. This is one area where effective policy interventions could be used to ensure that those without access to the means to enhance their skills at work, could be provided with other opportunities. These may take the form of formal courses which would help ensure that alternative avenues were provided to enable workers to develop their potential and secure more rewarding jobs later in their careers. Failing this there is a risk of new divisions emerging in the labour market.

In addition to the jobs that are characterised by a lack of opportunity to acquire skills, this research raises serious questions about the changes which are taking place in those jobs which do provide the opportunities for skill development. Thus, we found that in spite of the increasing use of IT and the general upskilling, there has been little or no increase in the autonomy enjoyed by the average British worker. While individual skill levels may be increasing it would appear that employers are not systematically increasing the autonomy and discretion such workers exercise in the workplace. This is an area where further research work is required in order to gain a full understanding of the changes currently taking place in skill levels.

One further issue which needs to be highlighted in any discussion of a 'learning society' is the responsibility of employers to create the conditions at work which will enable all employees to have the opportunity to develop their skills. Our research confirms the findings of many earlier researchers that suggests that education and training systems form only a part of the learning system. As we have seen, in what we have termed modern organisations, all groups of employees have increased their skills. This is important because it suggests that the way in which employers organise the workplace plays a part in shaping the skills of all employees. Given the right type of organisational environment even the unskilled can improve their abilities. However, something like two thirds of the work force do not work in such organisations. Public policy could help to extend the range of organisations which put effort into developing the skills of all their employees. Indeed, Investors in People has already shown how such interventions can operate. Yet the fact that this initiative is still restricted to a minority of organisations indicates that there is much to be done in this area.

Notes

[1] In a further round of institutional change TECs are to be replaced by Learning and Skills Councils in April 2001 (see Felstead, 1994; Felstead and Unwin, 1999 for a review of TECs).

[2] A small-scale study of how jobholders' perceptions of their jobs accords with (or differs from) the perceptions of their line managers was also carried out, and will be reported on in detail in a future study.

[3] In addition to the main strategy, we also resolved to push the self-report methodology a stage further, in attempting to gain information directly about the competences that individuals (think they) have. Another reason for taking this additional approach, despite the dangers of unreliable reporting, was that respondents might lack the skills required to perform the job, but still somehow have managed to hold on to their job. This approach is similar in spirit to that of Bynner (1994), although we phrased our questions differently and only studied those in employment. We attempted to minimise the dangers of low reliability of the competency responses through a careful phrasing of questions. Where feasible, we developed concrete, behaviourally-anchored items (Smith and Kendall, 1963) where respondents' attention was focused on actual work behaviour and specific performance. The intention was to reduce problems of ambiguity and social desirability associated with asking abstract questions about general constructs, potentialities or capabilities.

[4] While better educated people might learn a job of given skill level more quickly, learning time remains a good indicator of how high the skill level is.

[5] The SCELI sample was larger; it covered a range of areas in Britain and, although not designed to be representative of Britain as a whole, turned out to be closely representative in terms of the key socioeconomic and demographic variables (Green et al, 1999).

[6] We also found that individuals reported lower levels of detailed skills in the jobs they were in five years previously, compared to their current jobs (Felstead et al, 1999a; Green et al, 2000).

[7] At the individual level, the apparent mismatch is greater, since some hold qualifications that are not required, while others without qualifications are in jobs that would now require a qualification.

References

Ashton, D. and Felstead, A. (1998) *Organisational characteristics and skill formation in Britain: Is there a link?*, Working Paper no 22, Leicester: University of Leicester Centre for Labour Market Studies.

Ashton, D., Davies, B., Felstead A. and Green F. (1999) *Work skills in Britain*, Oxford: SKOPE, Oxford and Warwick Universities.

Attewell, P. (1990) 'What is skill?', *Work and Occupations*, vol 17, pp 422-48.

Banks, M.H. (1988) 'Job components inventory', in S. Gael (ed) *The job analysis handbook for business, industry and government*, volume 1, New York, NY: John Wiley.

Bertrand, O. and Noyelle, T. (1988) *Human resources and corporate strategy: Technological change in banks and insurance companies*, Paris: OECD.

Blau, F.D. and Kahn, L.M. (1996) 'International differences in male wage inequality: institutions versus market forces', *Journal of Political Economy*, vol 104, no 4, pp 791-837.

Braverman, H. (1974) *Labor and monopoly capital*, New York, NY: Monthly Review Press.

Bynner, J. (1994) *Skills and occupations: Analysis of cohort members' self-reported skills in the fifth sweep of the National Child Development Study*, mimeo, London: City University Social Statistics Research Unit.

Cappelli, P. (1993) 'Are skill requirements rising? Evidence from production and clerical jobs', *Industrial and Labor Relations Review*, vol 46, pp 515-30.

Cockburn, C. (1983) *Brothers: Male dominance and social change*, London: Pluto Press.

Daly, A., Hitchens, D. and Wagner, K. (1985) 'Productivity, machinery and skills in a sample of British and German manufacturing plants', *National Institute Economic Review*, February, vol 11, pp 48-61.

DfEE (Department for Education and Employment) (1997) *Labour market and skills trends 1997/98*, Sheffield: DfEE.

Eraut, M., Alderton, J., Cole, G. and Senker, P. (2000) 'Development of knowledge and skills at work', in F. Coffield (ed) *Differing visions of a Learning Society: Research findings, Volume 1*, Bristol: The Policy Press.

Felstead, A. (1994) 'Funding government training schemes: mechanisms and consequences', *British Journal of Education and Work*, vol 7, no 3 (September), pp 21-42.

Felstead, A. and Unwin, L. (1999) *Funding systems and their impact on skills*, Research Paper no 12, DfEE Skills Task Force.

Felstead, A., Ashton, D. and Green, F. (1999a) 'Justice for all? The pattern of skills in Britain', Working Paper no 23, Leicester: Centre for Labour Market Studies, University of Leicester.

Felstead, A., Ashton, D., Burchell, B. and Green, F. (1999b) 'Skill trends in Britain: trajectories over the last decade', in F. Coffield (ed) *Speaking truth to power*, Bristol: The Policy Press, pp 55-72.

Finegold, D. and Soskice, D. (1988) 'The failure of British training: analysis and prescription', *Oxford Review of Economic Policy*, vol 4, no 3, pp 21-53.

Fleishmann, E.A. and Mumford, M.D. (1988) 'Ability requirements scales', in S. Gael (ed) *The job analysis handbook for business, industry and government*, volume 1, NY: John Wiley.

Frenkel, S., Korczynski, M., Donoghue, L. and Shire, K. (1995) 'Reconstituting work: trends toward work and info-normative control', *Work, Employment and Society*, vol 9, pp 773-96.

Gallie, D. (1991) 'Patterns of skill change: upskilling, deskilling or the polarization of skills?', *Work, Employment and Society*, vol 5, no 3 (September), pp 319-51.

Gallie, D. and White, M. (1993) *Employee commitment and the skills revolution*, London: PSI Publishing.

Gatewood, R.D. and Field, F.S. (1990) *Human resources selection*, (2nd edn), New York, NY: Dryden Press.

Green, A. and Steedman, H. (1997) *Into the twenty first century: An assessment of British skill profiles and prospects*, mimeo, London: LSE Centre for Economic Performance.

Green, F. (1998) *The value of skills*, Studies in Economics, no 98/19, University of Kent at Canterbury.

Green, F. (1999) 'Training the workers', in P. Gregg and J. Wadsworth (eds) *The state of working Britain*, Manchester: Manchester University Press.

Green, F. and Ashton, D. (1992) 'Skill shortage and skill deficiency: a critique', *Work, Employment and* Society, vol 6, no 2, pp 287-301.

Green, F., Felstead, A. and Gallie, D. (1999) 'Changing skill intensity: an analysis based on job characteristics', European Association of Labour Economists, Annual Conference, Regensburg, 23-26 September.

Green, F., Machin, S. and Wilkinson, D. (1998a) 'The meaning and determinants of skill shortages', *Oxford Bulletin of Economics and Statistics*, vol 60, no 2, pp 165-87.

Green, F., Ashton, D., Burchell, B. and Felstead, A. (1998) 'Skill trends and pay determination in Britain', European Association of Labour Economists, Annual Conference, Blankenberge, Belgium, 17-20 September.

Green, F., Ashton, D., Burchell, B., Davies, B. and Felstead, A. (2000) 'Are British workers getting more skilled?', in L. Borghans and A. de Grip (eds) *The overeducated worker?*, Cheltenham: Edward Elgar.

Harvey, R.J. (1991) 'Job analysis', in M.D. Dunnette and L.M. Hough (eds) *Handbook of industrial and organisational psychology*, volume 1, Palo Alto, CA: Consulting Psychologists Press.

Hirschhorn, L. (1984) *Beyond mechanization: Work and technology in a postindustrial age*, Cambridge, MA: MIT Press.

Holzer, H.J. (1998) 'Employer skill demands and labor market outcomes of blacks and women', *Industrial and Labor Relations Review*, vol 52, no 1, pp 82-98.

Industrial Training Research Unit (1981) *CRAMP: A guide to training decisions – a user's manual*, Revised Edition, Cambridge: Industrial Training Research Unit.

Johnson, T.J. (1972) *Professions and power*, London: Macmillan.

Keep, E. (1998) 'Britain's VET policy and the third way: following a high skills trajectory or running up a dead end street?', Paper presented to the ESRC High Skills Project Seminar, Cardiff, 24-5 September.

Kohen, M.J. (1969) *Class and conformity*, Homewood, IL: Dorsey Press.

Krueger, A.B. (1993) 'How computers have changed the wage structure – evidence from microdata, 1984-1989', *Quarterly Journal of Economics*, vol CVIII(1), pp 33-60.

Lloyd, C. and Steedman, H. (1999) *Intermediate skills – how are they changing?*, DfEE Skills Task Force Research Paper 4, Sheffield: DfEE.

Lopez, F.M. (1988) 'Threshold traits analysis system', in S. Gael (ed) *The job analysis handbook for business, industry and government*, volume 1, New York, NY: John Wiley.

McCormick, E.J., Jeanneret, P. and Meacham, R.C. (1972) 'A study of job characteristics and job dimensions as based on the position analysis questionnaires', *Journal of Applied Psychology*, vol 36, pp 347-68.

Machin, S. and Van Reenen, J. (1998) 'Technology and changes in skill structure: evidence from seven OECD countries', *Quarterly Journal of Economics*, vol 113, no 4, pp 1215-44.

Marshall, R. and Tucker, M. (1992) *Thinking for a living*, New York, NY: Basic Books.

Murray, A. and Steedman, H. (1998) *Growing skills in Europe: The changing skills profiles of France, Germany, the Netherlands, Portugal, Sweden and the UK*, Discussion Paper no 399, London: Centre for Economic Performance, London School of Economics.

Parkin, F. (1974) 'Strategies of closure in class formation', in F. Parkin (ed) *The social analysis of class structure*, London: Tavistock.

Piaget, J. (1952) *The origins of intelligence in children*, New York, NY: Norton.

Primoff, E.S. and Eyde, L.D. (1988) 'Job element analysis', in S. Gael (ed) *The job analysis handbook for business, industry and government*, volume 1, New York, NY: John Wiley.

Primoff, E.S. and Fine, S.A. (1988) 'A history of job analysis', in S. Gael (ed) *The job analysis handbook for business, industry and government*, volume 1, New York, NY: John Wiley.

Reich, R.B. (1988) *Education and the next economy*, Washington, DC: National Education Association.

Saville and Holdsworth (1998) *Work profiling system, technical manual*, London: Saville and Holdsworth Ltd.

Smith, P.C. and Kendall, L.M. (1963) 'Retranslation of expectations: an approach to the construction of unambiguous anchors for rating scales', *Journal of Applied Psychology*, vol 47, pp 149-55.

Soskice, D. (1994) 'Reconciling markets and institutions: the German apprenticeship system', in L.M. Lynch (ed) *Training and the private sector: International comparisons*, Chicago, IL: University of Chicago Press.

Spenner, K.I. (1990) 'Skill, meanings, methods and measures', *Work and Occupations*, vol 17, pp 399-421.

Steedman, H. and Wagner, K. (1987), 'A second look at productivity, machinery and skills in Britain and Germany', *National Institute Economic Review*, vol 122 (May), pp 84-95.

Thompson, P., Wallace, T., Flecker, G. and Ahlstrand, R. (1995) 'It ain't what you do, it's the way that you do it: production organisation and skill utilisation in commercial vehicles', *Work, Employment and Society*, vol 9, pp 719-42.

Wood, A. (1998) 'Globalisation and the rise in labour market inequalities', *Economic Journal*, vol 108 (September), pp 1463-82.

Wood, S. (1989) (ed) *The transformation of work?*, London: Unwin Hyman.

Index

E

Economic and Social Research
  Council (ESRC) 19-20, 164
economists: on skills 196-7, 199-200,
  216
Education and Training (Scotland)
  114n3
education services: and people with
  learning difficulties 68-70, 74
Edwards, Tony 14, 36
Egerton Commission 63
11-plus examination 181, 184
emigration 107
'employability' 12, 69, 71
employers
  in Northern Ireland/Scotland 109
  and skills 5-6, 194, 197, 213, 214,
    222-3
employment *see* work
Employment Act (1945) 66
Employment Service (ES) 66
'empowerment': and people with
  learning difficulties 85
English, Susan 143-70
Enterprise in Higher Education
  (EHE) 161
Eraut, Michael 7
ESRC 19-20, 164
ethnicity: and learning difficulties
  80-1
Europe 23-6
European Area for lifelong learning
  26
European Charter of Basic Skills 26
European Commission 1, 26
European Union (EU) 26

F

family, role of 110, 180-1, 182
FE *see* Further Education
Felstead, Alan 5-6, 193-228
'festivals' of learning 1
Fevre, Ralph 8-10, 29-30, 171-92
Field, John 6, 18, 19, 22, 35, 95-118
52 week linking rule 65
Fleishmann Job Analysis System 199

France 25-6
friendships: of people with learning
  difficulties 77-8
Fryer, Bob 119-20
funding: and HE innovation 158,
  160, 163, 164
Furlong, John 8-10, 171-92
Further and Higher Education Act
  (1992) 139
Further and Higher Education
  (Scotland) Act (1992) 69
Further Education (FE) 29, 30, 36,
  69-70
  and credit-based learning 130-4,
    136-7
Further Education Unit 138
Future Needs Assessment 71

G

gender
  and credit-based learning 23, 136
  and learning difficulties 80
  and lifelong learning 62, 177, 180,
    183
  in Northern Ireland/Scotland study
    22, 101, 104, 110
  and qualifications 104, 218-19
  and skills 197, 207, 208
    inequalities 218-19, 221
    valuation (pay) 217, 220-1
Germany: care sector 22
Glasgow: libraries usage 106
Glasgow City Council 63-4
Gorard, Stephen 8-10, 171-92
Graham, Robert 29
Granovetter, Mark 19
Green, Francis 5-6, 193-228
'guided innovation' 20, 156, 161

H

Hadjivassiliou, Kari 25
Hannan, Andrew 143-70
Hargreaves, David 7

The neccesity of informal learning
Edited by Frank Coffield

The ESRC's programme of research into The Learning Society did not set out to study informal learning, but it quickly became clear to project after project within the Programme that the importance of informal learning in the formation of knowledge and skills had been underestimated. Policies to widen and deepen participation in learning need to concern themselves not only with increasing access and appreciating the different contexts in which learning takes place, but also with the different forms of learning. Formal learning in institutions is only the tip of the iceberg and this report constitutes an exploratory study of the submerged mass of learning, which takes place informally and implicitly.

Contents: *Introduction: The structure below the surface: reassessing the significance of informal learning* **Frank Coffield**; *Non-formal learning, implicit learning and tacit knowledge in professional work* **Michael Eraut**; *Informal learning and social capital* **John Field and Lynda Spence**; *Implicit knowledge, phenomenology and learning difficulties* **Stephen Baron, Alastair Wilson and Sheila Riddell**; *Formalising learning: the impact of accreditation* **Pat Davies**; *Necessary and unnecessary learning: the acquisition of knowledge and 'skills' in and outside employment in South Wales in the 20th century* **Ralph Fevre, Stephen Gorard and Gareth Rees.**

Paperback £13.99 (US$25.00) ISBN 1 86134 152 0
297x210mm 88 pages January 2000

Speaking truth to power: Research and policy on lifelong learning

Edited by Frank Coffield

In this collection of essays researchers discuss the implications of their findings for policy. They make positive recommendations for policy makers and those concerned to improve the quality of learning at work. Findings are also presented for the first time from a major new survey, commissioned by The Learning Society Programme, which examined the skills of a representative sample of British workers.

Contents: *Introduction: Past failures, present differences and possible futures for research, policy and practice* **Frank Coffield;** *The impact of research on policy* **Maurice Kogan;** *The impact of the manager on learning in the workplace* **Michael Eraut, Jane Alderton, Gerald Cole and Peter Senker;** *Young lives at risk in the 'Futures' market: some policy concerns from ongoing research* **Stephen Ball, Sheila Macrae and Meg Maguire;** *The costs of learning: the policy implications of changes in continuing education for NHS staff* **Therese Dowswell, Bobbie Millar and Jenny Hewison;** *Skill trends in Britain: trajectories over the last decade* **Alan Felstead, David Ashton, Brendan Burchill and Francis Green;** *Adult guidance services for a learning society? Evidence from England* **Will Bartlett and Teresa Rees.**

Paperback £13.99 (US$25.00) ISBN 1 86134 147 4
297x210mm 76 pages July 1999

Why's the beer always stronger up North?: Studies of lifelong learning in Europe

Edited by Frank Coffield

This edited report offers a fresh approach on lifelong learning and attacks the consensual rhetoric which has become dominant in the English-speaking world over the last 20 years. It provides a more convincing explanation of the high levels of non-participation in continuous learning, and sees lifelong learning as a new moral obligation and a new form of social control. The report suggests that lifelong learning may be better viewed as contested terrain between employers, unions and the state than as the new wonder drug which will solve a wide range of economic, social and political problems.

Contents: *Introduction: lifelong learning as a new form of social control?* **Frank Coffield;** *Lifelong learning: learning for life? Some cross-national observations* **Walter Heinz;** *Models of guidance services in the learning society: the case of the Netherlands* **Teresa Rees and Will Bartlett;** *The comparative dimension in continuous vocational training: a preliminary framework* **Isabelle Darmon, Carlos Frade and Kari Hadjivassiliou;** *Inclusion and exclusion: credits and* unités capitalisables *compared* **Pat Davies;** *Using 'social capital' to compare performance in continuing education* **Tom Schuller and Andrew Burns;** *Issues in a 'home international' comparison of policy strategies: the experience of the Unified Learning Project* **David Raffe, Cathy Howieson, Ken Spours and Michael Young;** *Planning, implementation and practical issues in cross-national comparative research* **Antje Cockriill, Peter Scott and John Fitz.**

Paperback £13.99 (US$25.00) ISBN 1 86134 131 8
297x210mm 88 pages January 1999

Learning at work

Edited by Frank Coffield

Learning at work is important in helping to transform fashionable phrases such as 'the learning organisation' or 'lifelong learning' into practical ideas and methods which could enhance the quality of learning in British firms. It examines the key processes of learning, as embedded in particular workplaces, in organisational structures and in specific social practices.

Contents: *Introduction: new forms of learning in the workplace* **Frank Coffield;** *Artisans in the making? Comparing construction training in Wales and Germany* **Peter Scott and Antje Cockrill;** *Jobrotation: combining skills formation and active labour market policy* **Reiner Siebert;** *Continuing vocational training: key issues* **Isabelle Darmon, Kari Hadjivassiliou, Elisabeth Sommerlad, Elliot Stern, Jill Turbin with Dominique Danau;** *Learning from other people at work* **Michael Eraut, Jane Alderton, Gerald Cole and Peter Senker;** *The Learning Society: the highest stage of human capitalism?* **Stephen Baron, Kirsten Stalker, Heather Wilkinson and Sheila Riddell;** *Skill formation: redirecting the research agenda* **David Ashton.**

Paperback £13.99 (US$25.00) ISBN 1 86134 123 7
297x210mm 76 pages September 1998